GOD OR NATIONS
Radical Theology for the Religious Peace Movement
William Durland

WIPF & STOCK · Eugene, Oregon

Wipf and Stock Publishers
199 W 8th Ave, Suite 3
Eugene, OR 97401

God or Nations
Radical Theology for the Religious Peace Movement
By Durland, William and Clark, Ramsey
Copyright©1989 by Catholic Worker
ISBN 13: 978-1-60899-055-9
Publication date 4/28/2010
Previously published by Fortkamp -- Cath Worker, 1989

ACKNOWLEDGMENTS

The direct quotations from Scripture are from the Revised Standard Version of the Bible, Copyright 1946, 1952, 1971, by the Division of Christian Education of the National Council of Churches of Christ in the United States of America. Used by permission.

Special thanks to Elizabeth Sanders who designed the cover, to Debra L. McConnell who retyped the original manuscript several times, and to George Hanst whose proofreading skills are proof that reading skills still exist among a remnant in Baltimore.

CONTENTS

vi Contents

GOD or NATIONS

To live as if the Kingdom has come.
To pray that the Kingdom will come soon.

FOREWORD

One is offered in *God or Nations* a journey of transcending
vision with a gentle and humble guide of amazing grace and
righteous purpose. Having wandered several times through the
ways and by-ways of this book, I urge the reader to thoroughly
live in these pages until the riches are deeply absorbed.

At the very threshold of this venture you will pierce the nearly
impenetrable prison walls of culture beyond which few people
ever see. Pindar told us: "Culture is Lord of everything, of
mortals and immortals king." To understand the message, you
must escape cultural confinement with a sonic boom and speed
beyond sound which limits our hearing to the reality that sur-
rounds us, disabling our capacity to wonder what might be,
what ought to be, to seek a better world. You will have to make
a leap of faith, to bear witness. Of the tens of thousands of
books you may touch in your life, all but a few score will work
safely in a small corner of their culture, some handsful will
stretch for its outer limits, and several will burst beyond cultural
walls to imagine the Kingdom of God. This is such a book.

The difficulty in realizing that a truth beyond culture exists
is perhaps the greatest single barrier to the life of love. Our
culture is permeated by violence, militarism, materialism, patriotism to nation right or wrong, the supremacy of force, racism, sexism. Most people, seeking approval of their peers, never
see how destructive these false values are. Here you are challenged to be dissatisfied with this cultural reality; to resist custom, habit, tradition, mores, social environment, even heredity;
to act on your own conscience, to reform reality, to return good
for evil, to love your enemy, to serve the oppressed.

Interspersed throughout this work of far-ranging scholarship,
William Durland gives us shards from his intimate efforts at
personal freedom which demonstrate the difficulty of the struggle. Like everyone born into our culture, he was taught to glorify
violence and revere wealth. He was, as he says, a militant, a

serviceman, a state legislator, a lawyer. He became a pacifist, a Christian. Read how he overcame.

I have often returned to a photograph of Gandhi's possessions at his death. Not everything is discernible; but a pair of spectacles, a book, sandals, a bowl, altogether not weighing a pound, can be seen. I think of Gandhi, the young lawyer, disembarking in Durban, South Africa, with his starched collar, stiff court suits, baggage, and law books, and I ask how he avoided becoming the intellectual dandy seeking personal wealth and power his society told him he must be, if he was to be deemed successful. I see him in his later life loving Christianity, if not accepting its insistence on miracles, and using with its Scriptures, his own Hindu, Buddha, Zoroaster, the Koran and other sources of inspiration for his evening prayer. Then I reread his autobiography seeking to know how he found the way, the will, the love to live as he did.

William Durland offers another example of this rare accomplishment. It takes great sacrifice, suffering, endurance, perseverance, learning, and plain hard work. Years and years of study, teaching, prolific writing, thought, and wonder lay behind these pages. His scholarship is of the highest order. This learned man teaches us there is nothing merely academic, i.e., irrelevant, about knowing the past, informing oneself from the widest range of speculation, idea, information, and observation available. He learns from others through a continuous dialogue with the thought of the past and the present. Never once is there a trace of mere pedantry, seeking power by showing knowledge. This is a quest for truth.

Beyond the books, the intellectual, the reliance on reason, Durland has plunged with equal enthusiasm into the world of experience. He intends to be a Christian in a world with little tolerance for such a dangerous pursuit. He knows that life is to be lived, that the Christian way must be acted upon, experienced, that this is the great teacher: to be personally involved in service to others, in nonviolence, in peace activism. You will find him in jail with those his culture imprisons, on the streets with those it impoverishes, confronting militarism, materialism, and cultural idolatry. He is abused, suffers, is hated, as are the poor, because he tries to be righteous and such is necessary to faith and understanding. The plight of the poor must be felt in the bones, he tells us. By study, meditation, and a life of principled acts, he has sought the truth and it has made him free.

He is painfully aware how long it took him to notice the awful justification of murder in the Wizard of Oz, and Snow White and the Seven Dwarfs. He is more painfully aware of how few Americans can see the degradation, even the wrong of violence in their culture. But he may be less aware of the all-pervasive celebration of devastating violence on TV, in popular books, movies, songs, and sports which saturates our children, because his life style spares him steady immersion in it.

Having broken his cultural bonds, Durland observes the tragic departures from Christian values in American mores. He contrasts the two through his work: service to others, not security for self through a kingship of force; a religious community, radical and pacifist, not an institutional church based on violence and materialism; voluntary poverty, not the idolatry of wealth; rural, not urban; faith in the Lord, not obedience to the king; a religion of the spirit, not of the Temple; not corrupt concepts of secular justice from law books, but law written in the hearts of people; the rejection of violence as the key to an alternative life of community, witness, and service, not law and politics based on institutional violence; resistance to the reign of untruth, greed, cruelty, and arrogance in the world.

It becomes easy for him to say no to a destructive culture, easy to identify the affirmative alternative, even easy to know what a Christian is supposed to do. The problem he tells us is finding ways that work to create the holistic community and to live a life of service that meets the needs of all.

To find the way to the Holy Nation we are taken through a fascinating, often brilliant analysis of the history of nonviolent communities, nation-states, and organized religion. This is followed by a study of ethical, legal, and philosophical theories of politics, law, government, justice and social contract based on force and property, and finally to nonviolent acts and advocacy in service to the oppressed.

The roll of religious figures and thinkers, from the earliest in the Old Testament through contemporary scholars and leaders who are called for testimony, is long. The lists of secular political leaders, law-givers, philosophers, historians, militarists and others are even longer. And each has a contribution to make to the unfolding inquiry.

Durland finds, perhaps as much by dint of imagination as from clarity in its text, that the purpose of the Old Testament stories is to chart the progression of human history from a covenant or gift of trust to a violent human effort to control events. He finds the early Israelites lived in a religious community in the wilderness where they obeyed God and were much freer than when they were later tied to land, and possessions, and when wealth was seen as a virtue. They preserved this history in their Scripture which records, he believes, the world's first commitment to an intentional community of God. Later, Israel shifted from God to king which by the time of Samuel made permanent the institution of war. Soon a king, Solomon, was seeking to house God in an earthly temple to harness His power to state will.

Durland observes Jesus did not institutionalize religious community during his life, but the early Christians did. Stephen saw the Church of God as being within each person, not at Solomon's temple. The early Christians rejected war, kings, and mammon, refusing to believe they offered security and not wanting it if they did. Their religious community lasted several hundred years.

The struggle between the Romans and the Christians provides a study of relations between state and church beginning in persecution. Christians who believed one could not be a soldier and a Christian at the same time and refused to serve the Roman armies gave way to an organized church that was co-opted finally by Constantine in what Durland calls the first triumph of Caesar over Christianity. By 380 it was the Roman Catholic church.

He is, with other scholars, harsh in his views about St. Augustine, agreeing that violence forms the firmest building-stone of his political thought and blaming him for adding to Cicero's philosophical support of the just war.

Durland's comments on the violence of the Crusaders, the real issues between Becket and Henry, the Inquisition, St. Francis, and Luther must be read. His humor and use of irony when he may be most outraged are illustrated by his comments on the Pope who today "lives in a castle like David, with a temple nearby like Solomon's, made secure by the economies of Vatican museums, treasures, and worldwide investments. From time to time he emerges ... to preach to the world about poverty, simplicity, and peace; then returns to its splendor."

He confirms Plato's *Republic* which finds an inherent tendency to war among nations. Most emphatically he agrees with Tolstoy that government is violence. He sadly rejects the submissions of Augustine and Aquinas that a religious person must pledge allegiance to civil authority in war. He also rejects Aquinas and Hegel who state coercion is necessary to control the antisocial elements in society. He patriotically decries the "false notion that the United States is a Christian nation."

Durland more than makes his case against the nation-state and the organized church. He concludes that nations are out of control and society must absolutely be changed. His arguments carry the day.

These are not the only idols he exposes. As a lawyer, learned in the law, he shows law as a form of institutional violence incorporating at its best, concepts of justice that are adversarial and give support to the theory of the just war. His attacks on cultural sin are never heavy-handed, but quite devastating in their insight. Of celibacy among the clergy and the exclusion of women, for instance, he observes "the church has allowed secular patriarchy to be idolized."

Primarily from the words and deeds of Jesus, the elements for the alternative, nonviolent religious community are identified. He finds a blueprint for it in "the historical records of the Israelites and early Christians." We must love our enemy, overcome evil with good, accept poverty and reject violence, live simply, resist power, employ civil disobedience, be pacifist, devote ourselves to service to the oppressed, reject force, coercion and security, recognize the importance of patience, endurance, and faith.

Durland describes in some detail how the alternative communities he has lived in work, as well as many of the better known efforts in the United States, Central and South America. He observes that the agape they radiate would seem "folly to the Greeks and scandal to the Jews." He calls for a social theology that takes the best from Marxism, liberation theology, political theology, and traditional theology to achieve the concept of the Christian community.

He envisions nonviolent religious communities that are viable, loving, and effective. Surely their increase to the largest consensual limits is desirable. For they are good, do good, and show others what is possible.

Still Durland concedes it is "beyond my ability and experience to describe systematically what living economically in the Kingdom would look like, primarily because it has never been done perfectly." If Durland cannot describe such religious communities, who can? Perhaps the meaning of this is that for all their love, their grace, and their good works, the alternative community is limited in its capacity, because all the service they can provide cannot begin to meet human need without institutional structure, regular function, and planning that may be incompatible with their nature. And if they became the larger community, what could happen to them, and what then would be the alternative?

Perhaps we must look beyond the critically important obligation to expand alternative religious communities to their natural voluntary limit and examine the possibility that violent institutions can change to conform to Christian values. If individuals can live nonviolent lives of service, can institutions? Need government function through violence, force, fear and fiat? Can we create institutions committed to act by consensus, persuasion without force, fear, or favor? Can law act by Christian standards of service, nonviolence, loving one's enemy? Can we find the law of Romans 12:10, "Love worketh no evil to his neighbor, therefore love is the fulfilling the law."

If the people who comprise the society and its government are capable of living lives of simplicity, poverty, nonviolence, civil disobedience, or obedience to conscience, of grace and righteousness, can their government function by the same values? Can we hope to meet the basic needs of the billions of poor on the planet, crowding into nearly uninhabitable megalopolises like Cairo, Calcutta, Karachi, Lagos, Shanghai, Bangkok, Rio de Janeiro, Mexico City without an early, urgent, organized effort? Can we stop nuclearism, the arms race, without world law and political institutions?

There is the further question of whether purely local communities, however effective, could hope to meet distant crises in the human condition caused by famine, flood, drought, earthquake, epidemic, and war. A truly Christian faith cannot create or accept forms of relationships among people that deny masses of humanity, or the least among us, the fundamental needs of the mind, body, and spirit.

Mohammed Iqbal, the poet-philosopher who dreamed of an Islamic nation of Pakistan, wrote in his book *Secrets of Collective Life* that "A nation is formed by a unity of hearts." This is perhaps close to a short description of the community we strive for. If a community can be created by shared belief and love in this way, why not a reformed nation and a community of nations? Aquinas also told us "War is inevitable among sovereign nations not governed by positive law."

Durland sees benefits in human rights' concepts despite their coercive potential. Indeed we are told the Bible depicts human rights, especially rights of the poor and oppressed, in ways that equal the best secular and humanist definitions. Surely this is an area where millions of people can agree to a more vigorous use of law based on nonviolent, social change and non-militaristic service to others.

Finally, Durland acknowledges that we must change not only our institutions, we must change ourselves. If we can change ourselves, we will find ways to create institutions like ourselves. If we can become righteous, nonviolent, loving, giving, non-materialistic, resisting, returning harm with good, we can create institutions, systems and ways to serve all God's children. Nothing else is worthwhile. Our capacity to provide ample service to assure health, food, education, spiritual growth and a good, simple, loving life for all is abundant.

William Durland has shown us how we can change ourselves. He did. This surely is the first and essential step to the radical change we must make in our institutions. Without individual change, institutions will remain the Temple of Force.

Individuals in the long and dangerous struggle for radical social change and peace, and human service must fulfill the promise of Gandhi's optimism:

"My optimism rests on my belief in the infinite possibilities of the individual to develop nonviolence. . . . In a gentle way we can shake the world."

Ramsey Clark
August 1989

PREFACE

For some time, beginning with the publication of my 1975 book, *No King But Caesar?* (Herald Press, Scottsdale, PA, which was influenced by the period of my life when I moved from state legislator to Christian pacifist), I was troubled by the implications of my transformation to Christian pacifism. I realized that becoming a pacifist could not be limited simply to an aversion to all wars, or just a negative refusal to use violence. Radically alternative values were called for. This included expressing them publicly, for such a life has political, religious, and economic consequences.

The reaction I received in teaching, in practicing law, in witnessing in the streets can be summed up by a feeling that to live a life of pacifism was seen as negative, as always saying "no"—"so, why don't you go to live in Russia, you Commies?" "You can't be a Christian anymore, because Christians support their government, love their flag, make military sacrifices, and the Christian churches support their government as part of the world's structures to be honored, as well as the economic system which gives us the most possessions, prosperity, and power in the world—all God's gifts. So are you against God's gifts?"

There was some truth to these challenges. I needed to write down my "yeses." What is the essence of this alternative Christian life in the religious peace movement today? Even before that question, how was it in the beginning when Christians emerged publicly as a radical sect? What did those first Christians look like? What debt did they owe their Israelite forebears? How did they lose their way? How can we recover it and present it as an affirmative, viable alternative to the existing misery of false security, to the way of life of the secular nations, and to the established religious, political, and economic institutions? My journey in the radical pacifist way of life has been accompanied by an increasing awareness that we who espouse this world view have a sacred obligation to attempt to offer positive visions along with our resistance to and rejection of the present world order.

To my joy there was already existing on a grass-roots level such Christian communities worldwide but little known. I discovered early on the writings of Jim Douglass such as *The Non-violent Cross.* Even by the time I undertook the final writing of this book in 1983, Christian base communities in Central and South America were little known, and in this country Doris Day was far more widely recognized than Dorothy Day and the Catholic Worker communities, even in Catholic schools. I had hoped to write a social theology for the religious peace movement. In the end that turned out to be too presumptuous. Instead I have settled for offering a glimpse of my own experiences in radical thinking as part of the movement.

Three events finally set me off on this undertaking. I read Morris West's novel, *Clowns of God,* wherein he describes how very important secret people among the western super-powers plan for survival in the final nuclear holocaust but make no arrangements for the safety of the little ones, the orphans, mentally retarded children who were entirely dispensable and disposable; rationale and reason run amok.

Secondly I watched the film "Becket" for a second time with Peter O'Toole as Henry II and Richard Burton as Becket. The assassination to which the bishop of Canterbury was willing to submit came about because Becket offered his entire allegiance to the King except in matters due God. For Henry that left nothing for the nations. As T. S. Eliot has observed, Becket probably died rightly for the wrong reasons, a martyr nonetheless, willing that through him the church would shed its blood. His wrong reasons may have been that the blood was shed to compete for secular power when the radical alternative way—that to which Becket alluded, God's will—was not found in mimicking the ways of nations.

The Clowns of God focused me upon the time remaining to live such alternative life. The film made me ponder prior attempts by the Christian church to experience such a life. That caused me to investigate the history of the church and the ways of the nations to see what went wrong in that attempt.

The third event was the more personal. My wife, Genie, and I were in a park in Colorado Springs on August 6, 1981, banging a drum, each beat representing another life that was ended at Hiroshima. A woman approached us who later identified herself as a Pentecostal Protestant. She was very friendly and asked why we were doing this. We said we were Christian pacifists and she said she was as well. We talked with her about our commemoration of the Hiroshima bombing and how religious and spiritual people needed to witness to the worldly powers which might result in tribulation, but that Jesus promised that those who endured to the end would be his disciples. (Matthew 10.) She said her pastor had taught her that she would be raptured with all real Christians (1 Thessalonians 4.), that St. Paul had said so, and that Christians would not have to experience tribulation or concern themselves about nuclear war or its consequences, because they all would be whisked away and saved before such events took place. When I mentioned the words of Jesus about witness and tribulation, she said that was "the Devil speaking" and scurried off.

She brought me up 800 years from the time of Becket rather quickly, from Catholic attempts to Protestant visions about religious community and social witness. I needed to collect my own thoughts. I needed to put together my own "yeses." This book is that attempt.

I need to say that if any of the criticism seems harsh, it is not of the people in the secular institutions, nor of the people, priests or pastors, of the religious institutions, but of the fallen structures which we have inherited and in which we live. I consider myself part of the ancient Catholic church, my Mother, and the Catholic Worker movement, as well as the people called Quakers, my brothers and sisters, who received a revelation from God in the 17th century, which has great bearing on all of this, but about which I have put my specific thoughts in another publication, *The Apocalyptic Witness: A Radical Calling for Our Own Time.* (Pendle Hill Publications, Wallingford, Pennsylvania, 1989.)

I have retained sexist language found in modern English translations of the Bible such as "Kingdom of God" (I prefer realm, reign or community) for the sake of historical continuity and not to indicate male preference, and I have attempted to eliminate such language in my own writing.

I want to thank the following who read the manuscript and/or supported it: Philip Berrigan, Liz McAlister, Sondra Cronk, Millard Lind, Stanley Hauerwas, Peter Sprunger-Froese, Art Laffin, Elmer Maas, Bob Smith, Bernard Haviland, Barr Swennerfelt, Paul Hood, Lilith Quilin, Ramsey Clark, Lyn Romano, Dorlan and Donna Bales, Anne Montgomery, Faye Kunce, Douglas Gwyn, Steve Levicoff, and the publishers who were willing to undertake a controversial piece of this magnitude. Thanks are due to Kandace Hawkinson of Harper & Row who could not accept the manuscript but who encouraged me to continue seeking a publisher. Finally, my wife, Genie, deserves much credit for editing the final draft copy, typing the many metamorphoses of the manuscript, and giving me unceasing support and encouragement. It would not have happened but for her. I wrote this book for the American religious peace movement, but especially for all the young ones of that movement, including my youngest son, Christian Francis Durland, who will inherit what we leave of this earth.

The book began as an enlargement of a talk given at Jonah House in the spring of 1979, which later became a monograph for the Center on Law and Pacifism entitled "Kingdom or Holocaust." That was inspired by the writings of Millard Lind,

Adolph Holl, and Jacques Ellul. Philip Berrigan urged enlargement of the monograph for publication and here it is. So it is
dedicated to Phil Berrigan and Liz McAlister, to Jonah House,
to the Catholic Worker Movement and to all the houses and
communities that make up the religious peace movement today.
I take full responsibility for all that I have written.

Bill Durland

The Lamb's Community

Erimias House

Cokedale, Colorado

October 4, 1989

The Feast Day of Francis of Assisi.

INTRODUCTION

THE WAYS OF NATIONS AND THE WAYS OF GOD

SAYING "YES" TO PEACE

With other resisters, I am demonstrating at the Pentagon. I hear the frightened and angry reproaches echoing in my ear: "You're lucky you can do this here! You can't do this in Russia! Why don't you go to your church to pray? Why don't you just go to church? If you say NO to us, ['us' may be the Army, the Air Force, the IRS, the Pentagon, General Electric, or any other defense contractor.] What do you say YES to?"

In that question lies the purpose of this book.

After twenty years of varied experience as an activist, twenty years during which I have wrestled often with that all-important question, I have decided to try to articulate what the YES may be. As long as the United States is my home, I have an obligation to speak out and to act. And speak out I do—with countless others—to witness to the hideous circumstance of impending world holocaust for which my country is uniquely responsible. As a Christian, I have an obligation to speak out and to act in love—love of myself, my children, my friends, my enemies. As a Christian I am accountable before God for my relationships with my sisters and brothers.

1

But what of the fundamental question? What do we say YES to? What are the alternatives to power, possessions, acquisitiveness, domination, the tools of wealth and militarism, growth, artificiality, distortion of community, the establishment and preservation of oppressive institutions?

Why is it so hard to say NO? Why is it even harder to find the answers, the alternatives? What are our YESES?

A few years ago I attended a delightful play presented by the students at my youngest son's grade school. The play was an adaptation of the perennial favorite, *The Wizard of Oz.*[1] The children were prepared for their presentation by their teachers at a school administered and operated by the Religious Society of Friends, the Quaker Society founded by George Fox in the 17th century.

George Fox prepared the way for Quakers when he said, "I lived in the virtue of that life and power that took away the occasion of all wars." When Fox met only conflict from his "occasion" of peace, he wrote in his Journal that "I told them that I lived in the virtue of that life and power that took away the occasion of all wars, and I knew from whence all wars did rise, from the lust according to James' doctrine. . . . Then their rage got up and they said, 'Take him away, gaoler, and cast him into the dungeon among the rogues and felons.' "[2]

Fox wrote further, "All such as pretend Christ Jesus and confess him, and yet run into the use of carnal weapons, wrestling with flesh and blood, throw away the spiritual weapons. . . . It is love that overcomes and not hatred with hatred, nor strife with strife."[3] Fox's words were greeted with hatred and strife. That was their immediate result. But Fox's life contains many instances in which he succeeded in overcoming evil with good, not violence.

The day of the *Wizard of Oz*'s production at my son's Quaker school, however, Fox's words were far from the minds of all of us, children and parents, as we settled down in the dimming lights for the fun that would follow.

"Ding dong, the wicked witch is dead!" the children sing. "We're off to see the Wizard, the wonderful Wizard of Oz."

After encouraging her three newfound friends to follow her and her little dog, Dorothy led the group on its way. The Tin Man wanted a heart; the Scarecrow, a brain. The Lion was cowardly, but Dorothy convinced him he could find courage from the great Wizard. Dorothy simply wanted to go home to Kansas.

After many adventures, they found the Wizard. When asked why they sought the Wizard's help, Dorothy answered, "Because you are strong and I am weak; because you are a great Wizard and I am only a helpless little girl." The Wizard replied, "But you were strong enough to kill the Wicked Witch of the East." Their reputation had preceded them! "That just happened," returned Dorothy, "I could not help it."

The Wizard told Dorothy that she had "no right" to expect his help in getting back to Kansas unless she did something in return. The "something" he wanted was for her to kill another wicked witch. He had her pegged as a successful witch-killer whether she liked it or not. When she claimed she could not kill the Wicked Witch of the West, the Wizard simply replied, "You killed the Wicked Witch of the East and you wear the ruby shoes . . . ." i.e., you've done it before and you've got the weapons.

There followed much lamenting and demurring on the part of Dorothy and her supporters, but in the end they agreed to kill. They agreed to kill because in spite of their apparent shortcomings—little-girlness, cowardliness, heartlessness, and brainlessness—they were all so determined to get what they wanted (and so sure that what they wanted would bring them happiness and wholeness) that they would attempt even another killing to get it!

The story is familiar to all of us. Dorothy narrowly escapes a hideous fate at the hands of the wicked witch and succeeds in melting her away with a bucket of water. Much rejoicing follows. The story—especially in its musical form—is so charming and apparently so innocent that it is completely seductive. Two generations of us grew up on it and we are lovingly handing it down to our children and grandchildren. The teachers and administrators of the very fine Quaker school certainly had no questions about it. This is a school where a well-developed social conscience with Quaker overtones is generally displayed and modeled.

There is much to be learned from this story. I am saddened by the realization that its message can so readily be embraced by little children; and I am sobered by the realization that its true message is lost upon little children and adults alike—until it is too late. When the music is silent and all the fantastic imagery is gone, what's being said is that it's all right to kill an evil-doer for a good purpose. "Wickedness" is not defined, but apparently it is in the hands of a phony Wizard to judge. Courage is one of the attributes for doing the killing, and courage is described in terms of retaliation.

The occasion of this play—refreshing my memory, as it did, about some details from the Oz classic—helped me to focus on the subtle and irresistible power of acculturation. How deeply we become seduced by and involved in the ways of nations— the ways of justified violence—before we attain enough maturity and discrimination to evaluate them for what they are!

Tolstoy wrote that Jesus absolutely denied the possibility of human justice;[4] yet our history, like our Oz story, is rife with concepts of just violence.

Whenever the question of alternatives to violence arises, the answer runs something like this: "I am a colonel in the military and I am a Christian. I go to church every Sunday. I'm doing what is good and right. It's not contrary to the Christian Gospel; my preacher tells me it isn't; I don't feel it is; I work with good people trying to end the threat of evil!" A basic fact of our culture is that when good people have problems, they often attempt to solve them by turning to violence and killing. Wickedness stands in the way of goodness, so goodness takes on the methods of wickedness to overcome wickedness. It is goodness, not evil, that chooses evil and justifies itself in overcoming evil with evil. It must be that way, unless we say that overcoming evil with evil is evil. And that's where our NO comes in. We *are* against overcoming evil with evil. We say NO to violence. We are in favor of overcoming evil with good. That's where the alternatives are. That's what Paul talked about—overcoming evil with good. That's what Jesus talked about in the Sermon on the Mount.[5] That's what George Fox talked about. And yet 2,000 years after Jesus and Paul, as Tolstoy noted, we are still trying to overcome evil with evil.

Resist not the evil-doer with evil, but overcome evil with good. That is our rule. The *Wizard of Oz* play did not demonstrate any new alternatives, but just applied the same old violent ones to a good end. At least, we assume the ends were good. Dorothy got back to Kansas. The Tin Man got a heart. The Scarecrow got a brain. The Lion received courage albeit colored by revenge. Two witches were killed in the process. But they were bad, so that's o.k. We don't know what eventually happened to the valiant four. Well, we do know a little bit about the Lion. He was primed to retaliate. We don't know what life in Kansas was like for Dorothy after her return. Maybe the Tin Man, who was heartless, remained heartless, even with a heart. Maybe a Scarecrow with a brain can come up with more rationalizations for a just war so the world can go on and on in the same old way.

This book is an endeavor to find ways not to go on in the same old way. It is an endeavor to flesh out some of the new—but eternal—ways.

A dentist's chair seems an unlikely place to begin the discussion; but a conversation that once took place in my dentist's office seems to me to contain all the elements of the beginning awareness of the confrontation we are dealing with. You know the scene in the dentist's office. The dentist has his or her hands and tools in your mouth and is asking you questions. How in the world can you answer? You've got to talk fast during the times your mouth is empty. My on-and-off discussion went like this: "What do you do for a living?" asked the dentist. "Well, I'm a teacher and I write. I'm teaching courses at a Quaker study center." "Really. What are you teaching?" "I'm teaching a course called 'The Ways of Nations.'" "Oh, what's that about?" "Well, we're trying to discover alternatives to oppressive structures and systems. Ones that haven't been tried. Perhaps can replace our need for violence, growth, wealth, power, war, and killing." That struck a note—killing—it always does. My dentist said, "Oh, do you talk about abortion?" "Yes, and capital punishment. But it goes deeper than that. It goes to the structures." "Well, I don't know about that. The only chance I get to think about morality is when I watch Phil Donahue. Otherwise nobody discusses it. What do you call what you teach?" "Theological ethics." "Oh, I never heard those words used together. What's it mean?" "We're questioning public morality, institutionally and systematically, from a religious point of view. For example, the legalization of violence. There comes a time when we have to stand up for our conscience and sometimes our conscience is not in accord with the law."

My dentist, who was struggling through all this (after all, her primary duty was to take care of my teeth) started to see the light. "You mean there can be a conflict between law and morality? You know, I think you're right! Sometimes our morality should not be determined by what law says."

"That's right. That's what we're trying to get to."

At this point, my dentist said she'd like to talk more but she put a tube in my mouth, the drill started up and we haven't talked about it again. But I've given much thought to it since then.

If we continue to say NO to the systems of power represented by military bases, corporate giants, government agencies, and "religious" institutions, if we continue to criticize their wealth, their militarism, their violence, we must also be able to envision alternatives, or we are not being fair to them or to ourselves. It is not even possible to protect our children if we cannot come up with another way. If we continually criticize people who are convinced that theirs is the only way, we must offer a powerfully salvific alternative; or we can do nothing for them or ourselves.

THE WAYS OF NATIONS

But why another way if the Wizard's way is so successful and effective? After all, the Wizard got what he wanted, the end of the wicked witches. And Dorothy and her companions got what they wanted. War and violence always seem to succeed—initially. But they are a quick fix. When I first began putting down some notes for this book six or seven years ago, it was Veterans Day (formerly Armistice Day, made a holiday in 1938 to commemorate the end of World War I at the eleventh hour of the eleventh day of the eleventh month in 1918). Could we be in the eleventh hour of the eleventh day of the world's lifetime? Looking us in the face is not an armistice or a celebration of veterans, but a potential nuclear firestorm and the destruction of all people. All those quick fixes, all those wars, all that violence have brought us to a point facing nuclear holocaust and annihilation of the planet. World War I was proclaimed the war to end all wars. But it was not and did not. Many wars have come and gone since then, all relying on lethal weapons which do not bring peace.

There is another way than this way of death. It is the way of life, the way of God; and there is a great difference between these two ways, and the way of God must now, in the face of nuclear peril, surely be practiced and lived. This difference must be discovered and understood. If only we can understand it, maybe we can work through it in our lives. Some secular philosophers have told us that the way of life is *through* the way of death. They say that if we only hold the right motivation and keep in our hearts the proper ends—peace, love, and happiness—then the manner or means by which we get from our motive to our end either does not matter, or can simply be characterized as just, even if violent and warlike. In other words, they say ends justify means.

For thousands of years we have tried the means of death, the means of lethal weapons, the means of destruction, the means of hell as a bridge between our good motivations and our good ends; and these means have utterly failed. They have been completely unrealistic and immensely irresponsible.

Under such circumstances it should not be too difficult to find other coattails to grab. The ones we have been hanging onto, whether Assyrian coattails, Roman coattails, American coattails, or Russian coattails, have not taken us very far. Over 2000 years ago Jesus and a small band of his followers, both men and women, decided to follow another way. They sought another power. Jesus proclaimed that power spiritual, and taught that it would undergird an alternative structure, another way, the way of God's Kingdom. Others who followed have called it Christian church. It too lost its original "way," but that is getting ahead of our story.

The *Didache* or "The Teaching of the Twelve Apostles" is thought to be the earliest handbook of Christian rules enunciating the way of living that Jesus and his followers undertook. It begins:

> There are two Ways, one of Life and one of Death, and between the two Ways there is a great difference. The Way of Life is this: "First thou shalt love the God who made thee, secondly, thy neighbor as thyself. . . . " The teaching of these words is this: "Bless those that curse you" and "pray for your enemies," and "fast for those who persecute you." For "what credit is it to you if you love those who love you; do not even the heathens do the same?" But for your part, "love those that hate you," and you will have no enemy.[6]

Christianity was originally called "The Way." But there was a long and rich tradition antedating this early Christian writing that informed the teaching of the twelve Apostles.

The Book of Jeremiah, from which this subtitle comes, says:

> Hear the word which the Lord speaks to you, O house of Israel. Thus says the Lord: "Learn not the way of nations, nor be dismayed at the signs of the heavens because the nations are dismayed at them, for the customs of the people are false. A tree from the forest is cut down and worked with an axe by the hands of a craftsman." Their idols are like scarecrows in a cucumber field, and they cannot speak; they have to be carried, for they cannot walk. Be not afraid

of them, for they cannot do evil, neither is it in them to do good."[7]

Jeremiah said to learn not the way of nations, the way of death, but rather to practice the way of life. From Jeremiah's time, 600 years before Jesus, until the time of the *Didache*, 100 years after Christ, the same message held true. Israelites and Christians alike were warned to beware of the nation idol.

What was the idol like? It could not speak or walk; it was inanimate and controlled by its creators under the compulsions of custom, culture, and political "reality." But the idol did have a human effect, which is apparent from the warnings and the rules of the *Didache*. It threatened enemies and neighbors, if not friends.

This was, and is, the way of nations—idolic death. The nation was and still is made secure through playing on hatred—Iran's of the United States, North America's of "godless communism," Nicaraguan school children learning to hate North Americans, Israeli hatred of Arabs and vice versa—a never-ending cycle fostered by the customs and traditions surrounding the nation-idol. It is an easy trip from the fantasy of a wizard nation to the nation ruled by president or presidium. The only difference is that the wizard's power is clearly shown to be illusory and his magic is dismantled. The fantasy and magic of our current nation-states have not been dismantled; the illusion has not been exposed—or has it? Nation-states are false idols. In truth we know this to be true; our Scriptural tradition and the life of Jesus make it clear. The illusion *has* been exposed. It remains for Christians to live in that truth.

Nations rely on inanimate weapons of war which have grossly horrible effects on the animate world. They are the price of security, we are assured, and yet today no one is secure. The idiocy of worshiping weapons is obvious. They cannot even fulfill their own purpose. Like the nation-states who build them, weapons too are false idols and they lead only to death.

THE WAYS OF GOD

Through the ages of history we have been called to a way of life that requires us to give up the false security offered by the nation-state and to take on the true freedom offered by loving God and neighbor and even enemy. We cannot love our enemies and kill them at the same time. We cannot love our enemies and even *plan* to kill, or *pay* for killing them, even if a worldly political situation seems to demand it. We cannot even threaten to kill by macho deterrence — the male ego universally run rampant—and expect that violence will not return tenfold.

So a choice must be made. We must recognize the conflict, reject this culture, commit ourselves to a new community—or rather, to an old one—to The Way.

What does this new community look like, shorn of the trappings of secular power, popularity, and possessions? We have a blueprint, and it is the holy nation described by Israelites and Christians alike, both of whom risked experimenting with it.

The story has it that after Moses disobeyed God in the wilderness, the Lord made a conditional covenant with him and his people, saying: "Now therefore, if you will obey my voice and keep my covenant, you shall be my own possession among all peoples; for all the earth is mine, and you shall be to me a kingdom of priests and a holy nation."(Exodus 19:5-6.) Peter echoes this: "You are a chosen race, a royal priesthood, a holy nation, God's own people. . . . " (1 Peter 2:9.)

God's people, the Israelites, sought to follow this calling to be a holy nation, a people set apart, living a holistic existence. But the world got in the way, as it might for any of us. The evil one, the powers and principalities of false idols, and human structures foiled them. They lusted after being like the other nations, they wanted what they could not have (James 4:2.) rather than being a light to the other nations—a task to which they were uniquely called.

Once the Israelites used violence to realize their ends, shortly after Moses' disobedience,[8] it was only a matter of time before violence was returned in kind. Those whom they opposed secured themselves from retaliation in war by means of kingship. The Israelites already had their King, but they became dissatisfied with an invisible God as King. The elders of Israel told the prophet Samuel of their desire to be "like the nations" and to have a "king to govern them." Samuel warned them of the ways of the king, but they took no heed. Forsaking their Divine King for another, they also forsook, step by step, their oneness with Yahweh, which was their wholeness, their Shalom. And God allowed it.

Their political house was in place in the figure of King David. (1 Samuel 8.) But David felt embarrassed. God lived in a tent and he, David, in a fine house of cedar, a palace. God should be treated better. So David approached Nathan, the prophet, with a grand idea. He would make God equal to himself, at least in accommodations. God would have a fine house, a Temple. But God would have none of it.

"Would you build me a house to dwell in? Did I speak a word saying 'Why have you not built me a house of cedar?' " God remained in control and promised that it would be God's son who would build a house which would be a kingdom forever. Nevertheless the Temple was completed. (Cf. 2 Samuel 7:4-11; Acts 7:44-50.)

Having secured themselves with political power and religious institutionalism coalescing side by side in Jerusalem, the Israelites could not heed the calls of Jeremiah and Hosea to move away from the city and back to the wilderness. The wilderness symbolized a return to economic simplicity—all that the city was not. (Jeremiah 2; Hosea 6.) God and mammon are in no greater conflict than in the urban milieu of technology and commerce—then, as today.

The political machinations of our own nation-state depend upon and cannot exist without economic and religious support. Those in power among the Israelites succumbed to the temptations of the surrounding culture and led the people to be less than the community of God.

But God did not forsake the people. God sent, as promised, a son who fought the same temptations of political, economic, and religious institutional power in the wilderness and emerged whole to found a new community dedicated to resisting the powers and principalities once again: a resistance grounded in living simply and loving neighbor and enemy alike.

Jesus, like David, was legally disobedient in the grainfields (Matthew 12.) and broke the Sabbath law when, if he had waited only a few hours, he could have healed infirm persons without legal incident. Life in the holy nation elicits suppression by the fearful nation-state and so creates witnesses, martyrs, arrestees, convicts, jailbirds.

THE CHRISTIAN FALL

The holy nation was once again alive in "The Way." And once again it fell. The Christians eventually "needed" Roman emperors to protect Christian possessions, and the simplicity and the pacifism of the earliest Christians were co-opted by the Roman empire. The lamb led to slaughter became the lion which devoured the world, and God's chosen, in the process. In their suffering as victims of Christian persecution, Jewish communities became whole again. They became a nation apart without secular king, land, or temple, and without Jerusalem— once the seat of this trinity of power. They had, instead, God's steadfast Spirit, only to be undone by the merciless mass violence of Christians turned Nazi. (The base, satanic root of "nazism"—the nation-state over all—far antedates Hitler, who was merely the reductio ad absurdum of all emperors, rulers, statists.) Nazism remains in all of us, Christians and Jews as well, when we violently confront our enemies.

Christendom, in its chosen, violent power, took its turn at apostasy and continues to do so. Such a contradiction cannot possibly incarnate the holy nation. Throughout its history, church has vied with state for secular control of the known world. A misguided, saintly Thomas Becket, seeking secular power, threatened Henry II's lust for the spiritual submission of God's priest. With the Reformation and Renaissance, the so-called Enlightenment placed absolute power in the hands of

the state, and the great experiment of Roman Catholic theocracy
failed for want of its roots. The social contractarians gave the
world a design for church-state relations that has dominated
political thought since the time of Hobbes. Now churches exist
in dictatorships and democracies only at the will of king, president, or presidium; for their original or authentic teachings
always threaten the basic structure of any state. Living a simple
life and loving enemies does not support either a growth capitalist economy dependent upon increased profit and exploitation of people and resources, or a state communist economy
wedded to materialism. The Hebrew Scriptures and Paul's writings teach us that if our enemies are hungry we must feed them.
(Romans 12:14-21; Isaiah 58:6-7.) Conversely, political rhetoric
insists that even if our enemies are hungry, we must bomb
them.

The ways by which people can live are two: one is the way
of life and is found in the teachings and lives of the Israelite
prophets and of Jesus and his followers. It is a way of religious
community embracing pacifism and simplicity, embracing resistance to the powers and principalities, embracing forms of
civil disobedience. It is an alternative community with hospitality and assistance even for "enemies." These principles of
the holy nation cannot be tolerated by any nation-state. Hitler,
Stalin and most U.S. presidents have equally feared the pacifist.
Reagan's "peace through strength" was not the peace of the
Scriptures.

Ultimately, the way of the holy nation will triumph over the
sad and insecure second way, the way of the sovereign nation-
state, the idol nation. For we are beginning to learn that killing
enemies kills ourselves, our community and our culture as well.
Gandhi's vision may indeed succeed in the end—Jews, Moslems,
and Christians will love each other, perhaps sooner than we
dare hope. Irish and English will lay down their weapons of
war, and the U.S. and U.S.S.R. will find themselves together in
a redeemed world no longer in need of super powers, but living
in the warmth of the way of the holy nation of God. But none
can find the way as Jew or Moslem or Christian, as Irish or

English, or North American or Russian. We will find the way
only as one people of God.

THE HOLY NATION

Our endeavor, then, will be to recover in detail the way of life,
the way of the holy nation, which can be the only genuine
alternative to existing secular institutions. To do this, we must
examine those institutions and communities that have attempted this before us to see what we can learn from them.
We will begin with Yahweh and the people of God, the first
nation of holy people, and see what happened to them. We will
look at Jesus and his Kingdom, proclaimed in the manner in
which Jesus and his followers lived during his lifetime and in
the early days of Christianity. We will examine the dissolution
of Christianity into Christendom (the marriage with the empire),
the events that transpired, and the meaning of those events
then and today.

Emerging from this empire and Christendom are the church
and the state, very much like each other, both infected with
idols and political agendas and competing with each other for
the worshipers of the idols. We will examine the nature of the
secular nation governed by the social contract of the Enlightenment philosophers and what that means for us and for the
world as it is. Finally, we will look at how we have been seduced
into living in sin, the sin of modern idolatry, civil religion. We
will see that we are born into it, so that we accept as normative
all those ingredients that make up the national and religious
institutions which have brought us to the present brink. Can
we fully grasp the reality of what it means to live in the land
of Oz, and to justify it at the military bastions? If we resolve to
find alternatives, we must confront that most basic question:
how do we live in the community of God while in the midst of
the world of nations?

We will look at radical religious pacifism and begin to define
the characteristics of community, the attributes of pacifism leading to resistance, simplicity leading to hospitality and service,

an alternative worship and religious community leading to a holistic, new model of life. Having formulated some guidelines for this life, we will ask ourselves: What then are the rights and duties of Christians living in secular society? What are the duties of Christians toward those whose lives are committed to the secular world and who yet are oppressed by that secular commitment? What is the Christian's responsibility in the nation-state toward the protection of human life on earth? If we accept an alternative for ourselves, what then is our relationship, not only to each other inside the community, but to the world and to those who are oppressed and suffering in the world?

We begin by explaining what we mean by "nation" since it is at the very heart of our critique and of our alternative model.

One need only pick up a Biblical concordance to find that the word "nation" is used in the Bible with great frequency from beginning to end. Its first use is in Genesis 10:5, a reference to the gentiles and "their nations." Its last use is in Revelation 22:2, again concerning the gentiles and "the healing of the nations." The healing of the nations is the message of this new radical community. The people of God saw their call to be separate from the people around them and in doing so they organized themselves in complete separation. Every time they came into contact with that from which they separated, they were corrupted, worshiping the idols of the secular nations. But the healing of the nations calls us to live within the midst of the nations without being corrupted by them. The meaning of "the nations" is central to our understanding of alternative community.

In the Book of Revelation, the reference to the nations necessarily includes both the religious and political nation.[9] Both have gone awry since God first talked to Abram and used the term in a religious-spiritual sense. God said, "Go from your country and your kindred and your father's house to the land that I will show you. And I will make of you a great nation. . . ." (Genesis 12:1.) That nation was not like a modern nation, divested or deprived of its religious sense, but a holistic nation, having political and economic aspects integrated with the religious. That nation, as the future promise of God to Abraham, came in an unconditional covenant (Genesis 15.) and is described in Exodus 19:6 as a holy nation, a holistic organization. The idea of a holy nation continues through the whole history of the Israelites, into the Judaism of the time of Jesus, and on into the Christianity of the first followers of Christ. It is referred to again in the First Epistle of Peter: "a holy nation, a chosen race, a royal priesthood," (1 Peter 2:9.) God's own people.

Our modern understanding of the concept "nation" is, however, heavily political. When we talk about a nation, we talk about an entity with geographical boundaries, with a politically organized government, with a leader such as a king or president, with courts enforcing compulsive directives. It is usually an entity having a military organization, a police force, and when there's enough money left over in the nation's budget, some social-service agencies. But the use of the word "nation" in the Hebrew Scriptures translates in the Greek to *ethnos*. Our English word "ethnic" is derived from this Greek. When we use the word ethnic, we think more in terms of the cultural and sociological aspects of a group or community. Actually the Greek word *ethnos* and the Hebrew equivalent is best translated "people." (The Hebrew word for nation is *goi*, and for people *cam*.)

The Theological Dictionary of the New Testament states: "There is no emphasis on the particular marks or bases of fellowship or relationship, on political or cultural connections,"[10] as in other Hebrew words such as tribe. (Cf. Genesis 10:31.) Over time the words, "the people" or the "nation" came to describe exclusively the holy people of God, the Israelites, and the plural of that "people" or "nations" became the technical term for the *other* nations, the gentiles. The Greek word which denotes political community is rarely found in the Hebrew Scriptures. So "nation" has a more cultural, holistic meaning than that which we are accustomed to in modern usage. It means a holy people, a people of God. *The rise of the other, that is, secular, "nations" is attributed to human sin in Genesis 11.* These nations come to play a significant role in the prophets' view of history. Hosea sees the nations as instruments of the wrath of God toward the holy nation of Israel which has gone astray and mimics the other nations. (Hosea 10:10.) Israel falls victim to God's wrath " . . . because they do not discharge their mission as a divine task. . . . "[11] But the God of Israel is nonetheless the Lord of all the nations, an important point to remember.

In Matthew 6:7, Jesus enjoins his listeners not to pray as the *ethnoi* (nations) do and contrasts the Jews and the gentiles in this way. As a member of the people of God, no true Jew belongs to the *cosmos* (world). (Luke 12:30.) It is these nations, the gentiles, that are conformed to this world. (Revelation 8:3.) By the time of the Fourth Gospel, we find that *ethnos* is not used exclusively for the gentiles but is used by John for the ruling class of Jews whom he thus equates with the *cosmos*, the evil world. Matthew 5:43 sets the *ethnicoi* in opposition to those who fulfill the law. No wonder Jeremiah has already prophesied that the word of the Lord says, "learn not the way of the nations."

The way of death in the *Didache* is the way of the nations in Jeremiah, the way of an empty idol. But why is it an idol? The Israelites saw themselves set apart from the nations (Numbers 23:9.); but they eventually chose to have a king and to be governed like all the nations (I Samuel 8:5.), making them untrue to their obligation to be a light to the nations. As their light goes out, their idols become silver and gold. (Psalm 135:15.)

It is to these nations that Jesus is born, and he finds both the once holy nation of Israel and the secular nations much alike. All nations, including Israel, are conformed to the world; all are following the idols of silver and gold. So he tells the chief priests and the elders who come up to him to hear his teaching: "the kingdom of God will be taken way from you and given to a nation producing the fruits of it." (Matthew 21:43.) One of those fruits is tribulation, for he prophesies: "they will deliver you up to tribulation, and put you to death; and you will be hated by all nations for my name's sake." (Matthew 24:9.)

As we look around the world today, it is difficult to find Christians who are not conformed to the world, who are hated by the nations for Jesus' sake, and who are suffering tribulation. Rather we find Christians behaving as some Israelites before their fall—idolaters conformed to the world and living in the midst of gold and silver while the world's poor become poorer. Yet Jesus promised power over the nations (Revelation 2:26.), and that through his followers the nations shall be healed. (Revelation 22.)

We will pursue three themes: One. How did the people of God, and later the community of Jesus, live together? That is, what was their community like? Two. What was the community's relationship to its society? How did it serve society in general? Three. How did the community relate to the powers in the time of Israel, to the other governments and nations through history, and in our own time to our own nation, to our own government?

In order to trace these three themes we will look at the manner in which Israelites and Christians lived in community and the manner in which today we live or fail to live in community. We will compare the way we live today in abundance with the call to the Israelites and Christians to live in simplicity; and we will ask from that perspective what the ramifications are for service to the world. We will examine these early communities to see how they dealt with confrontation and hostility and domination from the nations. In what ways did they use violence or refrain from its use? In what ways were they nonviolent and pacifist? These will be our guiding questions and themes as we search for a model, an alternative to the existing nation-state.

A BIBLICAL METHODOLOGY

Before we move on, however, we should say something about our use of the Hebrew and Christian Scriptures as the guide for determining the manner in which we live today. The basis for the view I will present is derived from my conception of the manner in which Jesus lived. There have been many perceptions of the historical Jesus. At one extreme, Brandon saw Jesus as a political savior, using all the tools of political power and violence. At the other extreme, Harnack saw Jesus as a person who emphasized the spiritual growth of the individual. Between Harnack and Brandon lie many images of Jesus.[12] How are we to determine what image of Jesus is more complete, more truthful? Obviously there is some truth in the image of Brandon, as well as in the image of Harnack. I will not undertake to provide a complete exegesis on each pericope which supports my Biblical thesis. That has been done elsewhere and I base my theological method on no particular passages or proof-texts, although texts are individually important. Taking the example of Jesus in particular, I look at his entire life as recorded in the Bible and other writings and I find a person who killed no one, but was himself killed by his enemies. More than anything else, Jesus was a person who lived what he taught. Theology must reach beyond scriptural statements and endeavor to reveal the essence of Jesus Christ himself.[13]

I look to what the exegetes call the *Sitz im Leben* of the text; that is, the setting in which the events took place in both the Christian and the Hebrew Scriptures. I move from a base of the plain meaning of the language, that is, its literal meaning, informed by the *Sitz im Leben*, which then determines whether the meaning of the words should be viewed as literal or amplified in a spiritual or allegorical or historical sense. I consider the possibilities of mistakes, the impact of myth or interpolation, and contradictions.

All theologians, whether they admit it or not, "pick and choose" what, for them, are the foremost priorities, the most authentic passages, and advance their choices as "objective." I act no differently, except that I make no claim to objectivity. I do ask that my methodology be understood, examined, and given some dignity. More than anything else, our own life informs us of what the Biblical words mean for us today. For example, I was once a militarist and now I am a pacifist.[14] I experienced a transformation that reordered my life to be more in conformity with the life of Jesus as I now understand it. It is my present experience, rather than any rational, theological method that forms in my gut a sense about the early Israelites and about Jesus that seems to hold true. This sense seems to

me to expose the cultural sin of our religious and political
institutions today and their own propagandizing of a distorted
life of Jesus which conforms to cultural morality.

It is not so much rational investigation but existential experience that opens us up to the truth of Scripture. To take to
the streets, to experience a form of suffering, to be arrested
and imprisoned, to be abused completes the necessary rational
base of theological methodology. Without experiencing what
the early Israelites and the Jesus-community experienced, i.e.,
imprisonment, suffering, alienation, our search for truth about
the historical Jesus is incomplete. Ironically, our search lacks
objectivity because it lacks subjectivity. Without a measure of
struggle and commitment, the process toward faith cannot be
complete. Suffering is a part of theological method.[15] Suffering
must be felt in the bones of those who attempt to tell us what
Jesus is about.

The traditional exegete places very strict rational and analytical demands upon herself or himself in the process of search-
ing for historical certainty. This is to be admired and supported.
However, there are other sources of truth which the religious
person experiences apart from rational and analytical methodology. These sources are revelation, inspiration, experience,
experiment; these are by nature difficult to establish or prove
by rational evidence.

Hence there is tension between the rational and the extra-
rational means of arriving at Biblical truth. Both have their
limitations from an objective standpoint. Objective methodology is not necessarily objective. Jose Comblin expresses well
the limitations of the academy:

> Academic theology believes that returning to the origins
> of Christianity—in other words, to the original documents
> of the church, as they are explicated by the historical
> method—is the only true road to the truth about God,
> Christ, and Christianity. . . . Academic teachers regard
> themselves as completely objective, as absolutely impartial
> conveyors of the universal principles and values of human

reason. They do not allow opinions, prestige, interests, emotive reasons, or prejudices to guide them. For them the university is the temple of criticism where the disciplines of the historical science are discovering the universal truth. . . . Far from all prejudices deriving from contact with practice, university theologians often believe that they are the only persons possibly able to distinguish truth about Christianity.[16]

But Comblin further points out:

"Sharing in action is a necessary pre-condition to discovering the reality of anything. . . . The new theologians think that only an active presence in the mission of the church can give an individual access to the privileged room from which it is possible to understand the reality of the gospel today. Consequently, they think that a mere academic theology cannot focus on Christianity. Such a theology will constantly make comments on the peripheral particulars, the outer shell of Christianity, but it will not convey the deepest meaning of Jesus' revelation."[17]

It is this sharing of action that connects us over the years with the Israelites and the early Christians. Without that connection "the absolute objectivity of the historical method is a myth."[18] Only with that relationship "is it possible to reach a suitable position for grasping the reality of the gospel."[19] This connection is achieved by those who practice street theology and experience the consequences Jesus predicted in doing so. For example, those who write about the model of an alternative community, must have in some sense already experienced it in part or in redemptive moments. It cannot be experienced by deduction or analysis. A head trip is no trip.

We cannot leave to scholars and theologians alone the determination of what Jesus's community actually was like. John Howard Yoder expresses a similar viewpoint. Jesus is the norm to be discovered by common folk like those with whom he lived.

"The Scripture scholars in their hermeneutic meditations develop vast systems of crypto-systematics, and the field of ethics remains as it was; or, if anything new happens there, it is usually fed from some other sources."[20] "It is safer for the life of the church to have the whole people of God reading the whole body of canonical Scripture than to trust for her enlightenment only to certain of the filtering processes through which the learned men of a given age would insist all the truth must pass."[21] This book, then, draws from both these sources of truth. The author has experience in both areas discussed—the so-called rational, and the experimental or experiential. I have lived in community, experiencing attempts at community and at alternative service and witness to the powers and principalities—the speaking of truth to power. My living in such community settings provides the basis and the daring for the writing of this book. All such experiments are incomplete and imperfect. But they create in one the ability to imagine the unimaginable[22]—something we miss living in this secular culture.

CHAPTER ONE

YAHWEH AND THE PEOPLE OF GOD

ABRAHAM AND NON-VIOLENCE

The key that allows us to enter an alternative life of community, witness, and service is the rejection of violence as a means to any end in life.

My own experiments and struggles with imagining and building alternatives have been deeply influenced by what I learned from the Biblical story. The spiritual journey of the ancient Israelites, chronicled so passionately in the Hebrew Scriptures, is inseparable from Israel's cultural journey. Political, military, economic, and religious history recounted there is unique because it is subject to a particular relationship with God.

In this chapter I review the history of the Israelites emphasizing how it has informed my images of alternatives. The relevance of such an endeavor is twofold: One, is that Biblical history—the stories of the ancient Israelites and of the community of the earliest church—*is* a history of alternatives. If it is nothing else, it is the story of succeeding groups of inspired people attempting to live in the world according to their revealed vision of an alternative to the world. Two, the key to the essence and meaning of the alternative lies in a life of

Biblical love and justice through nonviolence. Release from cultural imprisonment begins here.

Originally God is seen as Israel's warrior, allowing God's people to stand still and be rescued by God (Exodus 14:14). They lift no arms, they fight no battles, they do no violence. It is this Exodus experience of trusting in the Lord without violence that is the hallmark of the ancient Israelite nation. But while remembering this miracle, Israel forgot its meaning in practice: after the Exodus, Israel fights and God stands still. But from the beginning it was not so.

In Genesis 1:26-31, the people have been given no violent dominion over their brothers and sisters. They are all made in God's image. People have dominion over the fish of the sea, and the birds of the air, and over cattle, and all the earth, and every creeping thing. They are asked to be fruitful and multiply, not to kill and divide; not to conquer and destroy, but to fill the earth and subdue it. They have been given every plant yielding seed and every tree with seed in its fruit; but nowhere are they given authority over their brothers and sisters, for that is reserved to God. Psalm 8:5-8: "You have made human beings little less than God and have crowned them with glory and honor. You have given them dominion over the works of Your hand. You have put all things under their feet, all sheep and oxen, and also the beasts of the field, the birds of the air, and the fish of the sea." But nowhere does God give human beings authority over other human beings so they might dominate or destroy each other. There was no institution for vengeance, no "an eye for an eye." Stewardship, not vengeance, was God's alternative for all human relationships.

In Genesis, however, Cain does exercise domination over Abel and kills him. According to our cultural norms, one would think that God would punish Cain, an eye for an eye, a tooth for a tooth, violence for violence! But God forbears in this and banishes Cain for his use of violence. God protects him with the mark of Cain, even though God would have been "justified" in killing him. If anyone would slay Cain, it was for God to avenge. (Genesis 4:15.)

Genesis 6:11 reports that the earth was thereafter filled with violence requiring "vengeance" from Yahweh. God's vengeance here is not described as violence. According to Mendenhall, "vengeance" in this context is what the ancient Romans called *imperium*. *Imperium*, or sovereignty in English, is the Lord's. This means that God reigns over all power, including economic, political, and religious power. Genesis 9:6, which says "Whoever sheds the blood of man, by man shall his blood be shed; for God made man in his own image," is not to be understood as a command of God. This is the same as Jesus saying in Matthew 26:52, "All who take the sword will perish by the sword." These are not commands of God, but descriptions of the cycle of violence.

The nonviolence of Abraham and Sarah is amply demonstrated at the beginning of the patriarchal period. As John says in his Epistle (1 John 3:11.), it was not so from the beginning: violence did not reign at first. Many examples of peaceful relationships between Abraham and his flocks and the people round about are reported in Genesis such as the nonviolent distribution of land and the refusal of spoils. (Genesis 13:2-12, 21:22-34, 26:17 ff.) Although there is a break in the pacifistic practices of the patriarchs when Abraham routs the kings in order to deliver Lot (Genesis 14), Millard Lind contends that this rout is prior to the covenant and therefore not related to the loyalty due Yahweh after the covenant.[1] Nowhere does the covenant require violence on the part of Yahweh's servants. The covenant is a relationship between God and those people who know God. In its earliest forms the covenant is unilateral, initiated by God, and requires no response from the people. Violence is outside the covenantal relationship. Some believe that the story of Lot was inserted for no reason other than to indicate the power of God over pagan works.[2] In any case, Abraham's victory is not incredible, if it is understood "as nocturnal harassing activity by less encumbered men on the rear guard. The armies would have gladly relinquished a few prisoners and some loot to escape the annoyance."[3]

In Genesis 15, the unconditional covenant of God is announced to Abraham with the words, "Fear not, Abraham, I am your Shield." There is no obligation under this covenant, as there was in other ancient, Near Eastern covenants, for Abraham to fight for his benefactor. The covenant is an unconditional and unilateral promise of land given to Abraham as a gift after his call by God in Genesis 12 and 17.

The land is given in stewardship or trusteeship, not for ownership. This is an important point. Stewardship lessens the tendency to defend violently what one does not personally own, but what rather belongs to God. For example, we see a dispute over a well resolved nonviolently and the well is shared because "the Lord has made room." (Genesis 26:22).

Other rare examples of violence in Genesis are given as exceptions, again out of the covenant: when Simeon and Levi, Jacob's sons, avenge the rape of Dinah their sister. (Genesis 34:18 ff.) Later Jacob condemns his sons: "Weapons of violence are their swords." (Genesis 49). For the most part, the Genesis and patriarchal traditions are nonviolent, most unlike the surrounding ancient, Near Eastern war structures, the pagan war structures of the Greek world, and the secular-world systems which follow. The general tone is one in which violence *is not* taken for granted as an acceptable method of problem resolution. Violence is seen, rather, as a problem in itself which must be resolved.

MOSES AND VIOLENCE

The Book of Exodus begins with the killing of an Egyptian by Moses. This killing appeared to be justified but was not considered so by Moses' own people. The killing was condemned and Moses was required to flee. It was a long time before Moses regained his lost stature. By the time the actual Exodus from Egypt began, Moses had called upon the Israelites to "Fear not, stand firm, and see the salvation of the Lord which he will work for you today; for the Egyptians whom you see today, you shall never see again. The Lord will fight for you and you have only

to be still." (Exodus 14:13-14.) The Israelites trust in Yahweh
as their only warrior and only king. The Song of Miriam (Exodus
5:19-21.) describes how the Lord fought for Israel and won.
But by the time of Exodus 17:8, Israel had fought with the
Amalekites as Moses and Joshua chose men to go out and do
the fighting, with the rod of God in Moses' hands, but also with
the troops of Moses in the field. It is important to note that
immediately after this first use of violence by the Israelites to
gain what was given to them as an unconditional gift, the unconditional, unilateral covenant comes to an end. A conditional,
bilateral covenant takes its place. The condition is that the
Israelites obey the voice of God and keep God's covenant. In
return, they shall be God's possession, chosen from among all
the peoples. The covenant must be based on faith, trust, and
obedience; only then shall they be a realm at peace, a holy
nation.

What caused this change from unconditional to conditional
covenant? Prior to the move from the Wilderness of Sin to the
encampment at Rephidim, the history of the Israelites from the
patriarchs back to "Adam and Eve" had been essentially nonviolent and pacifistic. But an event took place at Rephidim,
before the attack on the Amalekites, in which the people found
fault with God, apparently necessitating the change in the covenant relationship from unconditional to conditional. (Exodus
17:1-17.)

The problem was this. Where they camped there was no water
for the people to drink. The people begged for water and found
fault with Moses. Moses asked them why they found fault with
him: "Why do you put the Lord to the proof?" So the people
began to murmur against Moses and asked him why he brought
them out of Egypt only to allow them to die of thirst. Moses,
angry, cried out, "What shall I do with this people? They are
almost ready to stone me." And the Lord, nearby, said to Moses,
"Pass on before the people taking with you some of the elders
of Israel and take in your hand the rod with which you struck
the Nile and go. Behold I will stand before you there on the
rock at Horeb and you will strike the rock and water shall come

out of it that the people may drink." This is what Moses did, in the sight of the elders of Israel, according to the Exodus report. He called the place Meribah because of the fault-finding of the people.

This report does not seem to depict an event severe enough to destroy an unconditional covenant. But a comparison with a report in Numbers of the same event (Numbers 20:1-13.) indicates that the problem was not only between Moses and the recalcitrant people of Israel, but a problem between God and Moses as well. There it is reported that as Moses and Aaron gathered the assembly together before the rock, Moses said, "Hear now, you rebels, shall we bring forth water for you out of this rock?" And Moses lifted up his hand and struck the rock twice and abundant water came forth and the congregation and their animals drank. The Lord was not happy about this. It is reported that God said to Moses and Aaron, "Before you did not believe in me to sanctify me in the eyes of the people of Israel; therefore you shall not bring this assembly into the land which I have given them."

God's specific instructions were: "Take the rod and assemble the congregation, you and Aaron your brother, and *tell* the rock before their eyes to yield its water." (Numbers 20:8.) In Exodus 17:6, Moses was commanded to *strike* the rock. In Numbers he was commanded to *speak* to the rock; no physical power was involved, only spiritual power. But Moses struck the rock in anger, and he did it twice. There was a note of "carnal self-importance and pride" in his inquiry, and he was punished for his "unbelief and disobedience."[4] Instead of a joyous event it became a sad one. Something broke down; some of the spirit was lost.

It is important to note that this first, concerted, warlike action of the Israelites took place in the defeat of the Amalekites (Exodus 17:8.) shortly after the Meribah event. Moses said to Joshua, "Choose for us men and go out, fight with the Amalekites; tomorrow I will stand at the top of the hill with the rod of God in my hand." This also is the first mention of the warlike Joshua. (The Amalekites were nomads of the Sinai peninsula and the Negev. They resisted the Israelites as intruders. In fact, they were distant cousins, coming from Esau's branch, or the tribe of Edom.) Moses apparently angered God by not following God's instructions and by playing a greater role than he was delegated to play. Organized and legitimized institutional violence began here, in this story. Violence crept into the covenant, and the covenant became conditional. Interestingly, all violence becomes conditional, even in the so-called just-war theories of today. If Moses had strictly followed God's commands, would his entry into the land promised to Abraham have been accomplished nonviolently? We know from the reports in Genesis that Abraham was able to infiltrate the land many years earlier in a nonviolent manner. Violence begins in our hearts, spreads to our social relationships, and eventually makes us depend upon its happening for our security. The weapons of war become the instruments of our violence through history. I am convinced that the purpose of these ancient stories in the Hebrew, and eventually the Christian, traditions is to chart the progression of human history from a gift of covenantal trust to a violent control of historical events. The stories are present in the tradition to illustrate the use of violence by human beings as usurpation of God's historical prerogative.

Taking on the violence of the nations around them, the Israelites lost a bit of that holy nation that was Abraham's and was to be theirs. (Exodus 19.) It was many years after they became accustomed to the need for violent armies before they took another step toward becoming like the secular, pagan nations. The history as reported in Exodus shows that God's commandment not to kill became qualified, no longer absolute, no longer unconditional. The amended laws of the covenant list numerous death penalties. (Cf. Exodus 21-26.) In Exodus 33:16, the Lord is no longer fighting *for* Israel alone, but *with* Israel, though it is believed that the weapons of the Israelites are inefficacious without the Lord's help. (Cf. Psalm 44.)

DAVID AND THE MONARCHY

In Joshua 6, Jericho falls when the only necessity for fighting is the "mopping up." In Joshua 7, Israel fights without God at

Ai and loses. The concept of *herem*, a type of sacrifice to God, emerges and holy-war motifs appear. Even though God's gift of land was unconditional, the Israelites seem compelled to pay for the land. Was this because they recognized their guilt for which the sacrifice might be an expiation? God was still fighting for the Israelites, even though the odds were against them. It is not the sword and bow, not the efficacy of the fighting of the Israelites, but God-on-their-side who wins the day, even against tremendous odds. The tremendous odds prove it is not the violence of the Israelites, but God's power that wins the day. Psalm 33:16-17 tells us the king is not delivered by an army or by war horses.

The primitive pacifism of the patriarchs is displaced by the idea of God fighting for the Israelites; then God fights with the Israelites; then the Israelites fight for God in holy war. This concept, in turn, is replaced by the national wars of David's dynasty, with David fighting for God. In David's time, furthermore, the use of hired mercenaries, Hittites, appears, putting a seal on the trend toward secular war-making. We see a movement from Yahweh's pacifistic servants to the holy warriors who fight for Yahweh to the essentially secular, nationalistic rule of the Davidic kingship.

It is my contention that the *herem* came about because of a misunderstanding of Yahweh's original gift, the unconditional covenant. The Israelites understood God had given them a gift, but they tried to repay the gift through works. Using violence and warfare to conquer land already granted necessarily constituted a type of works, an attempt to repay what God intended to give unconditionally and unilaterally. When the Israelites fought, they turned God's unconditional and unilateral covenant into their own conditional and bilateral agreement, using their own means to earn what God intended as a gift. The Israelites knew what they had conquered was a violation of Yahweh's intent; therefore a sacrifice was necessary to expiate the guilt. The sacrifice became the *herem*. Later this necessity was executed in the form of Temple sacrifice.

Assuming that God's will was to give the land without violence, were the Israelites attempting to pay back God for what they had taken against God's will? Was this why Hosea and Micah and other prophets, and later Jesus, said that Yahweh desires mercy *(hesed)* not sacrifice *(herem)?* (Matthew 12:9, Jeremiah 2, Hosea 6.)

Even though violence came to the fore in this early history, Israelite forms of primitive pacifism, violence, and holy war cannot be identified with existing structures of the time. Wars in the secular world, and all violence for that matter, were justified ethically or philosophically, rather than by a relationship with God. More typical of the Israelite motif, i.e., national violence based on a religious premise, is modern Iran, where a call to holy war (Jihad) is motivated by a certain vision of God's will and not by the self-interested ends of the nation as a secular structure. At least that is the theory. Secular societies make no such claims. Wars are waged by the will of the people. In Israelite society wars were attributed to the will of God and the power to win was found by trusting in God. There would be no victories without trusting in God no matter what the number of troops or the technology of the weapons. The Israelites, even when they forsook pacifism, still relied upon their belief that God would win the day for them. They would not accumulate weapons nor accept a king who would perfect their use. God was the ultimate Lord. Nothing the Israelites achieved without God could be seen as efficacious until the later, secular kingship of David. Then we find David waging wars for God rather than God waging wars for the Israelites.

This transition from total trust in God, as reflected in pacifism and *herem*, to the acceptance of war as a means to acquire God's gift of land, results in the establishment of the hereditary monarchy in Israel. War becomes its primary tool. Bruce points out:

[A] hereditary monarchy introduced a principle which was bound to change the character of civil rule in Israel. Hitherto they had been ruled by charismatic judges raised up by God from this tribe or that in His sovereign good pleasure; the hereditary principle meant that their rulers in future would not necessarily have the special spiritual endowments which had marked Samuel and his predecessors but would more probably resemble the kings of Israel's neighbors.[5]

It is ironic that the charismatic Samuel is the agent for this change of heart among the Israelites. Samuel makes it clear that the people's request for a human king marked a lack of faith in God, their only and true King. Why? Because it ended God's leadership of the people through those especially attuned to God's Spirit. The charismatic nature of the spiritual rule, even though infected with the violence of the times of the Judges following Joshua, preserved the idea of a person raised up and commissioned to lead in a quite different manner from that which comes about in David's monarchy. This tremendous change, far back in the history of Judaism, directly affects our religious and political relationships today. The way of a hereditary king or even an elected president is not the way of the holy nation of God. Kings and presidents: that is the way of the secular nations of pagans. Once we form a kingly or presidential institution to regulate legitimized violence, we must embrace Mammon; we must embrace a whole new economic system based on growth and urban technology, and characterized by dehumanizing priorities.

The Israelites exchanged a desert way of life for the agricultural economy of Canaan and later urbanization; a few, however, the Rechabites, resisted the trend. (Cf. Jeremiah 35.) This remnant continued to live in tents; they sowed no seed, planted no vineyards, and drank no wine; in fact they abstained from everything that had the remotest connection with the Canaanite fertility cult and were accordingly foremost in their detestation of Baal worship.

The connections seem clear. First comes a king out of violence, then the change of economy, all related to the religious institutions that permeated the area—the Baal worship and Canaanite fertility cult. The powers and principalities were at work even then, politically, economically, religiously. David was a victim of all three systems.[6] The living God of Israel's survival was not bound up with the fortunes of God's people; but the gods of the Assyrians and of the pagan states depended for their vitality and their very existence upon the continuing national identity of their worshipers. The God of Israel, the Living God, the God who gave the gift of the holy nation gradually became subsumed under the gods of the pagan culture. Thus a tremendous transformation in religious history occurred.

Today in North America we have no other kingdom than the kingdom of the pagan culture. Ninety-nine percent of all Christians and Jews living in this society have no knowledge of the effects upon us of this great transformation which took place thousands of years ago. It is hard to imagine an alternative society based primarily on religious rather than political or economic principles because we have lived so long in the politico-economic culture which has dominated Western civilization.

GOD AND VIOLENCE

Before we move on to a more detailed examination of the fall of the Israelite nation from the time of David to the time of Jesus, we must examine the violence which preceded that fall.

The fundamental question is not: "Was violence justified?" but rather, "Did not God sanction violence in the Old Testament?" The assumption is that if violence were allowed by God, then we may also use it for our own ends, for our own kings, for our own economic systems, for our own religious institutions, for our own religious institutions, for our own establishment's social purposes.

There are numerous reasons for concluding that God was not advocating the violence recorded in the Hebrew Scriptures. But even if God were justly violent, that does not justify our own use of violence. Only God knows the hearts of persons and therefore only God is in a position to act violently. We humans can never be in such a position, for we cannot see into our sisters' and brothers' hearts; we can only observe conduct. We cannot judge by appearances alone (John 7:24.); we are not morally or objectively free to use the final judgment of violence.

The question for us remains: Did the God of the Hebrew Scriptures sanction human violence? Is it possible that violence was not sanctioned from the beginning by God? If this is the case, we are able to show a consistency between the Old and New Testaments. If God did not justify human violence in the Old Testament, why does it appear that God was violent and that God's people were also? The answer is found in the Scriptures. We are not dealing with different gods in the Old and New Testaments, or a God who is inconsistent. We are dealing with the same God and with a consistent salvation history.

God works through nonviolence in God's first relationships with Adam and Eve. Nonviolence is illustrated through Abraham's relationship with the strangers in Canaan. God's relationship with Abraham is further illustrative of that nonviolence—a trusting relationship formed through a gift, asking nothing in return. There is a call for trust in God. There is no reliance upon force, sovereignty, or vengeance. Even when the Israelites use violence, they still hold onto that trusting relationship, albeit to a lesser degree, binding themselves and God. Nonviolence is a necessary component of the relationship of God's gift and human trust. If it is missing, something destructive happens to the relationship. There must be some element, some covenantal arrangement of gift and trust, which provides the courage and the impetus to practice nonviolence.

To summarize: God enters into an unconditional covenant with Abraham in which God promises to give to Abraham the land, no strings attached. The unconditional aspect of the covenant is better described in terms of God's *hesed*, that is, steadfast love, grace, and power. It is only this *hesed* that guarantees the unconditionality of the promise, that is, its character as a gift of love. Secondly, *hesed* also provides the power necessary to the effectual fulfillment of God's promise, that is, unconditional grace is both the impetus for the gift and the content of the gift.

God's action requires a response to affect history in conformity with God's will, a response as free and unconditional as the gift itself. The response is Abraham's trust. Abraham trusts God freely, God gives the gift freely. Abraham trusts God with Isaac; Moses trusts at the Red Sea. If trust is returned to God in thanks for God's *hesed* to the people, then obviously there is no need for violence; for human violence is used where humans do not have enough trust to rely on God and therefore take matters into their own hands for whatever reasons they deem fitting. God's *hesed*, God's grace and power, combined with human trust, makes violence irrelevant and unnecessary. Thus there is a covenant: God's *hesed* flows to the people and the people's trust returns to God. They take a risk with each other; both give spontaneously and not because of obligation.

When the people violated this covenant by using violence and then establishing kingship to organize that violence, God might have gone back on the promise of a land because the Israelites had withdrawn their trust. But because God had entered into an unconditional covenant, God provided the land to the Israelites despite their violence. The fulfillment of the promise, therefore, does not prove that God was violent or ever intended the Israelites to be violent. It simply shows that God fulfills promises even though human beings do not. The people lost their trust, but God fulfilled the promise anyway. (Deuteronomy 9:4.) God takes people where they are. This does not mean God justifies where people are.

The use of violence by the people of God interferes with God's gift and their trust. It creates a false relationship. Secular nations are incapable of trust. Political institutions cannot deal with gifts and trust. But the religious community, the holy nation, which started off on the right foot—with nonviolence and trust—lost its footing through the acceptance of violence and ended its early flirtation with a primitive pacifism. From that point, other events occurred in the cycle of violence—political, economic, and religious. The acceptance of violence was, in a sense, a new religious relationship. How do people live together? And with their God? They tried to build God a house;

they provided God with a government and a king; they created a society different from the one originally proposed.

THE POLITICAL TEMPTATION

The loss of trust in their Lord required a replacement of that trust with dependence on a human king. The Hebrews did not view their God as a god of a fertility cult; they recognized God as a spirit; and, at least at the outset, unlike the Mesopotamian and Egyptian models, as their only King.

The Lordship of Yahweh was supreme. Initially there was no human king in Israelite society as there was in the secular world of the ancient Near East. Yahweh was the only King until the time of Samuel, when the Israelites asked for a king like all the other nations. Then they became the slaves of kings who would fight their battles for them. The introduction of kingship makes permanent the institution of war in Israel. Samuel told the Israelites that God was their King. But they continued to seek a human king to imitate the secular regimes close by. Psalm 105 rebukes kingship, as do the writings of Isaiah, Jeremiah, Hosea, and Amos. Hosea states that God said: "They made kings, but not through me." (Hosea 8:4.) David's kingdom, the first full-fledged monarchy in Israel, arose under Philistine pressure. The king was required to institutionalize and legitimize the instruments of violence. The Israelites finally decided they wanted to be entirely like the surrounding nations. They had already taken on violence like the other nations. Next they would take on a king to implement and institutionalize the violence.

The Book of Samuel reports that the elders of Israel gathered together and came to Samuel at Ramah asking him to appoint a king to govern them like other nations. Samuel was displeased and prayed to the Lord. The Lord answered that Samuel should listen to the voice of the people. They had rejected God as their King, served other gods, and forgotten how God had brought them out of Egypt. God told Samuel to accept their demand and "Show them the ways of the king who shall reign over them." So Samuel told the people what God had said, and described the ways of a king:

He will take your sons and appoint them to his chariots and to be his horsemen, and to run before his chariots; And he will appoint for himself commanders of thousands and commanders of fifties, and some to plow his ground and to reap his harvest, and to make his implements of war and the equipment of his chariots. He will take your daughters to be perfumers and cooks and bakers. He will take the best of your fields and vineyards and olive orchards and give them to his servants. He will take the tenth of your grain and of your vineyards and give it to his officers and to his servants. He will take your menservants and maidservants, and the best of your cattle and your asses and put them to his work. He will take the tenth of your flocks, and you shall be his slaves. And in that day you will cry out because of your king, whom you have chosen for yourselves; but the Lord will not answer you in that day. (I Samuel 8:10-18.)

It is amazing that the people refused to listen to the voice of Samuel even after such a warning. "Oh no, we want this king! We want to be like these other nations. We want a king to govern us, to go out before us, to fight our battles." They had a Divine King who fought their battles. This relationship later evolved into the myth of "fighting God's battles" because of their failure to entrust their destiny to God. Samuel returned to the Lord and the Lord repeated, "Make them a king." And so he did. Thus they moved in the direction of a secular, political power and continued their rejection of the spiritual power of God. Not long after this, David became their king. Solomon and others followed him, but the history of Israelite kingship proved a great failure. It failed because the corruption of the kings became increasingly worse over time and finally the Israelites had no king at all. It failed for the Israelites as it fails for all nations, because of the futile spiral of violence and counter-violence and the endless political intrigue which is essential to the structure and power of any kingship, presidium, or presidency.

Jacques Ellul's description of God's response to such human willfulness is insightful:

> Man can create new situations which God does not will. And since the Lord does not give up, i.e., does not give up doing not his tyrannical will, but what is good for man and man's salvation, he changes his plans, he accepts the new situation and enters into it, and he draws from it certain consequences which man certainly did not expect or foresee but which will finally work for the actualizing of God's love.[7]

It cannot be said that God did not warn them. God gave through Samuel an extraordinary description of what centralized political power would mean—more taxes, military conscription, arbitrary police, the impossibility of limiting power. "This is the price the people will have to pay to have efficient political power and to reach the level of progress of other nations. . . . God does not press the point. He accepts this disobedience. . . . He does not give up saving the people in spite of itself. . . . We see here the mysterious strategy or adaptation of God, and we shall find this again and again."[8]

THE RELIGIOUS TEMPTATION

Following close on the heels of the acceptance of kingship is the replacement of the Lordship of God. This spells the beginning of the end of religious community. The acceptance of secular modes of political leadership puts God "in his place," and the relationship of God to God's people is radically changed.

David became the paradigm king and set up his kingdom and his palace in Jerusalem. But David was embarrassed. David was a king living in a palace, but God was still understood as being

invisible and abiding in the Tent of Meeting. David seemed to
have developed a sense that he was living better than God—
this, in spite of the long-standing tradition of not attempting
to confine God to a building. Now God had to be "up-graded"
to live as David did.[9] This meant that God had to have a huge
house, a Temple, so that God could appear equal to David who
lived in a palace. This time the characters are Nathan and David
and the story unfolds as follows:

> Now when the king dwelt in his house and the Lord had
> given him rest from all his enemies round about, the king
> said to Nathan the prophet, "See now, I dwell in a house
> of cedar, but the ark of God dwells in a tent." And Nathan
> said to the king, "Go, do all that is in your heart; for the
> Lord is with you." (2 Samuel 7:1-3.)

Nathan seemed to think that God would go along with this
since God, reluctantly, went along with the kingship. But the
same night the word of the Lord came to Nathan and the Lord
was not so willing. God said to go tell David:

> Would you build me a house to dwell in? I have not dwelt
> in a house since the day I brought up the people of Israel
> from Egypt to this day, but I have been moving about in
> a tent for my dwelling. In all places where I have moved,
> with all the people of Israel, did I speak a word to any of
> the judges of Israel, whom I commanded to shepherd my
> people Israel, saying, "Why have you not built me a house
> of cedar?" (2 Samuel 7:5-7.)

This time God said "No!" In fact God told Nathan to remind
David that he had been brought out of the sheep pasture to be
made king over the people; it is God who had made David's
name great and secured his power. Using the prophet Nathan
as messenger, God declares it is God who will raise up a house
for David, not David who should build a house for God. "I will
raise up your offspring after you, who shall come forth from

your body, and I will establish his kingdom. He shall build a house for my name, and I will establish the throne of his kingdom forever. I will be his father, and he shall be my son." (2 Samuel 7:12-14.)

The Lord was saying: Where does this idea come from, that I have to be in a house of cedar? It is not you who should build a house for me. I am building a community of people for you!

In spite of all this, the Temple was built in Jerusalem. Those who wished to build similar temples throughout the land were prohibited from doing so and were required to come to the one Temple in Jerusalem in order to fulfill their cultic obligations. Eventually everything religious was controlled from the Temple in Jerusalem and everything political was controlled from the palace in Jerusalem—except for the prophets who rose up anywhere and represented the continuity between desert and Jesus. (Cf. Deuteronomy 18.)

In Solomon's time Jerusalem also became the center of economic prosperity. Religious control, political control, and economic control were all concentrated there. Power was centralized in one location and completely controlled by the king, the political arm, under the guise of his also being a religious authority. Economic rules and regulations emerged from the same source. What resulted was a mutual affirmation between political and religious power or, as we describe it today, civil religion. What remained was simply to combine political and religious power with the strength of the city, the symbol of the nation, the force of urban technology. This had already been started by the trek from the wilderness to this high place and holy city and the eventual conquering of the land and the establishment of the nation and its boundaries. Solomon's great economic impact upon the whole ancient Near East is well documented. It was the final temptation and sealed the eventual fall of the Israelites.

THE ECONOMIC TEMPTATION

We have described how the Israelites changed in their relationship with their God, and in their political and religious relationships to government with their new king. We now examine the changes in their economic relationships and how these values were also corrupted.

There seems to be a later Old Testament understanding that the possession or accumulation of wealth was a virtue, or a least indicative of virtue. The prosperous person was seen as the one upon whom God's light shone. The Lord makes one able to become prosperous. (Deuteronomy 8:18, 28:11.) Perhaps the intention was that an egalitarian community would share property. That people had been given dominion over the land seemed to have been understood as an invitation to material acquisition. Job, the Psalms, and Proverbs indicate that wealth was seen as virtue. (Job 42, Psalms 1; Proverbs 14.) This is not to say that the poor were forgotten. Indeed the poor were well thought of. The rabbis indicated that they had no love of poverty. They thought that grinding poverty was one of the worst of human afflictions. They regarded riches as a blessing from God; yet they remembered the temptations of riches and gave warning about riches acquired illegitimately. They also noted that a poor Israel was more often faithful to God than was a rich Israel.[10]

In the Hebrew Scriptures the poor were always seen as the special charge of God, who would not forget them. (Psalms 9, 10.) God pities the poor, comforts them, and cares for them. (Psalms 34, 49, 107, 132; Job 5; Jeremiah 20.) God seeks social justice for the poor, and makes them the special concern of those who would do God's will. (Deuteronomy 10; 2 Samuel 22; Isaiah 25; Amos 2, 4.) There are many warnings against the oppressing of the poor in both the Law and the Prophets. The Hebrew Judges were to give to the poor full protection. (Exodus 23; Leviticus 14, 25; Deuteronomy 24, Ezekiel 22; Micah 2.) Interest was not to be exacted from them. (Exodus 22; Leviticus 25; Deuteronomy 23, Psalm 15.) The poor were to be allowed to glean the fields and vineyards. (Leviticus 19; Deuteronomy 24.) The tithe for the third year was for the benefit of the poor and needy. (Deuteronomy 14, 26.) Poverty should not exclude anyone from the joy of the festival. (Deuteronomy 16.) They were allowed to present less expensive offerings at the Temple. (Leviticus 27.) In humility they were expected to accept their condition, not because it was foreordained, but because God could bring it to good. The Old Testament King and Messiah were to be solicitous of the poor. (Psalms 22, 72; Proverbs 29.) To pity the poor was meritorious and brought blessings because one honors God by honoring God's poor. (Psalm 41; Proverbs 14, 17, 19, 31.)

Charity was considered a virtue throughout all Biblical history. The demand for charity was based on a remembrance of Israel's bondage. It was the duty of the rich to help the poor, of the strong to protect the weak, because it was understood throughout salvation history that this was God's way.

Few social differences existed among the early Israelites. They lived a life of simplicity. At first no social distinctions were made; simply there should be no poverty. Exploitation of the poor by the wealthy was forbidden. The development of the monarchy created new classes; kingship, with its attendant elitism, became responsible for social distinctions based on wealth. Amos prophesied against this phenomenon. (Amos 2, 4, 5, 8.) Nevertheless, wealth and possession of property was approved as a sign of reward for piety. (Sirach 40, 47; Proverbs 6.)

Not only in the Hebrew writings, but in many of the ancient Near Eastern texts, and even to this day in the Koran, there are countless references to respect for the poor as God's poor.[11] This contrasts sharply with the attitude which prevails in our society where the poor must bear also the burden of proof that they deserve our concern for them. In the Hebrew tradition the poor, the helpless, and the oppressed were helped simply because they were God's children and, as such, did not deserve their plight. After the establishment of the monarchy, wealth became a type of power in Hebrew culture, something to be sought after and not to be squandered. A person should be respectful of the poor if one were rich, because the poor were seen as God's special concern. It reflected one's piety and God's favor to share with them.

Nowhere, by the time of David, was there any semblance of an ethic of voluntary poverty. There is no longer a tradition of admonition to give up all wealth to follow Yahweh. Indeed, the follower of Yahweh was authenticated by the riches he or she possessed and by prosperity and old age. Wealth and property were to be sought after even in the laws of the Old Testament.[12] Solomon became the epitome of wealth as David was the epitome of kingship. But corruption was ahead!

Cain's sons were builders, building on the curse by which their ancestor was judged.[13] These builders brought Israel from a mobile, fluid society to a staid and static society, locked down in urban dwellings away from the wilderness. The city became a place where wealth could be accumulated, displayed, and held out as honor for kings. The classic symbol of economics is bread, or the exchange of bread. The device of the exchange is money, or as Jesus described it, Mammon, the idol of wealth. (Matthew 6:24.) The place for this exchange became the city. As described above, the prophets identified this economic temptation repeatedly in their writings.

In the 8th century Jeremiah chastised the Israelites for hundreds of years of assimilation of the ways of the economic technocracy of the urbanized nation. Jeremiah said that the Lord had called him to proclaim in the city of Jerusalem:

> I remember the devotion of your youth; your love as a bride, how you followed me in the wilderness, in a land not sown. Israel was holy to the Lord, the first fruits of his harvest. All who ate of it became guilty; evil came upon them, says the Lord. "Hear the way of the Lord, O House of Jacob, and all the families of the house of Israel." Thus says the Lord: "What wrong did your fathers find in me that they went far from me, and went after worthlessness and became worthless?" They did not say, Where is the Lord who brought us up from the land of Egypt, who led us in the wilderness, in the land of deserts and pits, in a land of drought and deep darkness, in the land that none passes through, where no man dwells? And I brought you

into a plentiful land to enjoy its fruits and its good things. But when you came in you defiled my land, and made my heritage an abomination. The priests did not say, Where is the Lord? Those who handle the law did not know me; the rulers transgressed against me. The prophets prophesied by Baal, and went after things that do not profit. (Jeremiah 2:2-8.)

The significance of Jeremiah's words is that the simple, wilderness life required dependence upon God for all things, just as trust and nonviolence required that same kind of dependence which was later lost in the violence of war. The assumption of technological, commercial, and urban characteristics of Canaanite city-life automatically meant a reliance on economic power and a drift away from dependence upon the power of God.

Hosea had a solution. Hosea called for a return to the wilderness where God would speak to the people tenderly and give them vineyards and a "door of hope." (Hosea 2:15.) God's people shall act as they did in the days of their youth. The Lord shall remove the idols from their mouths, and they shall be mentioned no more. And a covenant shall be made once again, " . . . with the beasts of the field, the birds of the air, and the creeping things of the ground; and I will abolish the bow, the sword, and war from the land; and I will make you lie down in safety. . . . And I will betroth you to me forever . . . and you shall know the Lord. . . . For the children of Israel shall dwell many days without king or prince, without sacrifice or pillar. . . ." (Hosea 2:18-20; 3:4.)

Hosea attempted to lure the Israelites back to the wilderness, at least symbolically and spiritually. He said that if they returned to their former lifestyle, their restoration would be accomplished. They would dwell many days in a new life without kings or princes lording it over them, without the enslavement of a growth economy encroaching on their lives. Later the children of Israel would seek the Lord their God for their needs and their protection, and that is what Hosea saw as the way out of their present situation. Their return was envisioned as a life where the beasts of the field and the birds of the air and the creeping things of the ground would lie down in peace with humankind. They would have no need for wealth and war. However, the Israelites chose instead to remain constant to the three temptations of cultural power—economic, political, and religious—and so their fall became complete.

THE FALL OF THE ISRAELITES

The kingship which Samuel warned against constituted the perennial political temptation to war and violence despite the presence of the institutional protection of prophecy. The Temple which Nathan warned against constituted the perennial temptation to civil religion. The need for an economics of growth and technology, the moving away from the simple life of the wilderness and the desert into the life of the city and nation-state constituted the perennial economic temptation. All gave rise to a perverse trinity of counterfeit power presented since to every generation of humankind.

Those questions we asked at the beginning, which could have been answered by those primitive, pacifist patriarchs, could no longer be answered in truth by the Israelites of less ancient time. In the centuries immediately before Christ, there was no longer a community of unconditional trust and covenant, no longer a community living together with God, but community living together only among themselves and in fear of the surrounding nations. Their king is no longer God, but a human king. Their community is no longer holistic but secular.

After the riches of Solomon passed, Josiah's covenant with God reflected the covenant of Moses' day. "It could not change the people's nature and would be kept with no greater success than the original covenant at Sinai had enjoyed. A covenant of a different kind—a new religious relationship—was called for. . . . "[14] In due course Jeremiah envisioned the new covenant brilliantly. He said, "This is a covenant I shall make with the House of Israel after those days, says Yahweh: I will put my law within them and I will write it upon their hearts; I will be their God and they shall be my people." (Jeremiah 31:33.) It is this covenant, bearing a new relationship and rising from the fall of the old, which gives us a hint of what a modern, alternative religious society might look like. Jeremiah saw the restriction of God to the Temple and the people to the city as blasphemy. "Has this house which is called by my name become a den of robbers in your eyes? Behold, I myself have seen it, says Yahweh." (Jeremiah 7:11.) Jesus echoes these words hundreds of years later—a den of robbers, indeed. (Matthew 21:13; Mark 11:17; Luke 19:45.) This topsy-turvy replacement of a holy nation by a worldly city is at the bottom of the problem.

The words of Jeremiah shocked the people. It was blasphemy to speak against the so-called holy house of Israel's God. The priests and cultic prophets clamored for his death. Jeremiah was put on trial for blasphemy and acquitted because the secular judges recognized that he had not spoken of his own volition but "in the name of the Lord our God." (Jeremiah 26:16.) They cited as a precedent the prediction of the destruction of Jerusalem and its Temple by the prophet Micah in Hezekiah's day. Micah was not put to death, they pointed out; on the contrary, king and people paid heed to his words and repented and so the threatened disaster was averted. (Cf. Jeremiah 26.) But this time the threatened disaster was not to be averted.

What is left for the people after the loss of the land and the fall of the Temple and the fall of the kingship is simply the Law. The worship of the Law contained in a Book is at the bottom of many of our spiritual problems today. Look at the dichotomy between power and spirit. The early Israelites were vulnerable as nomads in the wilderness; but there they were much freer than later when they were tied to land, property, and possessions, to security, to economics. God was Lord in the wilderness, but a secular king took God's place in the new land. The God of the Israelites was a Free Spirit; yet worship of that God was confined to a Temple in Jerusalem. Those who visited the Temple had to do so within the sphere of the king's political power. Finally the love and righteousness which motivated the early patriarchs was replaced by a concept of justice found in the Law. The worship of the law as an idol brought further blasphemy into the economic, political, and religious culture.

This gives us a hint about where to begin our search for radical community as a true alternative to the existing powers and principalities. We look not to the urban, but to the rural; not to the king, but to the Lord; not to the Temple, but to the Spirit; not to the law books (whether Hebrew or Christian) but to love and righteousness; not to corrupt concepts of secular justice, but to a law written on the hearts of people and practiced by them regardless of the consequences: the key to nonviolent community.

The fall of these people of God blurs, obliterates even, our connections with them. It makes it difficult for us to see a continuity between the Hebrew Scriptures and those of the Christians. John Bright's premier book, *The Kingdom of God*, asks the question:

> Is there in the Bible some unifying theme which might serve to draw its diverse parts together into a complete whole? Is there, amid its admitted discontinuity, any essential continuity?[15]

This is also our question. The complexity of the Bible is by no means to be minimized. Nevertheless we can recognize running through it a unifying theme which is not artificially imposed. Bright says, "It is a theme of redemption, of salvation; and it is caught up particularly in those concepts which revolve about the idea of a people of God called to live under his rule, and the concomitant hope of the coming Kingdom of God."[16] This is a note which is present in Israel's faith from earliest times, and which is found in one way or another in virtually every part of the Hebrew Scriptures. It also firmly links the Old and New Testaments; for both have to do with the Kingdom of God and the same God speaks through both.

Today this idea of a community of God as a different political, economic, or religious way of life is foreign to us. Bright points out that Jesus never once paused to define what he meant by the Kingdom of God, nor did anyone interrupt him to ask what he meant by this term. The idea was deep within the soul of every Jew. "It was something they understood and longed for desperately. To us, on the contrary, it is a strange term. . . ."[17]

What happened in Israelite history was the subsuming of religious power under the political state. The king gained power over the priests. When the veteran priest Abiathar was so ill-advised as to hew the wrong political line, he was summarily dismissed by Solomon. (1 Kings 2:26.)

> The state supports the cult, and the cult in turn exists for the state. It is the business of the cult to intercede with the Deity on behalf of the state, with the aid of its ritual, to maintain that harmonious balance which would protect the state from ill fortune within and without. If this be done, the state need have no fear; for it is God's 'kingdom' composed of God's chosen people, and ruled by his anointed 'son,' the king: God will externally defend the state. Thus are all the purposes of God in history equated with the existing order and made realizable in terms of it.[18]

Bright likens the hopes of Israel to America's continuing negative attraction to communism.

> Will we, like Israel, imagine that our destiny under God and God's purposes in history are to be realized in terms of the society we have built? The temptation to do so is subtle. After all, we may claim a Christian heritage from which human liberties have flowed; we have churches and support them lavishly; but communism, for example, is totally godless and so destructive of all that is noble in man that scarcely one redeeming thing can be said of it. Between the two there is simply no comparison. Surely

God, if he be just, will further our efforts and will defend us from his foe and ours—for we are his good Christian people! As for ourselves, we will labor and pray for the winning of the world to Christ and the victory of his Kingdom—for it is either that sort of world or a chaos in which nothing which we value will be safe. And if the victory of Christ—which we tend to equate with our own best interests—seems remote, we will turn to yet busier activity, for that is all we know how to do. Surely if we thus energetically serve him, God will protect us and give us the victory! To this hope Amos speaks a resounding NO! Let us understand his words clearly: God does not in that sense have favored people. No earthly state is established of God, guaranteed of God, and identified with his purposes. Nor has any earthly order, however good, the means of setting up God's order in terms of its own ends. On the contrary, all societies are under the judgment of God's order, and those that have been favored with the light doubly so![19]

These words of Bright's going back to Amos can be heard from time to time from the remnant and radical few who glimpse their meaning. Stanley Hauerwas, professor of theological ethics at Duke University, said virtually the same thing to a retired general in a Colorado church after Hauerwas had shared his understanding of God's Kingdom in relation to the political state. To the comment of the general that the Soviet Union was "godless," Hauerwas responded, "All nations are godless."

Does all of this mean that the prophets in those days or the prophets of our own time are urging that the existing institutions should be overthrown for other such institutions? No. It seems as if our calling is not to revolutionize, i.e., to overturn the established system, but to witness to the fulfillment of the Hebrew Scriptures, as Jesus urged. He did not come to abrogate or destroy, but to fulfill. (Matthew 5:17.) Imagine the impact of vast numbers of religious people forming alternative community, no longer having primary allegiance to the political state, changing that allegiance, not through the effort of destroying the state, but through the effort of creating an alternative, religious community. What would happen? A new realm, a new order, would replace the old—at least in those respects to which we are called to give to God and not to Caesar.

Paul Ricoeur recalls in his *Symbolism of Evil*, commenting on Isaiah, "If sin is the false greatness of purely human domination, Judah should not seek support in its might or in its alliances; if Judah had abandoned itself to unarmed obedience, without any reliance on itself, without defense and without alliance, Judah would have been saved."[20] Unarmed obedience, the true contrary of sin, is the first call to faith. The only way Ricoeur sees to practice faith and trust in God is to love God and neighbor as oneself, which presupposes pacifism. Ricoeur rightly understands that religious pacifism is not simply moral ethics, but faith and trust as a way of life. Josiah's arms brought only false security. This is why Jeremiah said, in spite of the false "security" of arms, the nations would be destroyed. (Jeremiah 23, 25.) Jeremiah's nonviolent resistance rose up accusingly against the false confidence of his day. He knew, as did Isaiah, in contrast to the priests representing the religious institutions, and the king representing the political and economic institutions, that "Israel must have neither soil, nor temple, nor king. In short, there must be nothing left of Israel from a human point of view, no room for political hopes, in order for the song of hope of the second Isaiah to be heard."[21] It is to this Song of Hope incarnated in the person of Jesus that we now turn. If any message comes from this trek through the history of the Israelites, it is that this loss of the soil, the Temple, and the king is at the same time, paradoxically, a return to the sacred beginning of its history when it possessed neither soil, nor Temple, nor king. God allowed the king, allowed the Temple, gave the land which v. .s misused in violence. In that violent misuse, the Israelites took on nation and kingship and Temple, and piece by piece lost these human inventions again, first the Northern Kingdom, then the Southern Kingdom, then the king, and finally the Temple and its priests. Without the Temple, there is no sacrifice, there are no priests.

When all was lost, a new king rose up in a conquered land who called himself "the temple." This temple is a new gift of God, a gift that could only be timed with the shedding by Israel of its power found in nation, king, and Temple; a time to return to the beginning, a time for the reign of God.

It is essential to remember that Israel preserved this history in its Scriptures, the sordid as well as the sublime. For this blessing we must be eternally thankful. Salvation comes from the Jews; for in addition to all the failures, they inaugurated the world's first commitment to an intentional community of God.

To sum up: We have examined the fall of a holy people from pacifism to violence as they adopted the ways of the pagans around them. We have seen this violence incorporated into their political, economic, religious, and legal institutions. We will continue our quest now with an examination of a radical Jewish sect which sought, unilaterally, to have a new relationship with society, a new relationship with government, and new relationships with each other and with God. This is the Jesus community.

CHAPTER TWO

JESUS AND HIS COMMUNITY

IN THE MIDST OF NATIONS

Our quest continues: How do we live in the light of the Kingdom of God while in the midst of the dark world of the nations? In its origins, Israel formed an intentional community, set apart from other nations. But Israel faltered when it succumbed to the temptations of land and power. Initially, the chosen people were pacifists; their lives were simple, embodying a holy poverty; and the least among them was comforted. But their holy poverty became uncaring wealth; their pacifism became dominating militarism; their community became an earthly kingdom.

In spite of all their failings, the religion and tradition of the Israelites gave birth to Jesus Christ. Next we look to Jesus' community to answer our questions. How did they live together? What was their community like? How did they relate to the governments and society around them, to Judaism and the Roman Empire?

Juan Mateos, a Spanish Jesuit and Biblical scholar, wrote an introduction to a Spanish edition of the New Testament. His comments were published in *Sojourners* magazine under the title, "The Message of Jesus."[1] He examines the Jewish world at the time of Jesus to establish the context of his writing. Albert Nolan, O.P., wrote a book entitled *Jesus before Christianity*.[2] Nolan, Mateos, and many others have observed that Jesus refused to identify himself with either the Roman political institutions or the existing religious institutions in his milieu. He rejected, for different reasons, the Sadducees, the Pharisees, the Essenes, and the Zealots—all religious parties or factions of his times. And, if as a carpenter he lived a middle-class life, he gave that up for a much poorer life and identified himself with those who were marginalized and dispossessed by society.

When Jesus was born, Herod the Great was an ally of the Roman Emperor; if there was a kingdom in Palestine, it was his, subsumed under the vast Roman Empire. Herod's sons inherited his kingdom upon his death in 4 BC. The Jewish government was represented by the Sanhedrin, composed of seventy-two members and headed by a chief high priest. The Sanhedrin was composed of three groups: the high priests, the lay senators or elders, and the scribes who were scholars and lawyers. The high priests were named by the Romans and controlled by them, yet the high priests were the official representatives of religion and worship and they administered the Temple which was the religious and political center of Israel. The second major group in the Sanhedrin was the senators and elders, lay people from well-to-do families, mostly landowners; they composed, along with the high priests, the Sadducees. This group was very conservative in both political and religious matters. They "played ball" with the Romans. They talked a lot about maintaining order and the status quo. Mateos describes them as realists who "accepted the injustice of foreign domination as long as it did not compromise their position."[3]

The third group in the council was the scribes, scholars and lawyers—experts in theology and canon law—the majority of whom belonged to the Pharisees. "Pharisees" means "separate ones," and that they thought they were, as they observed religious practices to the utmost detail. They wrote extensive commentaries explaining religious texts. Although the Pharisees and Sadducees were at opposite poles politically, they were traditional in their respect for existing institutions. Roughly, they could be likened to the conservatives and liberals of our own political and religious time. They differed in ideology but tacitly agreed in their support of the established powers.

There existed two groups that were neither conservative nor liberal. The Essenes and the Zealots would be described on a continuum of political and religious ideologies as radicals. The question is, were they truly radical? The Essenes "held that worship and the temple were impure because the priests were illegitimate, and they [the Essenes] took no part in the ceremonies nor did they collaborate with the establishment."[4] They saw themselves as unique and they lived a separate community life, breaking off from the Pharisees and moving to the banks of the Dead Sea, to an area we know today as Qumran.

The second radical group was, in contrast to the religious Essenes, a highly politicized group. They were nationalists called Zealots. Both groups saw the need for a radical transformation of existing political and liberal institutions. But, while the Essenes found hope in religious separation, the Zealots looked for change through violent revolution. As we know, the Zealots' day came twice, once in the late first century and again in the early second century, but only for them to find that their warlike ways brought on the total demise of the kingdom of Israel.

So the question was, for that time: What is this reign of God, this Kingdom of God to come, and who is this Messiah? Will he lead a Zealot revolution on a warrior's steed after the manner of David? Will he play ball, as the Sadducees, reminding everyone of Solomon and his syncretic approach to economic power? Or will he be a reformer, like the Pharisees, trying to pass new legislation in the Sanhedrin to make the world a place of law and order? Will he simply throw up his hands and take a small group out somewhere, perhaps again to the Dead Sea, and, like the Essenes, live in a model community separate from the world? No. No to all of the above.

The question then as now is: How do we live in the light of the Kingdom of God while in the midst of the dark world of nations? Jesus came to live the answer. He came to gather together a community of followers living and toiling in the world but adhering to the ethic of God's Kingdom. The Kingdom of God and the world of nations were intermingled temporally; they were together then as now. But for redemption to be accomplished, the Kingdom of God must be a light to the world, visible and apparent, and so Jesus took up his cross to show us this way.

Mateos sees the ruling classes as either collaborationists (Sadducees) or as inactive spiritualizers (Pharisees) who, while hating the Roman domination, did not present any serious danger to the status quo. The Pharisees dealt with outward religious forms but with no inward conscience or outward actualization of that conscience. All but the Essenes were drawn into violence, but even the Essenes were simply putting it off until the "time of the Lord." It was into this ferment that Jesus stepped.

As Jesus left his home to do what, in those days, was not so unusual—to go out into the wilderness to find out whether he was the Messiah—he must have pondered his world and its powers, and what it meant to be the holy nation of God. The powers then in Jerusalem and Galilee are the same worldly powers operating in our midst today under different names.

We grow up with and become acculturated to the worldly powers in our environment. These powers are easily identified with the religious, political, and economic structures within which we live. As these structures mesh in our culture, they form the basis for civil religion and politics. Paul talked about the worldly powers, forewarning us of where our real battle lies. In Ephesians 6:12, he says:

For we are not contending against flesh and blood, but against the principalities, against the powers, against the world of rulers of this present darkness, against spiritual hosts of wickedness in the heavenly places.

And in Romans 8:38:

"For I am sure that neither death, nor life, nor angels, nor principalities, nor things present, nor things to come, nor powers, nor height, nor depth, nor anything else in all creation, will be able to separate us from the love of God in Christ Jesus our Lord."

Hendrik Berkhof in *Christ and the Powers* popularized an understanding of what these worldly powers, as described by Paul and faced by Jesus in his temptations, mean for us.[5] They are religious and ethical structures which rule over human life outside of Christ, threatening to entice Christians away from Christ and thereby to reject his gift of power (grace) to witness to his way. We are told that his way disarms the worldly powers and is already at work among us. In Colossians 2:15: "He disarmed the principalities and powers and made a public example of them, triumphing over them in him." Jesus' life, death on the cross, and resurrection were a triumph over the worldly powers in the sense that he exposed them for our understanding, and exemplified the method by which they are to be confronted. To the extent we have not understood and accepted and acted upon that acceptance, we have rejected the resurrection, we have rejected the suffering and death of Christ, we have rejected Christ's life, and we have rejected God's gift.

Jesus, vulnerable as he entered the wilderness, took with him an understanding of these powers and principalities and an understanding of the Israelites' historical struggle with them. He was tempted by these same powers and principalities in the political, economic, and religious structures created long before his emergence as part of Israelite society. His temptations were presented by Satan who foresaw him as the Messiah, the Savior of his nation. Satan, the master of these demonic powers, knew the Kingdom of God announced by Jesus would be based on trust in God and not on Satan's wiles. The only way for Satan to ward off this cataclysmic challenge to his worldly kingdom was to tempt Jesus with the strongest possible seductions to sinfulness.

But what are these potent seductions to sinfulness? According to the majority voice in our churches today, we would have to believe they had to do with sex, alcohol, or drugs. Neither here, nor anywhere in the Gospels, do we find Jesus wrestling with sexual or other such carnal temptations. This is not to say that Jesus would not consider sexual promiscuity and other forms of physical overindulgence sinful. It is to say that these essentially personal or private sins do not constitute the powers. Private sins do not have in themselves the capability of foundering the Kingdom. Private sins are really manifestations of evil rooted in the fallen social powers; they are usually superficially addressed: straining a gnat while swallowing a camel. Moreover, private sins often cloud or block our understanding of the greater and deeper issues of structures and systems. We often spend time dealing with the private aspects of sinfulness while avoiding the greater and deeper manifestations of sin in our social world. This, in itself, is part of the temptation of Satan—to avoid dealing with the very temptations that he presented to Christ in the wilderness. Jesus' temptations, however, were entirely social in their thrust and meaning, just as his prayer to "our Abba" (intimate Parent) dealt with the social world and the eschatological meaning of the end times. (Matthew 6:9-13.)

THE TEMPTATIONS OF JESUS

Satan asked Jesus to command stones to turn into bread. Bread is the symbol of security in worldly life, the very first necessity of economics. There is a warning that when we store up our daily bread, and even more than what Jesus told us was our daily portion, we tend to possess and accumulate, thereby participating in acquisitiveness and the economics of growth at the expense of our neighbor. We begin to lust after the benefits of commerce, technology, and urbanization so prevalent in the Canaanite city-life to which the Israelites gravitated, but not found in the wilderness of their original, nomadic existence. We then want more than we give, a profit, interest, privilege.

The wilderness of the nomadic existence required the one element Satan could not deal with—trust in spite of a vulnerable situation. Instead of trusting in God, the Israelites dramatically changed their society. They were called to live in the Kingdom while in the midst of the nations, but they left the wilderness and took on a different economics grounded in the urbanization of the Canaanite cities, in the commerce and profits of Solomon's time. They lost their roots.

Ellul contrasts the example of Jesus' reaction to this temptation of Satan with our own reactions:

> He does not follow Cain's way. He builds no city, he finds no sheltered refuge, he settles in no one place. . . . What good are city walls? Jesus takes no part in the city. He rejects her money, arms, sciences. He ignores the capital and the progress of civilization. . . . Fence-straddling is impossible. Jesus' refusal to settle down in a city, to carry on there a pious ministry, shows us that to do this would be an unforgivable betrayal. It would, for him, be accepting the propositions of Satan. . . . When Jesus went to the city it was only to leave soon. Not only did he not reside there, returning each evening to Bethany, but he also left the city to die. He was, in fact, forced to leave it. The demons of the city could not tolerate the Son of God in their midst, and in fulfillment of the law they leagued themselves against him. . . . We have seen that the inhabitants of Sodom and Gomorrah were swallowed up in their ruin; there was no separation. In fact the city is one of man's treasures, and man's heart is possessed by the demon of the city. "Where your treasure is, there will your heart be also." . . . the desert is a place where human powers must be renounced. In the desert there can be no more trickery, no illusions as to getting out by one's own means, no possibility of placing hope in natural sources of help. Man is denuded of all his techniques, of all the possibilities of his civilization. He is alone, without arms or armor, and then he is both ready prey for the demons and in a position

to be helped only by God. The desert, then, appears as a
place of trial, because it is the place of honesty. Going into
the desert is the moment of truth. The desert is particularly
the dwelling place of the spirits, according to the older
texts of the Old Testament. This is where the scapegoat
is sent, bearing the sins of Israel, there to be the prey of
the demons.[6]

In the desert Jesus offers himself as the prey for demons,
perhaps even more so than in his dying on the cross. An understanding of the cross-likeness of the desert experience is
encountering death itself, and not over three hours but over
forty days. Our own temptation to the concentration of economic power is at the expense of our vulnerability and trust.
We refuse to accept the risk of giving more than we get. It is
a temptation to replace trust with worldly economic power, thus
providing a security not found in a trust that leaves matters in
God's hands. Instead, we find our trust in possessions, in inanimate objects, in accumulation of wealth, in insurance arrangements, in protection from others who may take our
possessions or lives away from us. Jesus did not turn the stones
into bread. He withstood the temptation to depend upon economic power rather than upon God for security and protection.
Jesus answered the question: How do we relate to society in
terms of simplicity, wealth, poverty, and acquisitiveness, in
terms of assisting others with less, and in doing hospitality and
service for those in need?

After Jesus left the wilderness and began his ministry, he
went so far as to declare himself the fulfilment of the Jubilee
Year, thus relating his witness directly to the great vision of
alternative economics from his own ancient tradition. (Luke
4:16 ff.; Leviticus 25.) For most of his hearers, he went too far.
Later we shall look at the consequences in greater detail.

The second temptation of Jesus was political. It poses for us
another question of Kingdom living. How did Jesus and his
community relate to existing governments? Were they pacifists
or militarists? Did they kill or were they killed? Did they forbear

their governmental rights, or utilize them? Were they nonviolent or violent? Did they live a life of holy obedience or a life more like that of the Sadducees, Pharisees, Essenes, or Zealots? The political temptation is to seek *for whatever purpose* all the authority and glory found in the political kingdoms of the world. Satan claims political power has been given to him and he can give it to whom he will; but the price is worship of Satan. Worship is the external expression of trust in Satan rather than in God. It is significant that Satan claims political power under his control. This should make anyone most wary of accepting political positions and the representation of that power. Jesus answered this temptation of Satan saying: "It is written, 'You shall worship the Lord your God and him only shall you serve.' " (Luke 4:8.) And him *only* shall you serve! "Give to Caesar what is Caesar's" and "give to God what is God's" must be interpreted in the light of this unequivocal statement. We are called *only* to serve God, and to owe no one anything but love. (Romans 13:8.)

It is significant that the words "authority" and "glory" are included in this temptation account. No person who has ever been in politics, whether in a democracy or in a dictatorship, can maintain power solely on his or her own authority. There has to be glory. This glory, in political terms, is commonly called "recognition." A politician's name must appear in the media. A politician must be effective and successful. Glory and recognition are the means by which a politician gains attention and increases his or her power over others. It is the means towards re-election; it is also the means toward domination.

Jesus is promised glory from all the political kingdoms of the world. He could readily use this power, not only for his own benefit, but also for the benefit of others. He could even free Israel from the yoke of the Roman conqueror. Jesus refused this power, but not just for himself. He refused it too for the possible benefit of others. His glory does not come from a political base; he will not accept it because he knows that this power is linked inevitably with the basic ingredient of all worldly, political power: violence, the ultimate expression of

un-trustfulness. Violence is born of fear and justified by short-
term success. The ends of violence are doomed to destruction
by the inherent dynamic of more violence. Modern political
empire thrives only by the manipulation of institutional violence, demonstrating that political institutions do not exist by
faith but by fear. Jesus, who tells us to "fear not," does not
accept this power even on behalf of others.

With the offer of political power in return for religious worship, we see how closely politics and religion are linked in the
mind of Satan. Politics can become a religion and religion can
become solely political, and in combination, they can become
civil religion which may be embraced by politicians and preachers alike. The truth contained in the temptation episode is that
all political power is ultimately in the hands of demonic power.
Ultimately political power subsumes what is left of religious
power, the end result being a civil religion in which politicians
speaking religious language dominate religionists speaking political language.

The final temptation of Jesus is religious. Jesus is tempted
by a cultural, institutional, religious power. The symbol here
is the pinnacle of the Temple, the very top, from which Jesus
is asked to throw himself down to be saved by a miracle. Jesus
answers: "You shall not tempt the Lord your God." (Luke 4:12.)
The conversation between Satan and Jesus closes with the statement that when the devil had ended every temptation, he de-
parted. These three basic social temptations encompass every
temptation. Certainly, the last one is a mighty one. For this is
the profession of Jesus—not economics or politics, but religion.
The Messiah is religious, the "Son of Man" is religious, in the
fundamental sense of one's whole life being given to God.
Miracles and healings are a very important part of the Gospel;
so this temptation to power fits the Messiah's own purpose
much better than the first two. The power of miracle runs
through the Old and New Testaments, and is still given much
attention in even TV ministries today. The power of miracle
is, for Jesus, one centered in trust, with faith and love overcoming the suffering of the one for whom the miracle is per-

formed. A miracle is not primarily a sign of the authenticity of its worker. Jesus did not need a miracle to establish his claim as a representative of God, as do many latter-day Jesus preachers, who ride in Cadillacs and live on million-dollar budgets. Jesus knew there were other miracle workers around and that such would be the case in the future as well. This particular temptation was to provide Jesus with an opportunity to prove his religious authority at the very seat of the traditional religious power of his day, the Temple. He refused, just as he refused many other times when he was asked to prove he was God by working wonders. Even on the Cross, by simply coming down, by simply doing something miraculous, he could have proved his religious authority. He refused. Cultural religious power is based on the ability to prove by something extraordinary that one is favored by God and thereby has power over the masses. But Jesus' power is more radical than that. The religious beast of Revelation calls down fire from heaven. Yet we know that when Jesus' own disciples, remembering Elijah, asked him to call down fire from heaven, he turned to them and said: "You do not know what manner of spirit you are of." (Luke 9:54-55.)

Jesus' power is more radical than burning enemies. It is more radical than proving himself a miracle-worker. His pinnacle is not atop the institutional church and his power-base is not some proof of his divinity. The radical religious authority of Jesus goes to the root of all religion. It is based in faith and trust, risk and vulnerability, downward social mobility, all of which are incompatible with proofs, with worldly power, with possessions.

Jesus resisted these kinds of religious power, these traditional, cultural underpinnings. He withstood the three social temptations which are all-encompassing in our personal as well as our public lives. He overcame Satan, emerged from the wilderness and the desert, and entered upon his ministry. His struggle admits the violence of these powers. He comes to it armed only with the nonviolent grace of God's approval and the power that comes from centering one's mission in trust.

That power we too have known to be our gift from Jesus. It is called the Advocate, the Comforter, the Holy Spirit.

The story of Jesus' temptations and the way in which he overcame them gives us more than a hint of how we should live together in the midst of the nations of the world. We do not accomplish this mission through a miraculous kind of priesthood, which he rejected; nor through a Temple built with human hands. It is accomplished with a community formed in the strength gathered from the wilderness event. That community lives simply, lives together, and witnesses to a way that is an alternative to the way of nations. Economically, the way of Jesus is to live simply; religiously, to live together; politically, to witness to the way of God as opposed to the way of nations.

THE TEACHINGS OF JESUS

In overcoming these universal temptations, Jesus in fact overcame the world. The world knew from the start that Jesus was a threat. When Jesus was born in Bethlehem in Judea in the days of Herod the Great, wise ones from the East came to Jerusalem asking for one who was born "King of the Jews." They said they had seen "his star" in the east and were coming to "worship" him. When King Herod heard that kind of language, he was troubled (to say the least) and called together the chief priests and scribes, those same authorities who were later to execute Jesus. Herod inquired of the wise ones where Jesus was to be born, and he was told, "in Bethlehem." (Matthew 2:1ff.)

Is not that enough to make any political ruler insecure, particularly one who is posing also as a religious ruler? Israel, a conquered nation, a nation which had succumbed to the temptations, a nation which had lost everything, finds in a baby born in a little town called Bethlehem, a ruler, not yet recognized by them, but known by seers from other lands who understood Hebrew prophecies. "And you, O Bethlehem, in that land of Judah, are by no means least among the rulers of Judah, for from you shall come a ruler who will govern my people Israel."

(Matthew 2:6; Micah 5:2.) Herod wanted no ruler out of Bethlehem; so a violent blood-bath with weapons of the secular nation was his response. He killed all the male children in Bethlehem and the surrounding area. Violence was brought about by the witness of the wise ones and the birth of the nonviolent one. Nonviolence does, at times, cause violence. There is causation, perhaps, but not culpability. The basis for violence is clear: the evil lusts of violent people to eradicate the threat of nonviolence for the security of the state or to perpetuate institutional religion which, as Revelation clearly lays out, mimics and lauds the state's use of violence. Here we have hybrid Herod, part Jew, part secularist, almost a king, subdued by the Romans, dominating the Jews. But his violence died, and so did Herod. The Nazarene lives on.

The Nazarene survived Herod to suffer the temptations of the devil and to emerge directly from those trials to teach crowds in the mountains his lessons for all people—the Sermon on the Mount. No oaths, no violence, no courts, no interest on money—whatever makes for violence is not part of his community. The hallmark of his community is love for all, including enemies, a sharing of wealth by living like the least. Jesus tells the people that what their tradition holds—"You shall love your neighbor and hate your enemy" (Matthew 5:43; Psalm 139:21-22.)— is not acceptable to him. The Kingdom comes through forgiveness, forgiving debts and trespasses, through loving enemies and living like the least in the Kingdom. The Kingdom does not come through the wealth of those living a special life as parasites off the poor, or through Mammon, security, or survival. In other words, Jesus teaches in the Sermon on the Mount that the economic, political, and religious ethics of secular society and its religious, institutional counterparts are all worthless. It is a topsy-turvy world and thus a great conflict will ensue. There is no syncretization between the secular world and the religious world of Jesus. There is no accommodation between the ethics of Jesus and the worldly powers. There is only conflict, tribulation, and division: heralds of the death of the secular state and the arrival of the Kingdom in full flower.

Everyone must go through this period of tribulation which cannot be ignored by religious fantasies or explained away by dogmas. (Matthew 24:9-14.)

Jesus tells us how the first tribulations come. He talks with the Centurion in Capernaum about how the sons and daughters of the Kingdom will be thrown into the outer darkness and there people will weep and gnash their teeth. Jesus found great faith in the Centurion, the outsider, the non-religious. (Matthew 8:5ff.) He did not praise him because he was a military person. But Jesus did praise the Centurion because he believed, whereas the sons and daughters of the Kingdom did not. There was a chance, then, for all to become children of the Kingdom—the secular Centurion as well as those who believed themselves to be "insiders." Jesus was very clear about the consequences of this conflict. He looked forward to a division and a fire upon earth:

> Behold, I send you out as sheep in the midst of wolves; so be wise as serpents and innocent as doves. Beware of men; for they will deliver you up to councils, and flog you in their synagogues, and you will be dragged before governors and kings for my sake, to bear testimony before them and the Gentiles. . . . Brother will deliver up brother to death, and the father his child, and children will rise against parents and have them put to death and you will be hated by all for my name's sake. But he who endures to the end will be saved. (Matthew 10:16-22.)

This will be a time "to bear testimony." Today, bearing testimony is described as being a "witness," "martyr" in Greek. The martyrs of that time and the witnesses of today are those who follow those initial teachings of Jesus. Tribulation will be experienced by anyone who accepts the faith, ethics, and plan of Jesus for living in the world but not of it. When Jesus tells his followers that he must go to Jerusalem and suffer many things and be killed, Peter speaks out: "God forbid, Lord, that shall never happen to you!" Jesus replies: "Get behind me,

Satan! You are a hindrance to me; for you are not on the side of God, but of men." (Matthew 16:23.) Jesus rebukes the demon of security and survival in Peter.

These followers shall be servants instead of rulers and the rulers will contest with them. "You know that the rulers of the Gentiles lord it over them, and their great men exercise authority over them. It shall not be so among you; but whoever will be great among you must be your servant, and whoever would be first among you must be your slave; even as the Son of Man came not to be served but to serve and to give his life as a ransom for many." (Matthew 20:25-28.) Service, not security! What a difference, what a conflict with the secular culture then and now. What Jesus is proposing is a new Kingdom on this earth, a threat to the existing secular and religious kingdoms, and one of the reasons why he was executed. This Kingdom of God will be taken away from the chosen religious nation which had been given its responsibility. The Kingdom of God will be taken away and given to a nation producing the fruits of it. (Matthew 21:43.)

Jesus, returning from the temptations of the devil, empowered, spoke first in the synagogue in Nazareth, where he read from Isaiah: "The Spirit of the Lord is upon me because he has anointed me to preach good news to the poor. He has sent me to proclaim release to the captives and recovering of sight to the blind, to set at liberty those who are oppressed, to proclaim the acceptable year of the Lord." (Luke 4:18-19.) He intentionally leaves off the concluding verse from Isaiah concerning vengeance. (Isaiah 61:2b.) Jesus' message here is a message of *hesed*, not *herem*. It is a message to those who are powerless and down-trodden, to those who constitute a threat to kingdoms—the poor, the captives, those who have need of assistance, the lame, the blind. All of those persons Jesus relates to so profoundly are the same ones whom we do not want in our way today. We want to execute the captives; we want to take away the social services for the poor and the blind; we want to label the oppressed "Communists"; we do not want to proclaim the acceptable year of the Lord. The message of Jesus runs counter to the message of the Caesar we worship.

While taking away the powers of wealth and violence and nationhood, Jesus says at the same time, "I have given you authority over all the power of the enemy." (Luke 10:19.) What kind of power is this if not nonviolent power? What kind of power is this, if not to speak on principle, to preach and teach? Is this not the ultimate power over the enemy? He tells them that what is exalted among people is an abomination in the sight of God. If only Jerusalem knew the things that make for peace! (Luke 19:41.)

Even after his death, his followers do not understand him. "Lord, will you at this time restore the kingdom to Israel?" (Acts 1:6.) Implied is expectation of a violent conquering of the land. Jesus replied: " . . . you shall receive power when the Holy Spirit is come upon you and you shall be my witnesses. . . ." (Acts 1:8.) And that is all. After that he was lifted up. Power, witness, authority, preaching, teaching, servanthood. There is no mention of Christians taking up arms to restore Israel then or now. Indeed Israel is not to be restored "politically" but a new Christian Kingdom, a new Christian community is to be inaugurated. Jesus refused to have himself made a territorial king. Nonetheless, it was Jesus' work to cast out the rulers of this world. Why was the religious institution as well as the Empire willing to pass sentence on him? The religious institution's stated position was that it is better for one man to die, so that the whole nation should not perish. The leaders saw that if Jesus were to live and his followers were to practice what he taught, the nation could not endure as it was then instituted. They gave their own answer: if they let him go, " . . . everyone will believe in him, and the Romans will come and destroy both our place and our nation." (John 11:48.) So they killed him for their own security and survival. The only effective way was legalized murder, and yet after his death once again what was left of their nation was lost; the rebuilt Temple was destroyed; the land was completely occupied by the Romans, and later by Islam, followed by the Crusaders, the Ottomans; today it is torn apart by Arab-Israeli conflict.

What easier task could we have? Jesus says, "Be of good cheer, I have overcome the world." His yoke is easy and his burden is light. (John 16:33; Matthew 11:30.) We have only to witness to what has been given to us, and still today we do not understand what that witness might be. Why was Barabbas more acceptable than Jesus to both the Romans and the Jews? Barabbas, after all, was a known revolutionary. Conservatively, however, he was within the mainstream of the cyclical appetites of human beings, both political and religious. He was understood and could be contended with straight away. In the long run, political revolutionaries are not great threats to existing institutions because the revolutionaries re-establish the same institutions in another form. Jesus though was a great threat because he cut through the sham of Satan's kingdoms of politics, economics, and religion. Jesus replaced them with something much more radical than violent, revolutionary governments can ever be.

Jesus' attitude and teaching toward secular society is expressed throughout the New Testament: "Do not love the world or the things of the world. If anyone loves the world, love for the Father is not in him. . . . The wisdom of the world is folly to God. . . . Do you not know that friendship with the world is enmity with God? . . . Therefore, whoever wishes to be a friend of the world makes himself an enemy of God." (1 John 15; James 4:4.) There must be acceptance of a radical alternative to the existing institutions.

THE COMMUNITY OF JESUS

The community of the friends of Jesus is quite different from the secular culture. His community is based upon these sayings put into practice: "Love one another as I have loved you . . . greater love has no one than this, that he or she lay down life for friends. You are my friends if you do what I command you. No longer do I call you servants, for the servant does not know

what the master is doing; but I have called you friends. . . . "
(John 15:12-15.)

Militarists and secularists see in this only a laying down of
life in the context of violence—a willingness to die only if one
goes down killing another. This could not be the message intended here. Jesus calls us to be killed rather than to kill. "They
will put you out of the synagogues; indeed the hour is coming
when whoever kills you will think he is offering a service to
God." (John 16:2.)

Paul's description of the community of God cannot be improved upon:

> "As servants of God we commend ourselves in every way:
> through great endurance, in afflictions, hardships, calam-
> ities, beatings, imprisonments, tumults, labors, watching,
> hunger; by purity, knowledge, forbearance, kindness, the
> Holy Spirit, genuine love, truthful speech, and the power
> of God; with the weapons of righteousness. . . . We are
> treated as impostors, and yet are true; as unknown, and
> yet well known; as dying, and behold we live; as punished,
> and yet not killed; as sorrowful, yet always rejoicing; as
> poor, yet making many rich; as having nothing, and yet
> possessing everything." (2 Corinthians 6.)

The first message of Jesus is to clear out all the garbage of
existing social institutions, structures, and systems into which
we have been born; and to be born again by freeing ourselves
voluntarily, as the Israelites could only do involuntarily, of these
powers and principalities.

Religious and political leaders know that what Jesus was calling for is so fundamentally radical that the destruction of the
temporal political state and the institutional church would take
place if his values were put into practice.

> [Jesus] . . . revolutionized the spirit of all law by teaching
> non-resistance. . . . How this works in modern life has been
> illustrated by Tolstoy, who says that the doctrine of the

gospel would do away with states, tribunals, property and individual rights. . . . The fact is that Jesus here, as well as elsewhere enunciates a principle that would destroy the structure of society. If no man can count as his own that which he has, there can be no such thing as private property. Anarchy would reign supreme and love would change into hatred. . . . How shall the conflict be waged? Only by the utmost abnegation, the completest self-denial on the part of all who despise the world and desire heaven. . . . The world claims justice, through the assistance given by oaths (for discovering truth). Justice is originally based on the principle that a wrongdoer must have as good as he gave. . . . The claim of the world that justice should prevail is denied by Jesus. . . . Judaism has rejected this view of the world.[7]

A Christian theologian agrees:

The exegete must follow that methodological principle that the utterances of Jesus are to be explained according to their literal meaning and context, by comparison with other sayings and the general pattern of his teaching as a whole. . . . Jesus was not only concerned with interior dispositions, but wanted his demands to be interpreted as real commandments that are to be converted into action. . . . [He also wanted] a new code of law, at least new guiding principles, and also to impose a certain pattern of behavior as obligatory. This emerges from the commanding tone of the antitheses, which have the same ring as the voice of the ancient lawgiver.[8]

Tolstoy's discovery of a loving command as the very base of Jesus' teaching—"Resist not the evil doer"—is confirmed by these comments. The call to activate the Jesus community opposed to the secular world is a clear, literal, and easily understood command. The message is clear. The problem is doing it. There is no problem in understanding what is being called for and exemplified by Jesus' teaching and life. The problem is in forming the community. The problem is in witnessing to the world. The problem is in living a life of servanthood in order to be of service.

There is nothing in the teaching of Jesus that indicates that secular kingship of any kind is to be part of his community. Rather the Lordship of God that preceded the kingship of David is reinstituted in the form of the Holy Spirit. The high priesthood is eliminated for all times. Jesus is the last high priest. (Hebrews 9:11, 10:11.) There is no need for high priests because there is no need for a Temple. There is no need for a Temple because there is no need for cultic sacrifice. Christians worship not in the temple of the Samaritans or in the temple of the Jews but in spirit and truth. (John 4:21-24.) Jesus' community is built around that understanding.

His teachings on poverty and wealth are equally clear. By accepting voluntary simplicity and poverty, the friends of Jesus live in a manner that helps to restore balance to economic community. If the rich begin to live like the poor and with the poor, then we not only have community with the poor but we have a community that truly shares once again. And if we truly share with the poor, not just from our excess but from our substance, we may find the miracle of the loaves and fishes taking place in our midst. We find all that we need, if not all that we want. If we begin by not being anxious, being willing to give up our possessions, we find that we possess something far richer. Jesus told us to have very few possessions, (Matthew 10; Luke 9.) and even to sell all and follow him. Our food is to do the will of God, and Jesus is our bread. There is power in his poverty. It is reported in Acts that when his followers lived this kind of life, they all had enough to go around. Poverty is not an end in itself, but voluntary poverty used as a means, results in balance and true community. The disciples lived together and had all things in common. "They sold their possessions and goods and distributed them to all as any had need. And day by day, attending the temple together and breaking bread in their homes, they partook of food with glad and gen-

erous hearts, praising God and having favor with all the people."
(Acts 2:45-47.) They were lovers of poverty and lived together
in that power.

"No one said that any of the things that he possessed was
his own, but they had everything in common." (Acts 4.) The
disciples' understanding of the gift of the land to Abraham was
as a gift for stewardship and not of inheritance nor ownership.
They predicted that in the last days people would be lovers of
money and would accept the plundering of property, but the
disciples had a better possession. The abuse suffered for righteousness' sake was greater than the wealth or treasures of Egypt.
Even in their poverty, they were considered rich by Jesus. Those
who said that "I am rich, I am prosperous" were the lukewarm.
They believed they needed nothing, yet they were poor.

Finally, there is no indication that Jesus' little band ever felt
it necessary, as David and Solomon did, as the Pharisees and
Sadducees did, and as the Roman Emperors did, to use violence
for any purpose. Violence, upon which political, economic, and
religious institutions are built, the very base of the power of
those institutions, is rejected at its source by Jesus Christ. Even
the arguments of Satan that we must use violence to defend
others, if not ourselves, are summarily rejected, without consideration, conversation, debate, or consensus. It's over. It's all
over. All violence is finished.

When Jesus talks about the least of his brethren, in Matthew
25, he is talking about his own people. He is saying, in effect,
"What you do to my poor followers, you do to me." Today,
we don't understand this context as we read Matthew 25. We
interpret it through the filter of our own culture: We suburbanites go down to the slummy part of town and give the poor
folks a glass of water—we, the Christians; they, the fallen-away,
down-trodden, certainly not as clean or well motivated as we
are. But we help them anyway, and as we do, we believe we are
following Jesus. That was not the message of Matthew 25. Jesus
was speaking to people outside his community and welcoming
them simply for their acts of service to his own small band of
poor, powerless people, who roamed the country spreading his

message. In time most of the Jesus people became rich and powerful, but continued to call themselves Christians; so we can no longer easily identify those Jesus was talking about in Matthew 25. He was talking about his friends. In those days they were truly nonviolent and poor.[9]

LIVING IN THE KINGDOM AMID THE NATIONS

Perhaps the clearest indication that Jesus came not to reform existing institutions but to proclaim a new world order is found in his claim of kingship. Jesus claimed to be king and doing so constituted high treason against Caesar. Treason, at that time, was any offense against the Roman Empire that affected the dignity or security of the Roman people. It is easily demonstrable that the teachings of Jesus were treasonable under Roman law. Although Pilate convinced himself that "Christ the King" was not a claim to earthly sovereignty, nevertheless, Jesus' teachings were inconsistent with the law of the state. Jesus, thus, was legally executed as a rebel against Rome—on a cross. The religious leaders of the time cried out to Pilate: "If you release this man, you are not Caesar's friend; everyone who makes himself a king, sets himself against Caesar." (John 19:12.)

Walter Chandler wrote the definitive *Trial of Jesus* many years ago. He looked at the threat Jesus posed to the secular world from a lawyer's viewpoint and he confirmed the acts of treason and sedition by Jesus.[10]

In a more recent study of Luke's Gospel, *Jesus, Politics and Society*,[11] Richard Cassidy asks the question: Was Jesus dangerous to the Roman Empire? He concludes Jesus did pose a threat to Roman rule—not the threat of rebellious, political zealotry; but his words and actions were nonetheless threatening. Nonviolence coupled with love of all, including enemies, is dangerous to statecraft and secular, political power. Jesus had a special concern for the poor, for the sick, for women, for gentiles: "He taught and acted in such a way as to explicitly or implicitly call for radical modifications" in the manner in which the powerless were treated. Jesus lived a simple life, praised others who followed in his footsteps, and took an extremely strong position against the accumulation of wealth. He traveled "with women not related to him or the apostles through marital or family bonds," and he insisted "that social relationships be governed by the themes of service and humility. Jesus rejected the use of violence and criticized the gentile kings for their practice of dominating their subjects."[12] Also, "he refused to defer to or cooperate with the various political officials who were responsible for maintaining these patterns."[13] Responding to the question concerning the paying of tribute, Cassidy writes: "Jesus took the position that the Roman Emperor and Empire were not to be accorded an autonomous or privileged position within the order of creation; they were rather to be evaluated on the basis of how closely they corresponded to the patterns desired by God."[14]

Jesus' kingdom was not an empire in any traditional sense, but a realm of truth; and his truth so conflicted with the Roman Empire that he became a problem for the empire. More will be said about Jesus' actions in violation of secular and theocratic law when we consider the form and practice of Christian community. For now the importance of these considerations is the way in which they demonstrate the nature of Jesus' revolution.

Cassidy agrees with other theologians that if large numbers come to adopt Jesus' stance toward the ruling political authorities, the Roman Empire (or indeed any similarly based social order) could not have continued."[15]

Civil religion, then and now, calls us to see the state as the locus of all public morality. And today fascism, autocratic socialism, or profit capitalism is the supreme civil religion depending upon where we happen to reside. For Jesus, to violate political, religious, and economic strictures and legalisms made him a marked man from the beginning, destined for arrest, trial, conviction, and execution. Jesus' claims were without authority, as authority was then perceived. To legitimize them, "to lay claim to the righteousness of God on behalf of those outside the law, and the transgressors of the law, was in contradiction to the traditions of his people."[16]

Jesus does not "anticipate the kingdom for the righteous . . . but paradoxically promises the kingdom to the unrighteous as a gift of grace and leaves the supposedly righteous outside it."[17] Today the "righteous" are usually the cultural Christians who see the justified use of violence, the accumulation of wealth and power, the idolization of the law as signs of God's presence in them. Jesus' poverty, the preaching of the Kingdom by a poor man, was from the very beginning not well received.

> From the very first Jesus received not merely support, but also hostility and opposition. The conflict which ultimately led to his death was inherent from the first in his life because of this opposition. . . . His execution must be seen as a necessary consequence of this conflict with the law. His trial by the guardians of the law was in the broader sense of the term a trial about the will of God, which the law claimed to have codified once for all.[18]

The fact remains, Jesus was in trouble with both the religious and secular powers. His punishment was not for blasphemy which would have been stoning, as in the case of Stephen. His punishment was crucifixion by the Roman Empire as a political, albeit nonviolent, rebel. Crucifixion was the punishment reserved for crimes against the state, for rebellion against the social and political order of Rome.

Jesus was civilly disobedient in relation to both the secular and religious authorities.[19] Any lawyer living at the time could easily have predicted that an individual behaving in the manner in which Jesus did would soon find himself subject to arrest, trial, conviction, imprisonment, and most likely execution. However, there are few living today, whether lawyers or not, who have this view of Jesus in spite of the Biblical history available to us. One such person is Philip Berrigan, who was asked in a prison interview: "Is there a temporal order (this side of the kingdom) which would not require resistance? If so, what would it look like?"[20] Philip's answer:

> No. Evil flourishes side by side with good, as Christ's parable of the wheat and the tares illustrates. Moreover, I agree with commentators that the First Horseman of the Apocalypse is Christ, riding with War, Famine and Death, but it is given to him to "conquer" them. There is no temporal order that would not require resistance—not even in countries like Tanzania, or in so-called models of the left like Cuba or Vietnam. By definition, the Christian is a resister of any government, civilization, body of law, culture. A close reading of the temptations of Christ or of the Sermon on the Mount should clarify this.

From Nero who threw early Christians to the lions to those who imprison resisters today, it is obvious that this clarity comes through to threatened non-Christians a lot faster than it does to cultural Christians.

Jesus' Sermon on the Mount is a distillation of his teaching. Here we find in clear and unambiguous terms that we should not resist the evil-doer, that we should walk the extra mile, give away what we own, let people borrow with no expectation of return, love our enemies as ourselves, not condemn or judge.[21] When Jesus spoke these words, he spoke for all people for all times. How is it that the Sermon on the Mount, then, has not been practiced by Christians who have preferred the sermons of the politicians? There are many excuses. Some of them are: That the Sermon applies only to a select group of priests or monastics. Not true. Or the Sermon does not apply to then or now, but only when Christ comes again. Where does he say this? Or the Sermon was not given to practice but only to convict us of our sins. How gloomy! There are many more, but this sampling suffices to communicate the fertility of human excuse-making over the years.[22]

The Sermon on the Mount was given as a political, religious, and economic exposition of what living in the Kingdom means as contrasted with living in the world. What we have attempted to do is to live in the world and apply the principles of living in the Kingdom only when they fit conveniently with our principles of living in the world.

To repeat, sometimes the clarity of the Sermon comes through to non-Christians a lot faster than it does to cultural Christians. Richard McSorley tells the story of a Jewish judge in New York who was hearing a case of a Catholic conscientious objector during the Vietnam war.[23] The defending lawyer thought he ought to instruct the judge a bit, so he said, "Your honor, I happen to know that you're a Jew, and you may be surprised to find that here's a Catholic applying for a CO status, because Catholics are not part of a peace church. You may not realize that their Church gives them good backing to be conscientious objectors." The judge responded: "Just a minute, Counselor. It's true that I'm a Jew. But I happen to know that this Jesus who you say was the founder of your religion was also a Jew and that he taught a doctrine of loving service. I have no trouble at all with anyone who says they're a follower of this Jesus who is opposed to killing and war. My trouble is with people who say that they follow Jesus and accept war, as I see Christians all around me doing. So just go ahead with your case, but you don't need to instruct me." It seems from the judge's response that the lawyer was also a Christian. The response of the Jewish judge makes the point.

So Jesus was ripe for trial and tried he was. A somewhat illegal trial at that; but judges then had wide discretion in the manner in which they held trials, just as judges do today. Historians have looked back on the trial of Jesus and found several instances where his case might have been appealed to a higher court, for due process was not honored; even the procedures of the day were violated. Jesus, however, was not concerned with reforming the legal machinery as much as he was with giving his witness, and so he did. The result of giving his witness was that he suffered great tribulation. He was scourged, he was crucified, and his followers were found out.

Thereafter his movement gained greatly in numbers through suffering and tribulation. Many of his followers ended up the same way he did. And they must have remembered what Jesus taught: if they would follow him, tribulation would follow them. (Matthew 10.) To deny Jesus' resistance to political and cultural norms, to deny his preaching of tribulation, to deny that he counseled nonviolence and pacifism, even as he actively and aggressively swept through the temple, is to deny the essential life and message of the founder of Christianity. It is to hide his message from those who are seeking to find the alternative "YES" to the "NO" of the nations.

The place of suffering and tribulation in the life of the Kingdom in the midst of nations brings to mind the conclusion of Kazantzakis' *The Last Temptation of Christ*.[24] In that novel, the author speculates that when Jesus begins his lament on the Cross, "My God, my God, why have you forsaken me?", the Tempter convinces him that he is not on the Cross, has not succumbed to the crucifixion, has somehow escaped it. Jesus, under this delusion, believes that he has returned to the bosom of his community and eventually takes on wives, Martha and Mary, and lives under the name of Lazarus in Bethany until he grows old, at which time he meets Paul and the original apostles. Jesus attempts to convince Paul that he did not die on the Cross. But Paul says it doesn't matter. As a matter of fact, without the fact of Jesus' death and resurrection, the followers of Jesus will believe Paul nonetheless, and Paul can fashion Jesus to his own making. Jesus sees this as a corruption of his whole life, but Paul says, "You have no reason to complain. You didn't die on the Cross. You said so yourself." Then, one by one, his apostles tell him how Jesus had led them by the wrong path, and Judas, close to killing Jesus, howls about how Jesus turned out to be a coward. Just at this point, in Kazantzakis' story, Jesus returns to consciousness on the Cross, concluding his statement: "My God, my God, why have you forsaken me?" and begins to feel the pain once more. The joy that fills him in knowing that he did not give in to this last temptation, that is, that he in fact is crucified and ready to die, the awful pain and tribulation that surrounded him give him joy, because he was true to his life, his principles, and his calling.

Theologians and lay people alike have been tempted over the course of hundreds of years to conjure up rational arguments so that the lifestyle Jesus presents in conflict with the religious, political, and economic institutions will not have to be such a burden. This last temptation, the temptation to deny the Cross, is probably the most serious one of all.

The most famous argument against Christian pacifism is found in an analysis of Romans 13 and is used over and over again by some theologians to convince Christians that God has ordained the state to be the judge of our entire society and to justify all acts contemplated and carried through by the state, whether religious, economic, or political. C. J. Cadoux, probably the foremost authority on early Christian attitudes toward the world, gives the best answer in refuting this claim to state worship. It is well documented that the early Christians prayed for Caesar and for the state. Cadoux states that Paul's words in Romans were written before the outbreak of imperial persecution in 64 AD and in order to counteract the strong tendency toward rebellious and aggressive anarchy in the Christian church, particularly in Rome. To this end Paul wrote what appears in our Bibles today as Chapter 13 of Romans. Nonetheless, Cadoux says:

> We are brought here to the very heart of the Christian problem of the State. Nothing could be more clear and explicit than the declarations as to the origin and purpose of civil government. It is an institution ordained by God for the purpose of restraining, by means of coercion and penalty, the grosser forms of human sin. If this view was a fixed datum in Christian political theory, the rule that a Christian must never inflict an injury on his neighbour, however wicked that neighbour might be, was also a fixed datum in Christian ethical theory: and the problem consists in reconciling these two apparently conflicting data. One thing is clear—that the fact of being appointed by God for

a certain work or permitted by God to do it, did not, in the Christian view, guarantee the righteousness of the agent or his doings. The Apocalypse says that "it was given to the Beast to have authority over all peoples and to make war upon the saints," that is to say, he was in some sense allowed or authorized by God to do it, for the achievement of some good end, such as the chastisement and discipline of the Church. But this did not mean that the Beast was righteous or that his persecution of the saints was not blameworthy. Eirenaias makes it fairly clear that he could as easily think of wicked rulers being appointed by God as he could of good ones. God uses the wickedness of some as a chastisement for others. But even this does not get to the bottom of the matter, for it refers only to the crimes of rulers, not to the just legal penalties they inflict. The key to the problem is simply this, that the just ruler who as the servant of God enforces the laws, punishes the wrong-doers and wages war against the unrighteous aggressor is, in the thought of Paul and the early Fathers, always a *pagan* ruler and therefore, though eligible for conversion, is yet qua pagan, not to be expected to obey the distinctly Christian laws of conduct or to exercise a distinctively Christian restraint upon wrongdoing. Not all the servants of God are necessarily Christians. God has a use for those in the sub-Christian stage of moral development, as well as for those who enjoy the full light of the Gospel. Paul evidently had a genuine respect for the nobler elements in the gentile mind, including that sense of responsibility for the peace and well-being of society, that love of law and order, that appreciation of the elements of justice which—with whatever admixture of baser motives and whatever crudity of unloving restrictive methods—formed the fundamental principles of the Roman Empire. In other words, the Christian justification of coercive government and of war, though real and sincere was only a *relative* justification: it was relative to the non-christian condition of the agents concerned. It therefore furnished no

model for Christian conduct and no justification for any
departure on the part of the Christian from the gentler
ethics characteristic of the religion of Jesus.[25]

In my opinion, no finer statement of this dichotomy has ever
been made. It should lay to rest the arguments of those who
are unwilling to take up the pacifist cross of Jesus and his simple
lifestyle, but who are constantly finding ways to turn Jesus into
a rich, political militarist through far-fetched interpretations of
the Biblical literature. It is ludicrous to believe that Jesus came
and went and the same institutions of political, economic, and
religious culture would continue with the only difference being
that a Christian would worship for a few hours on Sunday in a
different way and would try to perfect the natural morality of
Rome and of Israel in a somewhat reformed manner. No, Jesus
was much more than cultural Christians are willing to admit.
The challenge for us is to apply his radical teachings to our
common place lives, taking the risk of the consequences which
are sure to follow.

Biblical faith eventually forces one to adopt a radically alternative approach to existing institutions. Charles McCarthy
wrote that because the Christian is not of this world, but here
rather to practice freely agape service, Christian obedience to
the state comes to an end at the point where service becomes
impossible. The means of the world become antithetical. Violence, coercion, accumulation of wealth and political power,
defense of one's security and survival—all are at the heart of
the political commonwealth. Once we understand Jesus' teaching and life and compare it to the secular culture and its teaching, we are forced to conclude that the latter is fundamentally
incompatible with the will of God and the teachings of Jesus.[26]

In spite of God's love of humankind, in spite of God's extreme
humility in entering into human projects in order that people
may finally enter into their own design, one cannot but be seized
by a profound sense of the inutility and vanity of human action.
"To what end is all of this agitation, to what end these constant
wars and states and empires?"[27]

Once more we ask: How do we live in the light of the Kingdom of God while in the midst of the world of nations? How do we live as if the Kingdom has come while we wait for its final coming? For living as if our primary citizenship is with the world of nations is to worship the idol of the ways of nations. Jeremiah the prophet warned Israel against this; Jesus warned his friends against this; and we must once again raise the warning, and practice community. This worship of the nation-state has brought us to the brink of world catastrophe. What are the possibilities? To continue as we are? To quit and leave the country? To reform and legislate if we can? To terminate those we identify as evil-doers? Or to live as if the Kingdom has come? The first is to be a Sadducee. The second is to be an Essene. The third is to be a Pharisee. The fourth is to be a Zealot. The last is to be as Jesus.

Recent revolutions have fostered hope in some but *not all* "liberation theologians." Some seem to hope that violent revolution will somehow usher in the Kingdom. This is a bitter hope to be discarded, even in the depth of the understanding of the needs of the poor and the horrors of their present life. There is another way, as we are seeking to discover.

Robert Nolan in *Jesus Before Christianity* discovers that Jesus rejected these same choices but accepted John the Baptist.[28] John the Baptist came to a world where it was believed: prophecy was dead; God was silent; the end was near. A prophet appeared. A prophet is one who speaks not to individuals alone, but to individuals as members of a nation, and to leaders of nations. John's message to the nations, both political and religious, both fallen, was to call for repentance and baptism in response to a world heading for catastrophe. Jesus listened, was baptized, recognized the coming catastrophe, and the very first thing he did was to form community. He resisted authority by confrontations and advocacy. He practiced simplicity and voluntary poverty. He identified with the poor and with sinners. He preached first to the lost sheep of Israel who are described as the oppressed, those within Israel who had no future. And later his message was carried to others outside this fold. They heard both within and without; the "well off" did not. Jesus preached God's will to love God and neighbor in the form of compassion, liberation, conversion. The message was and is that the Kingdom of God is in our midst, within the nation, but it does not partake of wealth, prestige, exclusivity, or domination. Each one of God's people has a right to whatever all other members of God's people possess. When some are wealthy and some are not, when some have prestige and others do not, when some can exclude others, when domination becomes the prominent mode of human relationships, then we have followed the ways of the nations and we must change.

The Israelites, the people of God, were told not to live as those round about with kings and palaces and idols, but to be set apart, not separate but distinct, as a witness, a light to the nations. Christians, as children of that light, are people whose imaginations have been challenged by God who has invited us to an "otherwise unimaginable kingdom."[29] Imagination is formed by learning to live the story of Christ in a world of violence and despair.

So, we imagine now, that our light shines. Do not hide it under anything. Gather as community, not only to comment but to practice. What was original about the first Christians was not the peculiarity of their beliefs which nation-states can contend with, but their social inventiveness in creating a community which had an outward effect the like of which had not been seen before. Religion had surely become marginal, asocial, relinquished to the private and subjective realm. Our task, I believe, is to continue that creation of community, and not to let it die as we live, but to let it live as we, as individuals, must surely die. For it is in that living creation that we, as community, will also surely live eternally and be resurrected for that Kingdom which certainly will come.

We have not been left alone to discover this. We have already experienced Christianity as intended by Jesus from the beginning. We see that life and community in the experiences and experiments of the first Christians who, empowered by the Advocate and Comforter given them by Jesus, became a light to the nations some nineteen centuries ago. It is to that model and witness we now turn.

CHAPTER THREE

CHRISTIANITY AND EMPIRE

THE RISE OF THE CHRISTIANS

The new community that Jesus established finally came to understand what he meant by his rejection of the temptations of Satan. The "born again" Christian at the time of Acts was one who overcame the original sins of the powers and principalities, the sins of culture. He or she was washed in the spirit of a new birth. Those who first approached John the Baptist as prophet to the nations repented and joined the new community formed by Jesus as a radical witness to the idols of nations.

In Acts 1:6 it is reported that at first these disciples did not understand what Jesus had taught or what had happened. They asked Jesus, even after all that had taken place, including his resurrection, "Lord, will you at this time, restore the kingdom to Israel?" This was the crucial point to them. The kingdom, as nation, had been lost all those years. By the time of Jesus the Israelites no longer had a king—their political power was lost; they no longer had a free land—their economic power was lost; they were holding onto a temple that had been rebuilt by the pagan power of the Herods and which Jesus predicted would also be lost, and which in fact was destroyed by 70 AD. They

85

believed that Jesus, the Messiah, had come to restore the very institutional powers that were lost, so that Israel could be what it once was in the eyes of the world. But Jesus would not put old wine into new wineskins. He said Israel should not be what it once was. He said he would not restore a kingdom based on violent institutions lacking in faith, trust, and vulnerability. Jesus divorced himself from the sin of his own culture. This sin was truly the "misunderstanding of Judas"—"strength through force."[1]

Instead, Jesus prepared his community to live in the world armed only with the power of the Holy Spirit, the nonviolent example of the Lamb, and thus empowered, to create the Kingdom of God among the nations. Jesus had truly overcome the world and his followers no longer needed those powers which had been the nemesis of their forebears, the Israelites, who now saw the powers and principalities acting against them through Rome.

Little by little, Jesus' followers began to realize that this was a new kind of Kingdom, based on a spiritual power, the use of which had been absent since the rise of the monarchy, the marketplace, and the Temple. Complete divorce from that kind of lifestyle was necessary for them too. The new power operated in the political, economic, and religious realms but in a very different and radical way. Theirs was to be a Kingdom apart but a Kingdom within, based not on violent institutions and cultures, but on the radical truths of Christian nonviolence, love, and trustfulness. They also saw that not only were they not to restore the kingship, but economically, even though living in Jerusalem, they should live as if they were spiritually in the wilderness. For, as Acts reports, their life was truly spiritual, nonviolent, and simple. They possessed little except the immense power the Spirit had given them at Pentecost.

Just as they gave up the political and economic power of the world, they also gave up religious power, as we see in Acts 6 by the example of Stephen, the first martyr. Stephen was killed by the powerful Judeans. At that time there were great hostilities between the North, which was the original kingdom called Israel, and the South, Judea. Jesus, a Nazarene, and most of his followers, Galileans, were from the North. Northerners were considered second-class citizens; the Judeans in the South did not have much use for them and felt self-righteously superior. Jerusalem, situated in the South, the center of Judean power, had much to do with this false superiority. It is not surprising that a Messiah from the North would be unacceptable to the ruling religious, political, and economic classes of Judea.

Anyway, the Judeans were bent on killing Stephen for blaspheming the Temple. Stephen reminded them that though Solomon built God a house, God does not dwell in a house made with human hands. Here we have an obvious allusion to the story about Nathan and the building of the institutional church. (2 Samuel 7.) Stephen even added that the real Temple is the Holy Spirit within each person. This indicates that the early Christian community recognized the temple, or the house of God, within each individual as part of their community. When individuals gathered in Christian community, the temple of the Holy Spirit was born again in that community because it was born again in each one of the followers. As Jesus taught, it could not be destroyed. (Mark 14:58.) Jesus' resurrection provided the early Christians with the foundation of an indestructible "temple"—the body of the community. They recognized this message of alternative spiritual power and were able to witness to it, proclaiming Lordship instead of kingship, religious community instead of institutional church, voluntary poverty and simplicity instead of money, Mammon, and possessions. These alternatives fostered peace, love, and righteousness within the community. They rejected all wars, all human kings, and Mammon as a basis for their economic security. This ideal Christian community lasted for several hundred years; then, once again, it too fell as a replay of the history of the Israelite fall.

As they began to live in community, the early Christians carefully followed Jesus' teachings on the way of life. But theirs was a new community thrown into the midst of an existing culture which for thousands of years had operated according

to the way of death. The pagan nations, whose ways the Israelites adapted, in part, and which proved to be their ruin, were
also present to exert their influence on the Christian community. At first the early church attempted to accommodate itself
to the existing structures and not to resist them. It is at this
very early point that the process of acculturation and fall begins.
If there was a conflict, it was almost invariably with the established religious culture.

The Roman Empire, the political power, was perceived to
help, to stabilize, and protect the good from the evil. In particular, this was Paul's opinion, written at a time prior to the
political persecutions. Although Christians banded together in
community and answered the fundamental questions we have
posed about living together and relating to society, they seemed
to be lulled into accommodation with the Roman government.

There were, however, sporadic incidents with the political
authorities. In Ephesus there was a dispute over the impact of
Paul's teaching on the sale of Diana idols (Artemis, in Greek)
in the form of small statues. Apparently this was a lucrative
business. Paul seemed to have caused the wealth from this
enterprise to diminish and thus to have had an economic impact
on the Roman state. (Acts 19.)

The Romans were not directly angered; it was the town clerk
there who settled the dispute. However, the Christians were
aware that the persecution was no accident but arose out of
the faith-commitment of the church. This persecution was predicted by Jesus. It was a persecution that began here because
of economic conflict.

Rome eventually awakened to the lion of Judah in its midst.
The first official acts against Christians were the persecutions
of the Emperor Nero, which culminated in the death of the
religious leaders, Peter and Paul. Death penalties were pronounced against the Christians. A new sect had succumbed to
a superstition that was dangerous to the public.

The first holocaust report issues from Tacitus: "They were
clothed in animal skins and were torn to pieces by dogs (or
they were fixed on crosses or were buried) and when darkness

came they served as torches."[2] Christians were condemned solely for not renouncing their faith.

Were the Romans suddenly so intolerant of the religious beliefs of their subjects? No. Where the Romans did not see the interest of the state involved, they did not take any action. Perhaps the incident of the Diana dolls did not excite such state action. The Romans were known for their religious tolerance, and they practiced that religious tolerance toward the Jewish institutions in their midst. Rome did have an interest, however, in its own security. And when this Jewish sect of Christians began to cause more and more problems for the state, Rome had to face the situation publicly. A contradiction arose here which placed Christian belief, faith, and practice in conflict with the Roman culture—legal, political, and social—and caused persecution of the new community. The confession or admission of one's being a Christian was crime enough. But why? Why would describing oneself as a Christian be enough to have one's life taken? What was the great fear that emerged between the time of Paul and the time of Nero? Why was the proclamation of Christianity so threatening to Rome then but not before?

We know the early Christians considered the chief means for practicing their religion to be a deep and premeditated nonviolence or pacifism. Political, revolutionary resistance, in the style of the Zealots, was not associated with the Way of the early Christians. Pacifism or nonviolence was not simply a political ethic, but a religious faithfulness and way of life. It was essentially religious, in the best sense of that word, and so had potential political effects of the most fundamental and revolutionary nature. It took Rome a long time to see the threat as a much greater one—a moral threat to the values of empire, and beyond that to the basic structure and essence of its worldly power. It went to the heart of the powers and principalities, to the demonic core of its systems. The very systems and structures themselves were threatened, albeit nonviolently. Parts or aspects of the structure were not threatened by violent overthrow, hence the deafness of a state attuned to violence.

Even the Christians, including Paul for some time, failed to recognize the division that Jesus promised. The fire he longed for had finally taken hold. During Paul's period the church was considered politically loyal, because the kingdom which she expected was not of this world. Jesus was perceived as a non-political Messiah. The difficulty in finding something between the Jesus who would overthrow the Jewish state and the Jesus who, on the other hand, is completely apart, separate, and irrelevant to any political state, was as difficult for Luke and Paul to grasp as it is for many modern Christians. A non-political Jesus cannot be justified in light of history. How can a non-resistant church, not of this world, be a threat to anyone or anything? It took time for the Romans to perceive the answer to that question, and Christians today are still asking the question.

A THREAT TO THE NATIONS

This church's model, its image, its peaceful offer of an alternative Way automatically becomes a profound political threat. It need not lift the sword. The Psalms said it—the way was not by might or power, not by horses or chariots; and Jesus pointed the way clearly. (Psalms 83, 116:17; Matthew 5:17.) The Law and the Prophets would be fulfilled not militarily, through conquering, but by overcoming the world. And the Romans were being overcome. The Christians were to live as if the world recognized the presence of the Kingdom when, in fact, only they did. And then, after the Christians recognized it, the Romans recognized it; and they did not wish to be overcome.

The Christians' faith was necessarily activated in public and therefore it had a political effect while at the same time it was not political in principle. But for a politically powerful state, the distinction was irrelevant. Security is threatened by effect as much as by principle.

The Book of Revelation reveals that by the time of Domitian (c. 90 AD) the Romans had caught on. The consequences of the anti-worldly statements of Jesus were surely evident by this time. The increasing anxiety of Rome illustrates the real and deep conflict between the young Christian community and the Roman Empire in its death throes.

The conflict which emerged also speaks to the manner in which Christians carried out their beliefs in practice. Voluntarily and freely, Jews, gentiles, and Romans joined this new way of life. The threat became intolerable. Imagine hundreds of thousands of North Americans becoming conscientious objectors, refusing to fight or pay their war taxes, and living in intentional community based on simplicity and communitarian worship. Imagine them refusing to participate in capitalist institutions, creating instead a subsistence economy and living by such economic practices as barter. North America's security would be so threatened that Christians would be treated in a far different way than they are now. Supreme Court rulings would be decided almost exclusively as they now partly are—in a way that would preserve the security and survival of the state over against First Amendment "free exercise" of religion.[3]

With economic and political transformation come religious change and turmoil. Therefore the powerful civil religionists of our time who join with the U.S.A. in its fight for survival and security against the other nations of the world would also find themselves at odds with their own Christian brothers and sisters. The tranquility and peace they seek to preserve as a sign of God's approval of North America's culture exists only because Christians today have adjusted to a cultural concept of political peace. In this way their tax exemptions and privileged status with the state are preserved.[4] It was not so in the times of the early Christians, who had no tax exemptions or privileged status. They were threatening simply because they placed their faith in an alternative vision of security, and they were not co-opted by comfort and privilege.

The faith in community, the practice of peace and not war, the worship of the Lord and not the secular king or emperor, the placing of little value on wealth while living a simple life, the refusal to accept law as the ultimate social value, all are determining factors which placed Christians at odds with the political state. The Christian who looked to righteousness rather than pagan social justice and pagan moral values was ripe for persecution by both Rome and Jerusalem. The ultimate political act was the creation of community.

> Christ did not simply tell us to love one another. He "acted out" what he was talking about, striving with twelve to create a miniature model of the community he was fore-telling. Community energizes, injects spirit, sends out waves of hope, attracts, and finally disturbs ordinary patterns of thinking and responding, which is the reason an authentic expression of community often threatens the established order and in time finds itself in opposition to existing powers.[5]

The religious community sets itself apart while remaining within the midst of the nations to model love, and then returns that love to the larger community of nations. A community which simply refuses to fight poses a threat to the world at large, for it is free at last of worldly weapons. It does not need to *do* revolution, it *is* revolution. It is more than revolution, it is radicalization, transformation, *metanonia* (a turning around).

Yoder writes "The key to the obedience of God's people is not their effectiveness but their patience,"[6] as well "endurance." (Revelation 13:10; Matthew 12.) This key could also be described as "significance" or "faithfulness." But the state's business cannot exist if the citizenry occupies itself with useless, ineffective acts of faithfulness and endurance in place of "social responsibility" and practicality. The state cannot see the benefits it will derive from these acts, because the state is based not on patience but on "success."

The characteristics of community inherent in the life of the earliest Christians provided an alternative and holistic way of living in the world to which those Christians were called. This way conflicted with the way of death, the way of the pagan culture. Christians are called even now to be a nation set apart in the midst of the nations.

One of the key charges of Christian community life was to obey, in a broader, more extensive sense, the commandment of God to Moses not to kill. Phillips, in his *Law of Ancient Israel*, points out that human beings are the express objects of the commandment not to kill. The injunction did not apply only to violent acts, that is, intentional or malicious ones, but to all killing, regardless of the method or motivation. In Israelite times the prohibition was never used to describe killing in war and it applied only to the internal community of Israelites. Love of neighbor was confined to the community and never extended to the enemy, although eventually it included the stranger.[7] How did Jesus affect all of this? With the parable of the good Samaritan, he extended love to enemies; and by so doing Jesus taught that we may not kill our enemies if we are to live as Christians. Jesus' teaching embraced the cultural meaning of the commandments of Yahweh. The narrower meaning of "killing" had been in the culture for so long that it was considered Yahweh's absolute law.[8] Because he refuted it, Jesus had to be wrong, could not be the Messiah, and must be killed. To allow him to live would infect the nation with this false notion. If the nation-state may not kill its enemies, it cannot continue to exist in its present form. Jesus thus expanded the narrow confines of the earlier commandment of Moses and applied it to all types of killing, including war, and even to people outside the community, including enemies. How radical and revolutionary this was!

In practice love of enemy comes into conflict with our own security or survival. Jesus taught us how to die, not how to kill.[9] All nation-states teach us how to kill. The nation-state believes that by killing we are set free, but the first Christian community believed that by dying we are set free.

Another fundamental characteristic of the early Christian community was that it was organized on the basis of morality and not legality. So it was an anarchistic, voluntary society, not characterized by

the art of imposing one's will upon others. The saying of
Jesus in Mark 10:42-44 leaves no room for this within the
Christian community. ["Their great men exercise authority
over them. But it shall not be so among you; but whoever
would be great among you must be your servant, and
whoever would be first among you must be slave of all."]
If one believes the imposition of one's will is wise and
necessary, one must leave the Christian community to do
it. This saying is as close as the Gospels come to directions
on the Christian administration of political power.[10]

This saying is Jesus' call to be unlike the gentiles who thrived
on the exercise of authority over others. In secular society
service and servanthood do not count as stepping stones for
advancement unless we talk of service in terms of military service. Early Christians eschewed military service, profit, competition, and power. The state's values were the same in the
days of Rome and the early Christians as they are today. Practicing pacifism was and is a unilateral, gratuitous, and voluntary
act of Christian faithfulness. It was and is an anathema to the
state. From the state's point of view, it brings chaos unless
contained and controlled by legal definition and enforcement.[11]
For hundreds of years early-church discipline so formed Christian communities that they could neither kill for Caesar nor
follow compulsory orders. In an apostolic order of Saint Hippolytus of Rome it is written:

> The subordinate soldier may not kill. If he is ordered to,
> he may not carry out the order; nor may he take the military
> oath. If he does not agree, reject him [from church mem-
> bership]. An official with the power of life and death or a
> high-ranking civil official must either cease or be rejected.
> Catechumens or faithful who wish to enter the army are
> to be rejected because they scorn God.[12]

The early Christian community accepted this instruction.
What else could follow from loving one's enemies? For the first

one hundred fifty years after Christ, there is no record of Christian military activity or soldiering in the Roman army. Even as late as 300 AD, there were few Christian soldiers. At the beginning of the 4th century, the Emperors Diocletian and Galarius purged their armies of the few Christians they had, an indication that the numbers were small. Numerous disciplines of the church taught categorically that one could not be a soldier and a Christian at the same time. A church order from Egypt reads, "They shall not receive into the church one of the emperor's soldiers. If they have received him he shall refuse to kill if commanded to do so. If he does not refrain he shall be rejected."[13]

Of course, if one refuses to kill for Rome, one may likewise be rejected by Rome and perhaps martyred. The story of Maximilian is exemplary. Maximilian, a young African, was required, even though he was a convert to Christianity, to serve in the army because of a Roman law that the son of a military professional was obligated to perform military service. Maximilian refused and he died. He was killed by the Roman Empire which was threatened by the nonviolent love of one person's refusal to join hundreds of thousands of others in the army of Rome.[14]

Interestingly, there existed early on a direct relationship between ministerial leadership and martyrdom. Schillebeeckx writes that:

> Until well into the second century, "the witness" or martyr, i.e., a Christian who had confessed Jesus as Christ before the civil authorities . . . was qualified to be a church leader. . . . [15]

Rather than ordination, suffering and withstanding torture or derision "consecrated" one as "priest." The Christian who had suffered and been tested was the obvious one for community leadership and ministry.

Examples of radically alternative Christian community are so numerous that it is difficult to choose only one illustration. The early Christians were a light to the nations, living an alternative, religious, communal lifestyle while exemplifying hospitality, service, and voluntary simplicity in contrast to economic power, gain, and wealth.

Lactantius summed it up well:

> For what are the interests of our country, but the inconvenience of another state or nation?—That is, to extend the boundaries which are evidently taken from others, to increase the power of the state, to improve the revenues— all of which are not virtues, but the overthrowing of virtues; for in the first place, the union of human society is taken away, the abstaining from the property of another is taken away; lastly, justice itself is taken away. . . . For how can a man be just who injures, who hates, who despoils, who puts to death? and they who strive to be serviceable to their country do all these things. Is the Laurel of triumph made up of leaves, or of corpses? is it decorated with ribbons, or tombs? is it besmeared with ointments, or with the tears of wives and mothers, perhaps those of some men even [who are] Christians—for Christ [is] among the barbarians as well.[16]

THE CONSTANTINIAN FALL

Service to country was valueless to Lactantius. It was Christian idolatry, this killing for Caesar or partaking in secular economic values. Athanagoras had said it all before, "For it is not enough to be just (and justice is to return like for like) but it is incumbent on us to be good and patient of evil. . . . "[17] Early Christianity did not have a rule of reciprocal justice. Aristotle defined justice as giving "each man his due." In contrast, the early Christian ideal was one of servanthood and service, of hospitality, patience, pacifism, and community, all absent in the society into which the Christians came.

C. J. Cadoux, in *The Early Church and the World*, records the relationship of Christian social practices to those of the Jews

and Romans. The Christian aversion to the use of compulsion
and penalty, the glorification of poverty, and the deprecation
of wealth were all part of the structures and systems of early
Christian community.[18] The conclusion of all learned theologians and historians who have examined the progress of Christian community from the time of Jesus to the time of
Constantine is the same: though at first they followed the basic
principles of community, pacifism, and simplicity, somewhere
along the way the Christians lost their salt. They were overcome
by the world; they fell as did the Israelites before them. The
leaders themselves came to be poor witnesses. "Prosperous
ecclesiastics soon came to enjoy the possession of great wealth
and to live in great luxury while little account was taken of the
Gospel command to love one's enemies. . . . "[19] Perhaps they
were just dog tired of being the victims of holocaust. Perhaps
they would try their luck on reversing the roles.

> The common run of Christians . . . seems largely to have
> lost their Savior as the salt of society. What made things
> worse was the dreadful lack of charity and good-feeling,
> even of fair-mindedness and honesty. . . . Surely too, there
> was something amiss with the ideal of religious truth and
> value. . . . Somewhere or other the church had here missed
> its Founder's way.[20]

Christians at their lofty heights had died rather than kill, but
not without exercising the truth and love of holy resistance
before the powers and principalities. Theirs was an original,
holy disobedience unto death. They refused to pay taxes to the
temple of the state. They forbade the receipt of money for
magistrates polluted by war. "Numerous instances of this ob-
stinate and avowed disobedience to government orders are
mentioned."[21] Apollonias was told at his trial that the Roman
Senate had decreed that there were to be no Christians. He
replied, "But God's desire cannot be overridden by a human
decree."[22] Another martyr, in an address to the proconsul of

Africa in 180 AD, refused to recognize the secular government at all.[23]

Just like the Davidic fall, there was a Constantinian fall. Both resulted from the acceptance of kingship, the acceptance of wealth, the acceptance of an institutionalized temple. There was once again an apparent need for secular security, a need to eliminate risk, a need to be temporally successful; and it arose after seduction by the powers and principalities which pointed to secular structures as the gods to be worshiped. The pacifist, communal-living Christians slowly but surely began to long for the strength and security found in the political, economic, and religious powers. The beast thought dead, revived, as predicted in Revelation 13.

The temptation to economic power came in 305 AD as the Empire recognized Christians who, in return for economic protection of their possessions and property, swore allegiance to the state. I remember seeing a Catholic high school textbook which taught school children that what happened at the time of Constantine was the triumph of Catholicism over the Romans.[24] Hindsight shows us rather that it was the first triumph of Caesar over Christianity. A contract was worked out with Rome that was culturally and economically beneficial to the Christians: their property would now be protected; before, it had been destroyed or confiscated by the Romans. Indeed, the very ones who destroyed the property would now be its protectors. And so it happened. The church received protection for its lands and it began to accumulate them at a greater rate, protected now by the power of the state located in the city of Rome. Hundreds of years later, St. Francis of Assisi would abhor the accumulation of possessions, for he said that one would need to protect these possessions and ultimately the protection would be by means of weapons.

Politically, Christians were granted Roman citizenship and freedom from persecution; they were thereafter required to help defend Rome and Rome's possessions to the death in war. Once again, the political temptations of violence and kingship triumphed. But the change could mean only that someone else

would be substituted for the Christians and would go to the
lions. These new persecuted individuals were called heretics
and later included Jews who were often earmarked by the Christians themselves.

The worldly powers had always demanded measure for measure—worldly justice. So it was not a question of the lion lying
down with the lamb, but simply a question of whom the lion
would devour next. The Christian lamb became the Roman lion
and Rome triumphed, not only politically, but religiously as
well. The religious temptation finally triumphed in 382 AD,
when Pope Damasus added the word "Roman" to the word
"Catholic" and then assumed the Roman title *Pontifex Maximus*.[25]
The cycle was complete. The cultural religious power took on
the name of the political empire; and as that empire later collapsed, the Roman church took its place. The popes replaced
the caesars and lived in a castle like David, with a temple nearby
like Solomon's, later made secure by the economics of Vatican
museums, art treasures, and worldwide investments. Today the
pope emerges from this Roman Jerusalem to preach to the
world about poverty, simplicity, and peace; then he returns to
its splendor, the while supporting such obvious contradictions
as R.O.T.C. on U.S. Catholic campuses and state protectionism
in Poland.

How the Church moved from holy community to this fall
should be examined more closely. First, we look at community,
and the changing, internal structure of the early church—the
loss of its radical social structure in the midst of worldly culture.

The empire of Caesar Augustus claimed eternity here on
earth. The emperor himself claimed to be a god. Strikingly
similar Christian claims appeared at this stage. The Kingdom
of God would be eternal, but Jesus is God, not Augustus. The
work of Augustus was not in any sense novel; on the contrary,
it was merely the culmination of efforts begun centuries before—the efforts to create politically a world safe for civilization.
But the one thing Jesus did not promise his followers was safe
civilization. His followers agreed it was not possible to attain a
goal of permanent security, peace, and freedom through polit-

ical action, especially not through submission to the power or fortune of a political leader. "This notion the Christians denounced with uniform vigor and consistency. . . . In Christ, therefore, they claimed to possess a principle of understanding superior to anything existing in the classical world. By this claim they were prepared to stand or fall."[26]

Unfortunately, they fell. Caesar's gift to the world was to be civil law, following the Greek gift of philosophy. Paul had already warned against the lawyers and philosophers. (Colossians 2:8; Romans 3:19.) Cicero, the Roman legal philosopher, reiterated the theme that "the primary concern of those responsible for the conduct of public affairs . . . will be to make certain that every man is secure in his possessions. . . . "[27] Protection is the reason that states and republics have been created. Justice in the Roman state, one of its four great values, is described as the "bond and principle of civil society . . . to harm no one unless provoked by injury."[28] In contrast, the principle of Jesus and the early community was to harm no one *even* if provoked by injury.

Among the Romans economic values were also paramount. Fundamental was protection of property. "The first duty of government was to ensure through the machinery of law that every man should retain what he owned and that, while the poor and lowly should not be swindled out of their earnings, envy of the prosperous might not cause them to be robbed of their wealth."[29]

Christianity, however, by preaching the Gospel to the poor upset the Roman world. By 313 AD, the elements of opposition between church and state came to a head. "Christianity never preached or advocated the forceful overthrow of Roman order. Nonetheless, it regarded that order as due to extinction by reason of its inherent deficiencies, and it confidently anticipated the period of its dissolution as a prelude to the establishment of the earthly sovereignty of Christ."[30] The Roman Empire disintegrated; but by the time it did, *there was a different Christian community to replace it.* The Christians were no longer the possessors of Christ's sovereignty. The Christians had accepted

Constantine as "the champion delegated by the Most High to be the minister of his vengeance."[31] But where in the Gospels or the witness of the early Christians does it say or even imply that God, who told the Israelites not to put a human king in God's place, would find Constantine suitable as king?

It was Paul who first "conceded the fullest measure of legitimacy to temporal authority."[32] Nonetheless Tertullian later warned against a Christian caesar. "The fact that Christ rejected an earthly kingdom should be enough to convince you that all secular powers and dignities are not merely alien from, but hostile to, God. . . . For us nothing is more foreign than the commonwealth. . . . I owe no obligation to forum, campus, or senate. . . . We realize to enter Caesar's prison is to become free" since the world of self is a prison.[33]

By the late 2nd century, however,

> for the forms of their organization the Christian communities had made heavy drafts upon contemporary secular society. In the *civitas*, for instance, they had discovered a model for the *ecclesia*, its *ordo* (clergy) and *plebs* (laity) corresponding respectively to the *curia* and the *populus*. . . . The *ecclesia* had emerged as an antitype to the *civitas*. [The church had] an elaborate scheme for organized relief, . . . dispensed . . . uneconomically, according to the Christian law of charity, and was on this account to be stigmatized by the Emperor Julian as one of the principal snares for the poor and the weak.[34]

Christians were perceived still as atheists because they refused to accept the divinity of the emperor. Tertullian unmasked the Roman agenda for what it was, an "attempt to consecrate or set up purely secular values in the name of Augustus and Rome."[35]

The change of church attitudes toward Rome is no better contrasted than by Saint Hippolytus of Rome, who saw the Empire as a "satanic imitation of Christ's kingdom,"[36] and Eusebius, a bishop and historian, who said: "the empire was divinely ordained. And the Christian emperor, the church's defender against false gods.[37] Between the time of Hippolytus (d.ca. 210) and that of Eusebius (d.ca. 340), the empire became more autocratic and the Christian church became a professional organization and agency. It was no longer a community. By 321 AD, the church became a corporation permitted to accept gifts and legacies under Roman law; it also acquired tax privileges, the strongest weapon of the state for tempting the church to "mind its own business." In requiring the church to mind its own business, secular authority invariably reserves for itself the further privilege of defining what church business is.

THE DEVELOPMENT OF CHURCH POWER

Within the alternative religious community, a developing ecclesiastical institution emerged. Instead of the original Christian prophets, teachers, and other charismatic ministers, the bishops or priests gradually established themselves as the chief and eventually the sole leaders of communities.[38] Priests, who had converted to Christianity from Judaism and had given up their priestly titles, became priests again. The word "priest" is not used anywhere in the New Testament for someone who holds office in the church. It is a title given only to Old Testament, Judean dignitaries. "In his preaching Jesus does not use the image of the priest and the cult. . . . On no occasion did Jesus describe himself or his disciples as priests."[39] Priests were not mentioned as being among Christians, except in the Book of Revelation; and the cultic and ceremonial aspects of Judaism were thoroughly eliminated by the time of the first Christians. By the 4th century we see them emerging again in a priesthood, cultic sacrifice, and ceremony mimicking in religious terms the secular order of the Roman Empire.

The cultic instrument for the installing of the priests—ordination—is not mentioned in any of the Pauline letters, nor is any kind of ritual for appointing people to office. The word *eucharistia* or thanksgiving is not used in Scripture for the Lord's Supper and first appears later in the writings of the *Didache*.[40]

The oldest fixed formation of the ecclesiastical prayer comes from the time of Hippolytus(c. 200). The breaking of bread, however, existed from the time of Acts. The documents of Vatican II admit that "the word *sacerdos* is in Holy Scripture used only of Christ, the priests of the Old Covenant, and the whole Christian people. . . . "[41] In the New Testament the ministers are in general called *episcopoi, presbyters,* or overseers. Theirs was an authority exploding out of the original community structure. The hierarchical, ecclesiastical, paternalistic institution of priesthood came later and took on the trappings of the secular power structure which had been renounced.

Renunciation of power, however, is possible only for a person who has grasped something of the message of Jesus in the Sermon on the Mount. These demands of Jesus are not abstract ideas but relevant guidelines for the church and its governing.

The centralization of power through priesthood and hierarchy, ordination, sacrificial, presided-over Eucharist all led to a new type of professional, secularized, institutional church based on the archetype of Roman law and ritual, ready to vie with the soon to be fallen eagle of Rome for world power.

In the early church there is no special problem regarding who should preside at the thanksgiving Eucharist. In the house churches of Corinth it was the hosts who presided at the eucharistic meal, but these were at the same time leaders of the house churches.[42]

Hans Kung tells us that "the Eastern (and African) view of the Church did not start with a universal bishop, but with a fellowship of believers, with local Churches and their bishops, and was not so much legally as sacramentally, liturgically and symbolically oriented: a collegial, federated fellowship of Churches. But this older ideal of the Church found less and less sympathy in Rome as time went on."[43] The hosts of the house churches were replaced by bishops of far-away institutions.

Irenaeus, Cyprian, and others approved of church centralization in the West. They found the master design for centralization in the Roman, secular counterpart, thus giving birth to a Roman heresy which set the stage for the Constantinian take-over in the 4th century.

None of these changes had any Biblical basis. "In the beginning the leaders of the community *ipso facto* also presided at the Eucharist. . . . Anyone who is competent to lead the community in one way or another is *ipso facto* also president at the Eucharist. . . . In the course of history the link between community and ministry is narrowed down to an inner bond between priesthood and Eucharist."[44]

We know this to be true as we compare today's church institutions with the early Christian communities. Whether greatly concentrated in Roman Catholicism, or more diffuse in Protestant congregationalism, ecclesiastical structures today do not imitate those of the early church's religious community. It has been said that as a religion begins to "penetrate the official aristocracy," two significant developments must occur: first, the religion itself must experience a decline of eschatological emphasis, and second, the religion must embrace a traditional structure which renders it more acceptable to the upper classes.[45] This insight assumes that most religions—and certainly classical Christianity—are originally more attractive to less privileged, more marginalized people. In the beginning it was "the more of them are punished, the more do they increase."[46] But over time martyrdom would no longer be a valuable source of power because, while the religious community was changing itself to accommodate the culture, Rome was getting ready to offer the olive branch.

Through Constantine the empire did just that. No sooner done than the emperor found himself able to call church councils at Nicea with the Roman bishop presiding. This privilege was extended in gratitude for the protection of property and for the security the state now provided for the church; but the spiritual price eventually proved too high.

These immense religious and social changes were patently incarnate in the person of Augustine of Hippo (354-430) who also changed from pagan to Christian, from apologist for Christianity to apologist for Roman violence and power. By the time

Augustine died in the early fifth century, there already existed a state-sponsored Bible and a state-sponsored church institution.

It is possible that the church unconsciously took on the state's way of relating to the world. Christian inheritors of this massive switch are described more accurately today as secular humanists or classical naturalists than born-again Christians. The Book of Revelation seems to predict that the prophet Anti-Christ is the Apostate or Fallen Church which supports the pagan state, the first beast, Rome. (Revelation 13.)

THE AUGUSTINIAN MODEL

It is no surprise then that after the Constantinian break-in, a state-supported Bible became popular, but only after the burning of earlier texts. Eusebius prepared such a Bible as an emperor-admirer in 331 AD. Augustine came on the scene later in the fourth century, but after the paganization of Christianity and the Christianization of Rome. He began to write his best known works, the *Confessions* and *The City of God*, in the last half of the fourth century, but he remained prolific into the first part of the fifth century.

When Rome collapsed in 407, after 1000 years of existence, the Romans found their political influence ended. They blamed the Roman Catholic Church because of the bad luck which had befallen the Empire since its conversion in 325 AD. They thought Rome could not have been conquered if it had continued to worship the gods of old. Augustine, however, was sure Rome suffered because of its own wicked ways.

By the time of Augustine's birth, 354 AD, the Roman Empire was facing hard times in contrast to its glorious past. Perpetual warfare was the norm. Barbarians from the north and the east battered the boundaries of the sprawling provinces. The close ties between church and state are clear from the experience of Ambrose of Milan, who was sent to Rome as an imperial governor and was ordained as a Catholic bishop. The governor became an instant bishop. Ambrose's pupil, Augustine, became famous for his *City of God*. "The idea of a Christian fellowship in a 'City of God' . . . in the scattered elite of bishops and monks had become for Augustine a desperate hope, a hope deferred to a future life."[47]

The earth-bound church meanwhile had become very worldly indeed. It had become also very paternalistic and patriarchal, totally absorbed in the established patterns of secular life. Bishops were married, held civic titles, and were landowners on a large scale. The church in Augustine's North African city of Hippo owned much land.

Augustine personally rejected this pattern. After his conversion he followed a strict rule of poverty and celibacy based on the Christian Scriptures. He was on the right track, except for the exclusive male orientation of his practice and lifestyle. He illustrated his admiration of the Biblical imperatives by giving alms to the poor and by giving a banquet for the poor on the anniversary of his ordination. Alms-giving, however, seemed too impersonal to him. He preached against the rich, became a vegetarian, and absolutely refused female visitors.

Early in his career Augustine wrestled with Manichaeism, which held a worldview absolving God from any "wrong-doing" which might be construed from the Hebrew Biblical accounts. This was done by positing a dual godhead, one good, one evil, with responsibility for evil lodged in the evil god who had not quite equal power. Augustine eventually renounced Manichaeism forever. As bishop, Augustine also encountered the Donatist heresy. The Donatists claimed, "The church was a unique source of holiness, so no sinner could have a part in it."[48] "What was at stake," Brown writes in *Augustine of Hippo*, "was the attitude that the Church could take to the 'world' at large. . . ."[49]

> The Donatists thought of themselves as a group which existed to preserve and protect an alternative to the society around them. They felt their identity to be constantly threatened: first by persecution, later, by compromise. Innocence, ritual purity, meritorious suffering, predominate in their image of themselves. They were unique, "pure":

the Church of the righteous who are persecuted and do not persecute.[50]

In contrast, Brown points out institutional Catholicism reflected "the attitude of a group confident of its powers to absorb the world without losing its identity."[51]

Internecine warfare broke out between the Donatists and the Catholics in North Africa in 411 AD and continued for several years. Augustine's Catholicism saw the church in "co-existence with society as a whole: that it might absorb, transform, and perfect existing bonds of human relations. He was deeply preoccupied by the idea of the basic unity of the human race." But the Donatists regarded the church as "an alternative to society, as a place of refuge, like the Ark."[52]

We must ask of Augustine, in the final analysis, who transformed whom? Was it not already too late when he used Caesar's violence as the means to deal with the Donatists? From that point on the Catholic Church relied on the secular arm to enforce its doctrines. Once using the secular arm, it could not keep itself from taking on the image and likeness of Caesar. The emperors welcomed the church's use of the armies of Caesar to suppress the enemies of the church. The church became Rome's valuable ally. Both grew in numbers and worldly power. Augustine wrote that the emperor had a right to punish impious, fallen members who needed restraint.

The test of such an attitude is what Augustine thought might happen if ever the pressures of society were relaxed: "The reins placed on human license would be loosened and thrown off: all sins would go unpunished. Take away the barriers created by the laws!" Men's brazen capacity to do harm, their urge to self-indulgence would rage to the full. No king in his kingdom, no general with his troops, . . . no husband with his wife, nor father with his son, would attempt to put a stop, by any threats or punishments, to the freedom and sheer sweet taste of sinning.[53]

Augustine justified the use of secular violence and legal compulsion by the church in order to assure that the will of the church would prevail, and the Donatists provided the test. The Donatists were shocked by the way Augustine broke down the barriers firmly fixed in the minds of the early Christians between "the 'sacred' and the 'profane,' between the purely spiritual sanctions exercised by the Christian bishop within the Church and the manifold and at times horrific pressures of Roman society as administered by the emperors."[54] They said God sent prophets, not kings. The famous remark of Donatus is perceptive: "What has the emperor to do with the church?"[55] We ask ourselves why Augustine could not have followed the teachings of Jesus (Matthew 18.) and resolved the matter within the church, rather than resorting to secular authority in keeping with Paul's warnings. (1 Corinthians 6.) His decision could only pollute the internal structure of the church.

This political decision to utilize violence was followed by Augustine's rationalization of the institutionalization of wealth. He began to preach in this manner: "It is not a matter of income, but of desires. . . . Look at the rich man standing beside you: Perhaps he has a lot of money on him, but no avarice in him, while you who have no money, have a lot of avarice. . . ."[56] The idea that it is all right to be rich as long as one has a good attitude has become the traditional rationalization of the church. It thus avoids the hard questions and life-wrenching changes faced by the original Christians who confronted wealth with voluntary, evangelical poverty.

Augustine was the great secularizer of his age. Originally the pagans had accused the Christians of withdrawing from public affairs and of being potentially pacifist, but Augustine's life as bishop embodied a living refutation of this charge. "He knew what it was to wield power with the support of the Imperial administration. . . . In his dealings with heresy, lawlessness, and immorality, he had shown not a trace of pacifism."[57]

In the twilight of his life he wrote *The City of God* on a popular theme. Since the fall of Adam, humanity had been split into two great cities—one loyal to God, the other loyal to the rebel angel and his demons. These cities, now mixed, would be separated at the last judgment as Babylon and Jerusalem. Even though Babylon meant confusion, "a merging of the identity in the things of the world," the citizens of Jerusalem depended upon the world.[58] "The need to save one's identity as a citizen of Heaven"[59] is central to Augustine's idea concerning the relationship of the two cities. Augustine described Christians as resident aliens. He recognized the lust to dominate as one of the major forces of fallen people. Domination of Donatists, however, by Augustine and the church institution was apparently legitimate.

Christian empire replacing Roman empire was, for Augustine, the best possible state of affairs. His romance with the Roman state seems to have lost its earlier enthusiasm by the end of his life. His reliance on the state to quash the heretics proved to be his great fall. His view that "the army was the only effective police-force"[60] and was indispensable in suppressing the Donatists, infected Augustine with an equally "heretical" view.

Even in his waning years, Augustine journeyed to Numidia in order to keep a general at his post because of an urgent need for security. He said, "The Catholic communities need a strong man to act as their protector against the lightning raids of the nomads."[61] By 430 AD, Roman rule in Africa collapsed anyway. Augustine lived to see the very violence he condoned destroy his life's work in Africa. In the end his compromises with Rome proved to be valueless. The heavenly bishop had taken on too much of the earthly city.

Augustine's social theology in *The City of God* is far removed from the teachings of Jesus. The Christian ruler differs from the pagan, not in the amount of power he wields, nor in the nature of the state which he maintains. He differs only in his awareness of where his power stands in God's order, to what it is relating, what ends it must serve. Thus the Christian ruler is legitimized because of this tenuous difference.

Augustine's melding of church and state morality was more than welcome at the time. Christian ethics could absorb political life at a moment when pagans had begun to fear that Christianity had proved incompatible with Roman statecraft. Augustine's Christian ethics provided no answer to the question of why this form of political life existed at all. The lust for domination, typical of all political states, infected the church. As the Roman Empire died of its lust, a new state emerged, coming to life in the form of a religio-political institution. The new church-state then claimed the remaining Roman secular power and imitated the former Roman state in every detail, including costume.

Augustine's search was for an all-embracing community—a trap we all fall into when we form a religious community in terms of the broadest common definition. Augustine, like Hobbes, was a man for whom justified violence formed the foundation of his political thought. He was the first major Catholic writer to defend religious domination as a Christian concept. This justification was, of course, taken from pagan, Roman sources, mainly Cicero. It would also in time provide the basis for the just-war theories which informed and served Christian civilization from this point onward.

CHAPTER FOUR

CHRISTENDOM AND THE NATIONS

THE RISE OF PAPAL POWER

Since the time of the early Christians, the world has seldom seen basic Christian communities living the way of Jesus as if the Kingdom has come. Overcoming religious institutional temptations, those earliest Christians lived together as sharing communities led by the Holy Spirit. A lay federation of priests, they made decisions based on consensus. Overcoming the economic temptations of wealth and acquisitiveness, they related to society with voluntary simplicity and poverty, living like the least as described in Matthew 25, offering themselves as servants for assistance and hospitality. They respected the rights of others while forbearing their own. They worked out their relationship to existing governments by becoming distinct and separate from them while living in their midst. They understood the distinction between legitimizing political institutions by seeking official status in them, and affecting politics by their radical religious practice of pacifism and alternative values. They overcame political temptations and were empowered to witness to the authorities and resist the intrusion of Roman violence and coercion. All this was lost once again as the temptations to honor the powers and principalities returned. The warning of James, "you desire and do not have; so you kill," (James 4:2.) went unheeded. The Christians wanted what they did not have and in getting what they wanted, they lost what they had and needed.

Religious institutional power substituting for the base Christian community is best seen in the development of papal political and economic power. Once again a religious institution like the temple takes for itself kingly power in the image of David and worldly wealth in the image of Solomon and re-institutes a "community"—this time not in Jerusalem but in Rome.

Some forbearance of violence persisted even beyond the time of Constantine and Augustine. The refusal of Christians to fight in defense of their security or for the survival of the state perpetuated the tension between church and state even after the Constantinian break-in and the Augustinian cover-up.[1]

Canon 12 of the Council of Nicea in 325 AD said, "As many as were called by grace . . . having cast aside their military girdles but afterwards returned like dogs to their own vomit, . . . Let these be three years hearers and ten years protestors."[2] The Christian church, even though holding on to its anti-war stance, adopted coercive means to enforce that end.

Canon 22 concerned willful murder. In the time of the Patriarch Luke, a certain bishop gave absolution in writing after a very short time of penance to a soldier who had committed voluntary homicide. The synod subjected the soldier to a canonical penance and ordered the bishop to cease from the exercises of his ministry for a prescribed period of time. The *First Canonical Epistle of Basil*, archbishop of Caesaria (c. 370 AD), required ten years' penance for abortion (Canon 2) and three years' exclusion from the Eucharist (Canon 13) for those who killed in war. "He who gives a mortal wound to another is a murderer whether it is done in aggression or in self-defense." (Canon 43.)[3]

As the contractual agreement between Constantine and the church became operative, clerical church order emerged as distinct. For example, Canon 11 of the Council of Antioch (341 AD) forbade clergy on their own motion from appealing to the emperor for redress of differences. Here church discipline was threatened. Church discipline in regard to the relationship between clerics and lay people was also threatened; hence the need for specific canons to preserve the power of the clergy over lay people. But this sharp distinction between clergy and lay people is an example of church order that did not exist in the early centuries. Married priests were the rule as late as the Council of Nicea. Canon 4 of Gingrea pronounced anathema for one who hesitates to receive communion from married presbyters.[4]

In the earliest centuries the house churches were hosted by lay people, and the host usually presided at the Eucharist or breaking of bread. Later priest functionaries came on the scene but they were often part of the family of lay people through marriage, through their wives. Church polity evolved in such a way that this connection of male priest/clergy and female wife/laity became an intolerable pattern that had to be broken. There were two reasons for this: one, because of the conflict of interest between the allegiance of the male to the church hierarchy and his allegiance to his wife and family (and through them to the existing lay community); second, because the laity was also female, in influence and in numbers. Rules adversely affecting women were strengthened as the years progressed, illustrating the powerful influence of a patriarchal, secular culture.[5]

The attitude toward women and slaves as underlings in the secular culture is interesting to note as we see a hierarchy in both religious and lay life emerging. Anathema was warranted for anyone who persuaded a slave to leave his or her master under pretense of religion. The emperor's permission was now needed to free slaves in the churches under an African code of 419. But if slaves claimed that they were forced by their masters to offer incense to idols in their masters' homes or workplaces, they were commanded to perform one year's penance. In regard to women, Canon 30 of the Synod of Laodicea of 343 AD states: "It is an abomination to bathe with women." Bathing at that time was done in the nude in public baths. Canon 44 stated that women may not go to the altar "polluted" by menstruation. Canon 65 of Quinsext prohibited women to speak in the liturgy. The *Apostolic Canons* of 325, by Dionysius, bishop of Alexandria, decreed in Canon 2 that menstruous women ought not come to the church at all. Women, however, were a step above Jews, with whom Christians were to have nothing to do whatsoever, according to Canon 11 of Quinsext!

As women and slaves were separated from the original sharing community by the male, clerical hierarchy, the hierarchy itself set rules to preserve its own elitism. A priest could not be present at a privately gathered religious meeting without the consent of the bishop, and without such consent the whole gathering would then be prohibited. Bishops previously chosen by the people could no longer be elected democratically by "seculars," according to Canon 13 of Antioch in the year 341. The Synod of Laodicea decreed that the oblation could not be made by a bishop or a president (presiding priest) in any private house.

All these proclamations came out of church councils which were declared ecumenical, that is, "the decrees of which have found acceptance by the church in the whole world."[6] In fact, many of the councils were held in the eastern world without any western representation from Rome or elsewhere.

As "ordinary" lay folk were ranked in descending order: men, women, slaves, Jews, ascending esteem was given to the civil authorities during this patristic period. The council of Ephesus in 431 AD referred to civil authorities and leaders as "our most religious emperors." At Chalcedon in 451, Canon 18 stated that "the order of ecclesiastical parishes will follow civil and public forms." "Ordinary" lay persons were prohibited entry into the sanctuary, but the emperor was welcomed there.

A canon of 419 proclaimed that it was permissible for the Roman Catholic Church to ask for secular protection against the Donatists because Paul had sought the help of the military against the lawless in the book of Acts. (Cf. Acts 21.) So this lay hierarchy of men, women, slaves, Jews, had civil authority at its top, and the community of lay religious who had formed the essence of the early Christian church was now relegated to an inferior position.

How did the church change in its internal and external relations? The changes that came about militated against the continuation of the small, grass-roots, base communities that once formed its style and life. Since these internal and external changes were intimately interdependent, we will look at them simultaneously. The fundamental characteristics of the external relationships continued beyond the period of fundamental internal change and these characteristics seemed to solidify by the end of the patristic period, i.e., by 500 AD. These hallmarks of the ecclesiastical establishment may be identified as hierarchy, paternalism, concentrated power, and the use of institutional violence in the internal governing of the Christian community.

In the course of its 2000-year history the (Roman) Catholic Church has changed its stance dramatically. "At first, it was a private fellowship surrounding Jesus. . . . From a persecuted sect, the Church became the official religion of the Roman Empire."[7]

We shall see that the church, from that time until the Reformation, was the inheritor of the place and status of the Roman Empire of the caesars. It was eventually unseated from its lofty, imperial perch and thereafter relegated to a primarily "spiritual" role. But that is getting ahead of our story. The key to the internal change is the separation of the masses into classes. The original, egalitarian community was replaced by a superior-inferior, internal arrangement at the same time that the church and state moved toward a more cozy external relationship. That relationship lasted for only a short time, after which church and state vied to take each other over so that one might become the sole deposit of spiritual and temporal power.

As to the emerging, internal arrangement, Ullmann writes:

The distinction between ordained and unordained members of the Church, between clerics and laymen, was a distinction which was not only to give medieval society its peculiar imprint, but also to make the problems of this society, that is, of Latin Christendom, accessible to understanding. The distinction—not between Church and State, but between clergy and laity as parts of one and the same unit—is a thread that runs throughout the medieval period.[8]

Through ordination a most important distinction is drawn between lay and sacerdotal members—constituting together the *unum corpus*.[9] The body was spiritual as well as earthly and thus needed direction in the form of authoritative government. The clerics finally chose the monarchic form, for the designs of the nations about them were monarchic. Once again the leaders of the community of God chose to imitate the nations at the expense of the majority of the lay people, and at the expense of the egalitarian structure of the early, radical community. The male hierarchy emerged to perform functions which previously had been performed by a less monarchic, more communitarian order.

Lay people were no longer seen as prophets or charismatics, receiving the Biblical gifts of the early church. Instead a more administrative and practical leadership emerged, from *presbyter* and *episcopoi* and oversecr to monarchic priest, bishop, archbishop, cardinal, and finally pope, all contrary to the writings of the New Testament and the practices of the early Christians.

On the model of the secular, Roman government, the ordained members were said to form the *ordo*, which together with *ordo laicalis sacerdotalis* composed a monarchic *ecclesia*,[10] if indeed it could be called *ecclesia* at all. It was no longer an assembly, but rather a theocratic, legalistic government ruled by succession instead of by the Spirit of God left as Jesus' gift in place of his followers' plea to restore the kingdom of Israel. (Cf. Acts 1.)

Pope Clement made the first clear declaration of Roman, papal primacy based on the Petrine commission (Matthew 16:18-19.) in his letter to the Corinthians (ca. 90). Monarchy in the church was fixed for all time (at least to the present) by the fall of Rome and the pontificate of Leo I in 440 AD. As imperial Rome died, Roman Catholicism rose, taking on the mask and movements of the beast thought dead (Cf. Revelation 13.), mask and movements at the expense of its own inherent and spiritual nature. Political power was embraced by the so-called *ecclesia* to deal more effectively with friends as well as enemies. Having established its own internal power to deal with its flock, it was ready to do battle with Rome. It justified its need for Rome because of its inability to enforce its decrees through its inability to use violence. It failed to remember that such inability was intrinsic to its earlier pacifist and communitarian nature. Such inability should have been desired rather than rejected. The deal with Rome was, at its root, contractual. Each party to the contract needed the security and power of the other.

The imperial Roman government needed the institutional Roman religion to preserve unity throughout the empire. The Roman church therefore became the principal focal point in the Roman empire and was particularly privileged under Constantine. He offered economic benefits for religious ones. He initiated construction projects and protected the church's accumulation of wealth. The bishop of Rome was given a palace fit for the bishop of the first city of the empire. Construction of St. Peter's Basilica was begun in 318 AD following imperial designs.

> On the imperial model a chancery was established. . . . Furthermore, as a result of imperial legislation, the clerics of the Roman church begin to enjoy a great many privileges which amounted to exemption from public burdens, especially taxation, as well as from the jurisdiction of the imperial courts in all cases involving faith, . . . and discipline.[11]

CHURCH AND EMPIRE IN CONFLICT

However, there was a trade-off, a *quid pro quo*. The emperor, by these agreements of toleration, committed the Roman church, like any other church, to become subject to the Roman law. "The constitutional right of the emperor to convoke a church council and to intervene directly in the affairs of the Christian church, as 'supreme priest' designated by his title of *pontifex maximus*, continues."[12] Retaining this power of *ius in sacris*, the traditional Roman monarchic imperial government thus received an enormous boost."

Ullmann emphasizes that the feud that later unfolded was directly related to the constitutional, legal framework of the Constantinian settlement. The deal made with Rome was as wrong for the church then as in our own time. In 1933, Pope Pius XII, only a few months after Hitler came to power, signed a concordat with the Third Reich which stated in Article 16:

> Before bishops enter upon the government of their dioceses, they are to take an oath of fealty either to the representative of the Reich government in the provinces or to the president of the Reich in the following words: "Before God and on the Holy Gospels I swear and promise—as becomes a bishop—loyalty to the German Reich and to the . . . state. I swear and promise to honor the constitutional government and to cause the clergy of my diocese to honor it. In the exercise of the spiritual office entrusted to me I will endeavor, with due solicitude for the well-being and interests of the German state, to prevent any harm which might threaten it."[13]

William Langland wrote of Constantine's "gift": "When the kindness of Constantine gave Holy Church endowments in lands and leases, lordships and servants, the Romans heard an angel cry on high above them, 'This day *dos ecclesiae* has drunk venom and all who have Peter's power are poisoned forever.' "[14]

After the toleration and legitimization of the Roman church between 313 and 330 AD, the emperor Theodosius, in 382 AD, declared it the only religion of Rome. Pope Damasus returned the favor by renaming the church "Roman."[15] The removal of the seat of empire to Constantinople and the eventual collapse of the western empire left the keys of secular power with the then enthroned popes in Rome. It was the "employment of jurisprudential principle which enabled the papacy to become an institution of government charged with the direction of Christians with the means of the law."[16]

Even though the church canons still prohibited the study of law by lay persons under penalty of being "cut off," excommunicated, the institution became essentially legalistic.[17] The popes copied the Roman institution in yet another matter—its decrees were patterned after Roman usage, and so were recognized conversions. Conversions were no longer based upon inner spiritual conviction but were accomplished by legal fiat. Every citizen of Rome, *ipso facto,* became a Christian upon Christianity's official adoption by Rome and this without benefit of previous baptism or voluntary consent. Many legalistic parts of the Old Testament were used by Rome in its terminology enforcing ideas of law and religion.

Pope Celestine I declared, "The law . . . should be our master and we as recipients should not try to master, but serve, the law."[18] The Christian was asked to be a servant of law rather than love. The model for the imperial design of the papacy was Moses, who, in Exodus 8:22, set up judges and reserved "any great matters for himself."[19] By 418 AD no appeal was made to any other authority. "The people should be led. It should not lead itself."[20] And the leading was reserved to the clergy through ordination. Pope Leo I solidified these claims when he applied the Roman imperial term of *principatus* to the papal claim of jurisdictional primacy over not only its own people but now over the empire as well.[21] *Principatus* was originally a constitutional term used by the Romans to describe imperial sovereignty.

These two political giants wielded power side by side while tension grew between them. With its internal organization complete, the Roman church continued its quest to replace the Roman empire. The church's claim of jurisdictional power encroached upon the empire's power, while the empire's claim of *pontifex maximus* invaded the prerogatives of the church. In Con-

stantinople, the patriarch of Constantinople, the highest religious authority, was an appointee of the emperor. However, in
Rome, with the disintegration of the western empire, the church
occupied the power vacuum as the empire moved east.

Ullmann points to the basic problem which arose: "Who . . .
was to govern, that is, to direct and orient the corporate union
of Christians?"[22] Religion calls for the whole spirit, while government must govern the whole body; thus the dilemma ideo-
logically was enunciated and felt by the two superpowers of the
day. It was this lust after superpower that overshadowed spirit
and body and became the source of the violent confrontations
of church and state.

In order to understand why each power—political and religious—vied for total power, we need only look again to the
original model of the base Christian community. It took for
itself total power, but in a totally different way. It exercised a
political effect upon governments but did not seek political
power. It was a religious community, not a religious institution.
It was founded on economic simplicity, not economic wealth.
It organized itself as a holistic body and spirit, a complete
community. In short, it rejected the values of secular society
while existing in the midst of it. The empire had been a self-
sufficient power before the emergence of the Roman church.
It had its own religion inherent in its political community and
its own unique economic, political, and legal system. It tolerated
other religions as long as its own was not prohibited or dish-
onored. The Roman church, too, as it shed its original characteristics, pictured itself as a whole—not only a religious, but
a political community as well. Thus, neither superpower could
tolerate the powers found in a competing organism of equal
scope.

None said it better than Emperor Justinian, "The empire is
a divinely instituted guardian of peace and order. . . . Just as in
the celestial cosmos there was only one who combined all
power—Christ . . . so there was in the terrestrial cosmos only
one monarch."[23]

The empire had always been seen as a divine entity and it continued so as Christianity became institutionalized. Its buildings were sacred and had the looks of cathedrals. Keep in mind that both church and empire had entered into a contract to share ultimate world power. Each entity, however, attempted to encroach upon the other's power and increase its own. The papacy tried to keep a lid on the ability of the empire to wield power over the church. At the same time the church received the benefits from the violence the empire offered in the papacy's defense. The papacy spoke to the Romans in their own language. The church claimed final and supreme authority in any matter. To prepare for the empire's rebuttal, the church formed itself more tightly into a complex institutional, hierarchical structure.

Various forged and fictional documents began to appear reinforcing papal power. One known as *The Legend of St. Sylvester* by an unknown author, which appeared around 480 AD, made the claim that no one may sit in judgment on the Roman See, neither emperor, nor clergy, nor kings, nor people.

By the end of the 6th century, the papacy was the biggest single landowner in western Europe. As the property of the empire declined, the property of the church increased. With such economic power based in patrimonies or gifts of land, the papacy under Gregory II (715-731) moved toward complete emancipation from the Roman Empire. All had forgotten Augustine's warning, "Business is in itself evil;" and Jerome's saying, "A man who is a merchant can seldom or ever please God."[24] To make money out of money by charging interest was usury. Capitalism, the ultimate institution of corporate profit, was later based on usury. However, it was taxation, not usury, that brought the power issue to a head. Pope Gregory II refused to execute the taxation decrees of Emperor Leo III. The pope could openly obstruct imperial laws, although theoretically and constitutionally he was bound to obey these decrees.

The eastern emperor was having trouble holding on to his lands in Italy, and the pope saw himself as the emperor's viceroy there. However, the emperor did not agree to this arrangement and threatened to prosecute the pope for treason. This proved an empty threat.

Meanwhile other forged and fictional documents such as *The Donation of Constantine* continued the propaganda war advancing absolute papal supremacy.[25] The papacy began looking around for another partner in violence. It hoped that its continuing troubles with the eastern empire might be avoided by finding a more cooperative consort in the Frankish kingdom closer to home.

The historical era that followed, of course, involved a powerful and popular figure known to most school children—Charles the Great, Charlemagne. Charlemagne's power was primarily created by the pope. He became the Holy Roman emperor and wore that crown only because the pope agreed and approved. The eastern Roman emperors were in effect decrowned by the pope and Charlemagne. Charlemagne had sought equality with the east, not supremacy. He did not lust after emperorship, but the papacy lusted after the power he could bring under papal control.

Apart from military support the papacy desired legislative decrees to be promulgated in conformity with its will. Charlemagne conceded "the magisterial primacy" but not jurisdictional primacy which included legislation. "The teachings of the Roman church are enforceable, not because the Roman church has given them the force of law, but because the monarch Charlemagne in his autonomous function surrounded certain magisterial expressions of the Roman church with the halo of an enforceable rule."[26] The church's view obtained during the reign of Charlemagne: the purpose of the king was to exercise terror to preserve justice. Does that have the ring of Romans 13 about it! A king is a watchdog to keep peace. Only when the word of the pope proved inadequate would the king exercise his function of violence. "He does not bear the sword in vain."[27] This came to mean that he wielded the sword only when the pope decreed.

The pope sought to dominate the emperor so that he would be reduced simply to a lay person subject to the functions of those ordained to greater hierarchical status. The king, as a lay person, should not interfere with church land for this reason. Lay people were protectors and not administrators of such property. The new king saw himself, however, as a new or second David. The papacy chose, but the king ruled—this became the understanding and practice of the Frankish political domain. There could be only one monarch as far as the emperor was concerned.

As far as the church was concerned, ordination was the final criterion of all power. "The function of the Ruler is the extermination of evil and for this he receives the sword."[28] The determination of what is evil and what is not evil must necessarily be left to those who are deemed functionally qualified to pronounce it, namely the *sacradotus* or, in secular terms, the pope.

The early church had called upon all the Scriptures to describe its power. The empire relied upon its legalistic interpretation of selected parts of the Old Testament. On what then did the pope rely? Certainly not the New Testament. The Roman church in the final analysis had to rely upon its own authority—the very kind of understanding for which Jesus was accused of blasphemy. Jesus possessed the right from God to do so. The religious institution of Roman Catholicism possessed no such authority from God to ignore the obvious Scriptural prohibition against such extension of power.

After the empire's collapse, only the church offered an organizing principle for political success. Society cannot stand a vacuum, cannot abide anarchy. So the church moved in the direction of taking on all temporal authority by imitating "the ancient curia of Rome."[29] With feudalism as the new economic system, "the king or prince had to surrender [his land] into full papal ownership . . . and received it back as a fief. . . ."[30] The king had to pay tribute or provide military protection. The pope became the strongest feudal monarch. He now had his own personal troops under his direct control. Later, at the instigation of Bernard of Clairvaux, the pope instituted the crusader who was given exemption from ordinary duties of feudal land taxes in order to fight for the Roman church in the Holy Land. Crusaders also received indulgences granting after-life absolution for sins committed in this life, particularly those committed while engaging in warfare.

With the change from empire to nation, from Constantinople to the Frankish kingdom, there was another shift of power, so that once again each superpower, religious and political, vied for exclusive control.

The Crusaders provided the impetus for this shift. A modern book designed especially for young Roman Catholic readers, *The Crusader*, states " 'God wills it,' cried the men of the Third Crusade. . . . Even as a young prince, Richard loved adventure, and horses, armor, war machines, and castles. . . . He learned the skills and knowledge necessary for a warrior knight."[31] The inside cover pictures two Crusaders stabbing a Moslem with a spear. This book, considered acceptable for modern young Catholics, illustrates the manner in which the church at the time of Bernard of Clairvaux saw violence as a tool for the aggrandizement of the religious institution.

The book tells young Catholics that love of military might was born in Richard the Lionhearted, who received the sacred lance of St. Hilary. Being a valiant soldier assured one's admission to heaven. When these Crusaders killed, shouts of frenzied delight filled the air.[32] Richard lost the lives of 26,000 men in this endeavor. He had set out to kill unbelievers as a military necessity. St. Bernard, who was influential in forming the Knights Templars for such military violence in the Lord's name, influenced the pope to take such action for the sake of suppressing evil. By the time of the Crusades, the pope was even described as king.

> The pope is the king of the earth, lord of the heavens, because the apostolic see is "singularly distinguished by divine and royal privileges." Christ Himself was supreme priest and king. . . . The pope is His vicar and hence as the supreme monarch . . . of this universal civitas sancta,

he disposes of kingdoms and empires and presides over the princes, nations and people.[33]

It was Bernard who authored the change of the pope's title from "vicar of St. Peter" to "vicar of Christ" and who, in pleading for the Crusades, urged the pope "to draw both swords," because he alone had the power of both. Now the pope had his own military sword to execute that which his spiritual sword was incapable of achieving.

By the 11th century, under Pope Gregory VII, the church had become the sole ruler of Christendom: "If the holy and apostolic see, through the principal power divinely conferred upon it, has the right to judge spiritual things, why then not secular things?"[34]

The last great confrontation of power between church and state took place in the latter part of the 12th century. This power struggle came to a head in the great battle between Henry II and Thomas Becket. Their struggle offers a thumbnail sketch of the quest by both church and state during the whole era for ultimate secular power.[35] We tend to sympathize with Thomas Becket because he was cruelly murdered in his own sanctuary as he prayed and refused to take up arms against his assassins. But this confrontation of the late 12th century (c. 1170) was not a simple one.

The struggle is imaged in conversation between these two representing temporal and spiritual power:

Henry: Have I not raised you from poverty and lowliness to the summit of honor and rank . . . ? How is it then after so many benefits, so many proofs of my love for you, which everyone is aware of, you have so soon been able to blot from your mind, so that you are not only ungrateful but oppose me in everything?

Thomas: Far be it from me, my Lord. I have not forgotten your favors—which are not yours alone, for God deigned to confer them on me through you. For that very reason, far be it from me to be ungrateful or oppose your will in anything that accords with the will of God. You know how loyal I have been to you, from whom I expect only a temporal reward. How much more ought we both to be faithful and honest servants to almighty God, from whom we receive temporal rewards and hope for eternal goods? You are indeed my lord, but He is my Lord and yours. It would be useful neither to you nor to me if I were to neglect His will in order to obey yours. For on his fearful Day of Judgment you and I will both be judged as servants of ONE Lord. Then neither of us will be able to answer for the other and no excuses will avail; each of us will receive his due according to his acts. Temporal lords must be obeyed, but not against God. As St. Peter says, "we must obey God rather than men."[36]

This exchange between Henry and Thomas clarifies the conflict of church and empire. The emerging church, a weaker entity than the powerful Roman Empire, entered into a contract for its very existence. As it grew and the empire waned, the church sought to expand and enlarge its power. A time came when it was all-powerful. Then the empire was replaced by nation-states which in turn began to accumulate new power, and the church was threatened with dethronement. Becket, unhappily, was martyred for an earthbound institution no longer true to its original heaven-sent communitarian design and severely challenged by the emerging nation-states of the 12th century.

In *Thomas Becket* David Knolls sums up what this death really meant:

Was his death, then, really that of a martyr? If we use the word in its original Christian sense, we must say "No." He did not die as a witness to the Resurrection of Jesus, or in defense of any specified article of the creed or point of Christian morality. It has indeed sometimes been said that he died for a novel extension of canon law, or to recover Canterbury property, or because he had upheld an unessential right of the archbishop of Canterbury. All these, and other matters, formed some part of the large issue of rights which he was defending, but neither individually nor as a group were they the crucial point at issue. That, reduced to its simplest terms, was the demand of the king to treat the affairs of the church, apart from its credal and sacramental aspects, as under his sole jurisdiction.[37]

The demands made by Henry, Knolls says, were less than those of Charlemagne. But Thomas, in his own mind, was martyred "for the freedom of the spiritual authority of the church."[38] The plummeting of church power after Innocent III (d. 1216) would bring the church so low that not even its spiritual authority would be intact in many parts of Europe. This was particularly true in England where Henry VIII would later unite temporal and spiritual power not in a pope of the 12th century, but in a king of the 16th.

THE EMERGENCE OF THE NATION-STATE

Living without the awe of papal spiritual supremacy over the world gave birth to the notion that such spiritual authority was no longer universally needed. The idea that power could come from a community of people, once truly a religious idea of Jesus, was given life once again, but in a counterfeit, secular form, limited to political community alone. This would emerge as the idea of the social contract, a concept we will examine later. It was a creation of nature, a creation of people seeking sovereign power. In order to be a state, it was not necessary for a community also to be Christian. The state thus emerged as autonomous and sovereign.

Near the end of the long period of church-state power struggles in the Dark and Middle Ages, two men appeared as reformers of the church—both confronted the history traced in these reflections: Francis of Assisi and Martin Luther. The former failed in a worldly sense; the later became the father of the Reformation.

By 1302 the pope was saying, "It is altogether necessary to salvation for every human creature to be subject to the Roman pontiff."[39] Once having achieved this summit of secular and religious power, the popes were unable to hold on to it for very long. As papal power began to decline in the 13th century, the Inquisition emerged. Dominicans and Franciscans were sent forth to seek out heresy, the disease threatening papal power.

[A] number of friars were employed in administering the laws of the Inquisition, one of them, Angelo of Assisi, producing in 1361 a manual for the use of inquisitors which gives some idea of the principles upon which he and his colleagues worked. . . . For example, under the heading of *appellare* the inquisitor is told that heretics have no right to appeal, and under that of *destruere* he maintains that any house in which a heretic is found must be immediately and completely destroyed without hope of rebuilding.[40]

However, according to the ideal of Francis, his followers were supposed to "wander the world to do good, to walk barefoot among the poor and the outcasts bringing Christian love to the lowest, to beg for the necessities of life in kind, never in money."[41] Paradoxically, Francis formed an order which, having rejected property, received the support and donations of the wealthy because the order seemed in its purity to offer the assurance of holiness.

The order thus acquired land and riches, built itself churches and cloisters, and developed its own hierarchy, all in opposition to its founder's intent. Francis understood the process. Replying to a novice who wished to have a psalter, he once said: "When you have a psalter you will wish to have a breviary, and when you have a breviary you will sit in a chair like a great prelate and say to your brother, 'Brother, bring me my breviary.'"[42] Luther later rejected this simplicity which the Franciscans had sought about three centuries before.

Luther's search for reform was narrower than Francis' and was limited to the extravagances of the institutional church without radically confronting its political, religious, and economic power. He wrestled with a new model for church. Once having overthrown the old model, he missed the opportunity to restore its original sense and form.

People seemed unable to respond to the newly liberated Word, and seemed to be as hungry as ever for some organization, some law to tell them what to do and thereby to assure themselves that all was well. They looked for formulas, rules, conventions to fill the spiritual gap which should have been filled with the metanoia, that repentance, that new charity, that faith which alone can produce effective, overflowing good works. They looked for new authorities to provide the new guidelines.

Luther and his friends were, often against Luther's wishes, being used as these new authorities, having to make judgments on everything from new liturgical texts and styles to the details of the organization of the Poor Chest in some distant town. They were the new authorities providing the new norms, and acting willy-nilly as an alternative church—or as he began to say simply as members of the True church. He was indeed happy to act as a *local* Church authority and his understanding of the Church allowed for that. But he was not happy as his authority, and that of other Reformers grew and grew. He began, at times, to question whether what he had done, whether the revolution he had loosed, was right. And in any case, if it was, what to do? How to manage and control Church life, Church property, relations with political authority?

Jesus of Nazareth had proclaimed the end of conventional religion and the ultimate irrelevance to people of faith of all worldly standards. So, although organization was still apparently needed, its structures must be functional, at the service not of an exclusive religious group but of the People of God. The community itself, that People of God, remains primary. This quite simple idea of the Church as a community is the key to Luther's message for us. Organization there has to be, but it must always be at the service of the community.[43]

Perhaps this is the key to understanding the recurring disintegration of organized religion. The organization that emerged from early Christian community into Christendom and Roman institutional religion was not an organization fundamentally designed to be of service to its members. It was an organization for and at the service of the hierarchy and the patriarchal power structure. It was an organization that served, at times, the Roman Empire more than it did its own people. It was an organization that practiced repression—especially of women and slaves—rather than liberation. It was an organization that took on the mightiest political power the world had yet known, the Roman Empire, and for a time became its master.

For a time the church also controlled the emerging nation-states under the allegiance of the Frankish kingdom. Ultimately it lost that battle, for the battle was not its own. The church was misplaced; and as Francis witnessed to its misplacement, Luther aided its misplacement. Becket in sincere delusion attempted to keep the balance of tension between church and state constant, but no longer could such an arrangement continue. With the emergence of nation-states, the powerful religious institution's time came to an end. It had its chance, as did Israel; but Israel went to its Babylonian captivity and final obliteration. The same fate became that of the Christian community turned monstrous institution: its power became confined to an internal, spiritual realm, having little to say about the world's political, economic, and religious concerns.

To recapitulate: the infant Christian community followed essentially in the footsteps of its founder for several hundred years. But it sought to end its persecutions and sufferings and to find worldly protection. In embracing protection from the state which persecuted it, the church entered into a contractual relationship with the state, a trade-off which essentially became the Constantinian break-in.

A contract emerged where all the benefits seemed to flow to the state rather than to the Christian community. But at the same time the Christian community absorbed the state by mass baptisms, and the state became "Christian" through this new transformation. The Christian priest became powerful and imitated the Roman emperor.

Finally, the empire fell and as it appeared to die, much as in the story in Revelation 13, a new beast emerged in the guise of a new Christian state imitating the trappings of the old Roman state. Yet the Roman state did not completely die and vied with the Christian state for power. The Christian state absorbed all power, at one point, and triumphed, only to be consumed by its own lust for domination and to lose its grip once again.

The Christian state was weakened by personal struggles such as that of Henry II and Becket and finally toppled by the combined forces of Luther's Reformation, political realignments in Europe, the Renaissance, and the Enlightenment. The new states appeared with no need for spiritual guidance or dependence. Final temporal and spiritual power resided in the people themselves who made up the state and who entered into a social contract with the state.

All looked well in this new relationship. The people eventually became sovereign in their democracies, and spiritual authority, even though remaining paternalistic, became devoid of any kind of temporal power. As in repeated instances throughout history, the "ways of nations" once again became dominant. This time it was under an arrangement known as the "social contract."

THE GREEK BEGINNINGS OF THE SOCIAL CONTRACT

Although it seems that for some the ultimate duty of the political state is to protect its citizens from harm within (from criminals) by the death penalty, and from harm without (from enemies) by war, for others the ideal moral responsibility of the state is securing justice for its citizens. For most citizens these are one

and the same thing. Secular justice should not be confused with
Biblical justice, however, even though secular justice is often
described as the first virtue of social institutions. Justinian defined justice as "the constant, perpetual disposition to render
to every man his due."[44] Toullier defined justice as "conformity
of our actions and our will to the law."[45] Justice for Plato was
a part of human virtue and a bond which joins *men* together in
the state. And the Greeks truly meant *men*, not women or slaves.
Aristotle saw justice as the fair rendering to every man his due.[46]

The tension between justice as law, (or might enforced by
law), and justice as virtue is the subject of Plato's *Republic* and
the discussion ensuing therein between Thrasymachus and Socrates.[47] Thrasymachus' contention is that justice consists in serving the interest of the stronger. By this he means that what is
just or right is what benefits those who hold power, the establishment, the ruling class. His reasoning is that justice in any
society consists in conformity with that society's laws, and those
laws are made by the ruling party in its own interest. His position
is the classical denial of a distinction between *de facto* and *de
jure* social control. It is also summarized in the slogan "Might
makes right."

Socrates attempts not only to refute him, but to develop his
own theory of institutional justification formulated as a definition of the just state. He presents his theory of an account
of why people would establish organized society in the first
place and contrasts it with an alternative view advanced by
Glaucon. According to Glaucon's account, which foreshadows
one given by Thomas Hobbes in the 17th century, organized
society arises from humanity's need for security. Organized
society more than compensates one for the loss of liberty by
the security gained from everyone else's loss of liberty. He says:

> First I will state what is commonly held about the nature
> of justice and its origin; secondly, I shall maintain that it
> is always practiced with reluctance not as a good in itself,
> but as a thing one cannot do without. . . . What people say
> is that to do wrong is, in itself, a desirable thing; on the

other hand it is not at all desirable to suffer wrong, and the harm to the sufferer outweighs the advantage to the doer. Consequently, when men have had a taste of both, those who have not the power to seize the advantage and escape the harm decide that they would be better off if they made a pact neither to do wrong nor to suffer it. Hence they began to make laws and covenants with one another and whatever the law prescribed they called lawful and right. That is what right or justice is and how it came into existence; it stands halfway between the best thing of all—to do wrong with impunity—and the worst, which is to suffer wrong without the power to retaliate. So justice is accepted as a compromise and valued not as good in itself, but for lack of power to do wrong; no man worthy of the name who has had that power would ever enter into such a compact with anyone. . . . He will be moved by self-interest, and the end which it is natural to every creature to pursue as good, until forcibly turned aside by law and custom to respect the principle of equality.[48]

Socrates' view is that the advantage to organized society lies not in security but in a division of labor or a type of community. One person alone cannot adequately do all the jobs required to satisfy various needs. These jobs will be done adequately if everyone does just one of them, the one he or she does best. So one's needs are best satisfied when there is a division of labor which organized society makes possible. Justice according to Socrates and Plato is itself a kind of division of labor. A state is just provided it is organized so that everyone does his or her proper job, the job for which nature has provided suitability.

Obviously, the state must be given the power to force this division to arise. That power is found in the nature of the state. The state, *polis,* is a perpetual, indissoluble, and sovereign community governed by laws. It is sovereign because it is the location and deposit of ultimate political power. It is perpetual and indissoluble because it exists indefinitely and has as a primary goal its own perpetuation. The government is the ruling

authority of the state and the law is the means by which the
ruling authority enforces its rules.

Robert Nisbet comments that Plato's *Republic* "has had the
effect of making the ideal of politics, of political power, of the
political bond, of the political community, the most distinctive
and most influential of all types of community to be found in
western philosophy. The intellectual line from Plato to both
the democratic and totalitarian states of the 20th century is a
clear and direct one."[49] But he goes on to say that whatever
the differences are between the two types of modern states,
democratic or dictatorial, "what they have in common is the
ascendancy of the political bond over all others in society; of
the political role over all roles of kinship, religion, occupation
and place; of the political intellectual over all other intellectuals;
of political authority over all competing social and cultural authorities; and finally, the proffer of the political state as the
chief protection of man from the uncertainties, deprivations,
and miseries of this world."[50]

There is a common theme through all of this. Whether it is
Plato, Socrates, Glaucon, or Thrasymachus, we are dealing with
an idea of foundation for community that is the antithesis of
the Gospel of Jesus. The idea of enforcement, the idea of security, the idea of protection, all are foreign to the Gospel. Only
Plato's notion of a type of community where labor is divided
has any relationship whatsoever to the original Christian community. But Plato's insistence on necessary enforcement by a
hierarchical, secular state obliterates the egalitarian nature of
the Christian community.

While Plato sings the virtues of justice, Aristotle trumpets
the virtues of law. In the *Nicomachean Ethics*, Aristotle discusses
different kinds of justice and says, "The law enjoins us to fulfill
our function as brave men (. . . not to throw away our arms)
as self-controlled men (. . . and not to commit . . . outrage) as
gentle men (. . . not to strike or defame anyone.)"[51] Aristotle's
justice is not egalitarian reciprocity, however. For example, "if
a magistrate strikes a man, it is wrong for the man to strike him
back; and if a man strikes a magistrate, it is not enough for the

magistrate to strike him, but he ought to be punished as well. The very existence of the state depends on proportionate reciprocity, for men demand that they will be able to repay evil with evil."[52] The Biblical admonition to requite evil with good or love does not follow from this pagan, Greek understanding as it was later incorporated in Roman law. Aristotle hardly calls us to suffer injustice voluntarily.

THE ETHICS OF DOMINATION

We have all been conditioned to view Machiavelli as the epitome of political evil; but there is nothing in Machiavellian politics that differs much from Plato, Aristotle, or Hobbes in terms of fundamental political considerations.[53] A prince should be feared rather than loved, for "men have less scruple in offending one who makes himself loved than one who makes himself feared."[54] The only difference in Machiavelli is that he really understands the internal mechanisms that result in outward violent manifestations. For Machiavelli there were two methods of fighting—law and force—which he equated with humans and beasts. If the first does not work, one should resort to the second. It is well for a prince to know how to be a man and a beast. Whoever desires to found a state must start by assuming that all persons are bad and ready to display their vicious nature whenever opportune. Thus for Machiavelli a political state become a mechanism for the control of the wicked aspects of the populace. Power, rather than justice, emerges once again as the Beast personified.[55]

In Machiavelli's view a justified social institution must *seem* to reflect the will of the people. It was for Hobbes and Locke and Rousseau and others to determine that a justified social institution must *truly* reflect the will of the people.[56] For a social institution to be just, the reflection of the will of the people must be part of its structure. The traditional philosophical statement of this idea is called the social contract theory. Perhaps the most respected and influential of modern social and political philosophers, the contractarians, held that society's control over the individual is justified only if it is or could be the product of some sort of unanimous agreement by the members of society—that is, a social contract. The 17th-century English philosophers, Thomas Hobbes and John Locke, and the 18th-century Frenchman, Jean Jacques Rousseau, are the persons most frequently associated with this theory of the state. All three philosophers held that a state must be the product of a social contract entered into by members of society.

THE ENGLISH AND FRENCH SOCIAL CONTRACTARIANS

Hobbes' social contract is a mutual agreement by the people to subordinate themselves unconditionally to a sovereign who may be either an individual or a legislative assembly. The only qualification for this office is the power to govern. The sovereign is not a party to the contract. The people agree with one another to obey the sovereign. The sovereign agrees to nothing. The contract imposes no restrictions on what the sovereign may do.[57]

The government established by Locke's idea of the contract acts as trustee for the people's sovereignty rather than as absolute sovereign. The people give up their freedom on condition that if they obey the government, it will protect and respect their natural rights to life, liberty, and the estate. The trusteeship is voided when this condition is not met and the people are no longer bound. Hobbes' social contract, then, is simply an agreement among people to submit to monarchic or governmental authority under certain conditions, not an agreement between the people and the sovereign. Locke's is a two-part agreement consisting in first, an agreement among the people to constitute themselves a corporate union, a commonwealth, and to institute a government, and second, an agreement between the people as a corporate unit and the instituted government defining the government's powers and responsibilities as trustees for the people's sovereignty.

Under Rousseau's contract, both the citizen and the government are subordinate to the collective.[58] The government is neither sovereign nor trustee for the people's sovereignty; it is the hired servant of the sovereign people. 'Its job is to administer 'the general will'—the will or interest of the people, taken as a whole. Rousseau thought the people incur no real loss of freedom in entering into the social contract, because the sovereign established thereby consists of the people themselves, taken as a collective unit."[59]

Why would one enter into a social contract and agree to restrictions on one's liberty? Hobbes answers that without a sovereign to restrain them in their pursuit of personal advantage, people would find themselves in a state of war, a war of all against all in which the lives of individuals are solitary, poor, nasty, brutish, and short. Because there are no institutions of social control in this "natural state," (Hobbes called it the "state of nature") one person can take unlimited advantage of others. But what is gained thereby is more than offset by the losses incurred as others also press personal advantage. Sovereign force prevents one from taking advantage of others.[60]

THE NATURE OF SECULAR POWER

The power of the nation-state is rooted in kingship, war, wealth, and law, the antitheses of the Christian community. In a democracy, there is a type of king, usually called a president, or premier. The president exercises the sovereign authority of "kingship," usually delegated to him (rarely, her) by the will of the people. The secular model moves from the basic premise that the will of the people is knowable and can be actuated. Sovereignty is located in the people and the king or leader is the sovereign representative of the people instituted to fulfill their will. It is not God's will, but the people's will which operates the secular state (the democratic form considered to be its best version). Although we will see in the next chapter that through the processes of civil religion, the state has made Machiavellian ethics look like God's will, the state is nonetheless founded upon, at best, the people's will and, at worst, the will of a dominating minority.

The sovereign power is located more or less in the "king" or the people and nowhere else. There is no higher authority for the secular state. There are theologians who say that there exists above the state's positive law a natural law and a divine law. But, of course, this is not recognized by secular states which no longer listen to the theologians of a church which abused its power in its attempts to form a religious community that ultimately mimicked the empire model and thereby lost its right to be a spiritual authority.

Conscience is thus seen as the root of chaos for governmental rulers, and those who stand upon conscience, even religious conscience, are sent to jail or prison as threats to the state.[61] Plato at least admitted in his *Republic* (Book II) that the state has an inherent tendency which compels it to go to war.[62] Augustine, in Book IV of his *City of God*, wrote: "To carry on war and extend a kingdom over wholly subdued nations seems to bad men to be felicity, to good men necessity."[63] But, what, after all, is the difference?

Kingship is always surrounded by war, and hierarchical power is always found in kingship. It should also be mentioned that war always requires the relinquishment of one's conscience, for the warrior must submit to the will of the state and follow orders without hesitation.

> In time of war or other danger everything has to be done quickly. There is no time to win over subordinates, to give a moral vindication of the authority of officers, or to secure consent to hazardous mission. To attempt that would be to abandon the initiative to the enemy. Orders simply have to be given. That is why in the military there is a particular danger that force will predominate and that subordinates will be degraded to mere objects.[64]

Given these understandings, it seems self-evident why the early Christians could not serve in the existing political structures or the military. Acts otherwise illegal or immoral, in war become acceptable, even required. War is simply violence intended to compel an enemy to fulfill another's will. As such, it is surely a tool of human will, not God's. At the same time war requires the abdication of individual conscience and subordination of individual will to a military superior. Nonetheless Thomas Aquinas (d. 1274) justified this form of institutional violence as within the sphere of the civil authority to which the religious person must pledge allegiance.[65]

Added to kingship and war a third empowering attribute of the state is its corporate wealth or economic self-sufficiency. The accumulation of wealth has been an incentive promoted by the secular state since its inception in the 16th century. Wealth is a threat to those without, a protection for those within. Wealth is power, a major tool of the secular state. Economic growth for its own sake is one of the "ten commandments" of capitalist culture.[66] Soviet state socialism has proved quite capable of imitating and adjusting to such western greed. In the United States the entire tax system is constructed to benefit those already wealthy and hinder those who are not. Nation-states are based on the accumulation of wealth and no secular state has ever proposed that its citizens practice voluntary poverty or simplicity as a way of life or even that wealth should be held in trust or relinquished voluntarily in some measure. It has, of course, taken away the wealth of persons unfriendly to the state as a form of punishment.

E. F. Schumacher, in his masterful *Small Is Beautiful: Economics As If People Mattered,* comments on the American politico-economic system:

An industrial system which uses forty percent of the world's primary resources to supply less than 6% of the world's population could be called efficient only if it obtains strikingly successful results in terms of human happiness, well-being, culture, peace and harmony. I do not need to dwell on the fact that the American system fails to do this, or that there are not the slightest prospects that it could do so *if only* it achieved a higher rate of growth or production associated, as it must be, with an ever-greater call upon the world's finite resources.[67]

Finally, the nation-state, economic, political, and religious structures are all interconnected by the protection of law as the enforcer of state morality. Law has been worshiped by the Roman religious institution ever since it took over the trappings of the Roman Empire. Augustine, and later Aquinas, not only argued for a just war but also a just-law theory of the Christian state. A Christian theologian has written:

The specific character of law lies in this, that it constitutes the rule of external conduct and provides the power to ensure this conduct by force. Hence law differs from morality in two respects: first, it has regard only to external relations; second, it empowers the community to enforce compliance with its claims. Law, then, is directed only toward external conduct, not toward inner attitudes. Morality, on the contrary, is also concerned with man's intentions. Social order must establish ordered autonomy of action in accordance with the responsibility for existential ends. Such order is guaranteed when the external actions of the members of society are in harmony with law. The social order is not directly affected by the fact that the motive for these actions is respect for others or is fear of punishment. . . . The external conduct demanded by law must be realized if social order is to exist. Hence the law is essentially bound up with the power to secure this conduct by the application of physical force through social cooperation. St. Thomas [Aquinas] and Hegel agree that the title to compulsion is then an essential and necessary constituent of law both for the same reason, that it is so because of the unsocial element in society.[68]

The characteristics of the nation-state today are so far apart from those of the early Christian community that it is a wonder

that anyone can see how the two can be joined together in a
universal morality which a Christian may follow while being a
citizen of a state. At its worst, law is only a rule of enforced
command. In this form it is generally unacceptable. Law, at its
best, can be seen as enforced justice. As such is it acceptable
to the Christian citizen of the nation-state?

Leo Tolstoy was a prolific 19th-century writer, well known
for his novels *War and Peace* and *Anna Karenina*. He is less well
known for his writings on religion and morals.[69] Tolstoy was
born into the Russian aristocracy and his family attended the
Russian Orthodox Church. He grew up honoring the existing
institutions of his time, the Russian Orthodox Church, the tsar
and tsarina, law, the war machine, serfdom, gambling, and pros-
titution. His experience in later life led him to a spiritual conversion. He then saw these institutions as corrupt in substance
as well as in form.

Tolstoy took seriously the words of Jesus in the Sermon on
the Mount to resist not the evil doer, to turn the other cheek,
to love one's enemies. (Matthew 5:38-48.) He studied the lives
of the early Christians and found that their version of Christianity was indeed quite different from what his church taught
and from what he later voluntarily accepted as true. In Russia,
the church, as a national church, was controlled by the political
institution (much as it is today in our country). Tolstoy's analysis
of this situation told him that the underlying premise of the
legal institution, whether that of the church or that of the state,
necessitates the use of force and ultimately violence for whatever purposes it deems to be just. The very fact that laws are
enforced made them immoral as far as Tolstoy was concerned.

Force is generally used to require people to kill or to enslave
or to do violence, whether that violence is psychological, economic, political, or religious. Further, justice, although a moral
virtue, is not the highest virtue, since love is that. Tolstoy rightly
saw that no government can love or institute the practice of
love. At its best the government can do justice in neutral situations not involving questions of deep religious morality, and

at its worst it does much less than this. Generally it operates far below even the level of justice.

As a man of intense moral concern, Tolstoy was naturally drawn to the belief that attitudes and motivation count far more than behavior and conduct. He believed that a change in behavior and conduct caused by laws and penalties constitutes no moral change at all; therefore law is morally ineffective. Since all law is based on force, law must also be seen as essentially immoral. The answer is to follow another order, a nonviolent order. For Tolstoy, the ultimate expression of that order was the teaching of Jesus Christ in the Sermon on the Mount. The one who would voluntarily practice these moral teachings would, in effect, be able to live with neighbors in peace and love. The Christian would suffer blows and turn the other cheek, and resist not the evil doer with evil retaliation. The Christian would free all from jail, make war against none, and practice only the law of love toward others. According to Tolstoy government is violence and Christianity is meekness, nonresistance, and love. Government therefore cannot be Christian and a person who wishes to be a Christian must not serve government.[70]

THE DEMISE OF THE MODERN STATE

Governmental power, even if it suppresses private violence, always introduces fresh forms of violence into the lives of people and does this increasingly as it grows stronger. Governmental violence, expressed not in strife but in the demand for submission, is less noticeable than individual violence committed by members of society against one another. Violence exists nonetheless and generally to a greater degree than in former times. This type of violence we call systemic or institutional violence. Although this impersonal violence is subtle and often covert, it is as powerful as personal violence was ever thought to be. It is the violence that permeates the nation-state today. It is the violence that perpetuates dictatorships throughout the second and third worlds. It is the violence that convinces the

United States and other superpowers that they must manipulate and exploit their weaker neighbors for their own aggrandizement.

Nisbet believes that the key to western cultural life has been its quest for community.[71] He considers several communities—political, religious, military, ecological, revolutionary, and pluralist. He concludes, as we have noted, that the political has dominated. "It is sometimes said that political nationalism is the contemporary man's substitute for religion in the ordinary sense. And it has to be admitted that during the past two centuries the political state has taken on many of the attributes medieval man found in the church alone."[72] Nisbet observes that we have come full circle. Our modern sovereign states are now mimicking the religious community ideal. In the past, it was the religious community, turned religious institution, which mimicked the empire and political state.

However, the fall that overtook the bloated religious-institution-turned-state now awaits the arrogant nation-turned-religious-community. The latter will also face disintegration, as did the Roman Empire, and the Roman religious institution that followed it. But we must not judge the nation-state too harshly. It is an inanimate object; it is a structure and system; it is a power and principality given power by our own deeds and infected with our own malevolent spirit. The present sovereign state even in its demise continues to be true to its own political values, not seeing that those values are now impossible to implement. At its inception, under the political contract theories, the political state had seen itself as the protector of its citizens' society, economic possessions, spiritual lives; it legitimately—i.e., following its own laws—used violent weapons as the means to defend its citizens from their enemies, with the blessing and acquiescence of those same citizens. It justifies as a necessity, if not an ideal, the destroying of fetuses, innocent children, adults, men, women, total populations, civilian and military for its survival as an institution. The utilitarian political state now finds itself at this impasse: its weapons no longer guarantee survival. Nuclear weapons can only mean total destruction and yet the political state calls upon us in its death throes, in its last hope, to build, or wield, or pay for weapons that surely will bring destruction, not survival. The political state no longer can fulfill nor honor its promise, yet it fights the threat of violence with the only means it has ever known, violent retaliation in kind, unable to realize that its power is spent. The great idolatry and hypocrisy is that the peoples of the world may go down fighting with and for the sovereign nation-state, no longer sovereign, no longer with power to protect its citizens, ultimately loyal to those political values that have no final victory.

This study provides us with a basis for a clear understanding of the relationship to the political state as it exists today: the protector of traditional religious, political, and economic values. Now the state requires our total allegiance, causing us to succumb to the very temptations of institutional political, economic, and religious power which plagued the ancient Israelites and the early Christians. Today the temptations take such forms as Trident submarines, corporate imperialism, and religious phariseeism.

The answer to all of this is the acceptance of a life of radical religious power in a community of people of the Holy Spirit. This does not become a call to separate but a call to witness. This life of love in action is described in Luke 4 as the resisting of oppressors and the freeing of the oppressed, the essence of the Jubilee Year. (Leviticus 25.) Again, in Matthew 25, as broadly interpreted, it is seen in the doing of the works of mercy, feeding of the hungry, clothing the naked and helping those in prison. As Christians following the teachings of Jesus, we must love not only our friends, but strangers and enemies as well, finding our strength not in our culture but in Christ. In living this life we must live the way of voluntary poverty and creative nonviolence characterized by our resistance to war and to cooperation with its system, our resistance to capital punishment and imprisonment, our resistance to abortion and to all that justifies killing as Godlike and expedient. To kill is to judge, to condemn, to usurp God, to fear, to lack faith and trust, to exploit. It is the ultimate sin and it is usually justified in the name of religion, politics, or economics. We are called to live and do otherwise and therefore to fulfill the prediction of Jesus that we will be dragged before Caesar, arrested, and persecuted as our earthly reward for our witness.

We must, nevertheless, strive for the kind of spiritual power that comes from alternatives to cultural, economic, political, and religious power and principalities: a spiritual power which makes us so strong that we need to kill no more. Nor need we depend on the culture for bread or glory. We must continue to live in this world and at the same time exercise the spiritual power which directs our consciousness to the true relationship between our religious commitments and our society. And so we must first divest ourselves of the cultural idolization of kingship, of national boundaries and possessions, of temples and pinnacles, of money and possessions, and rely rather on the power which comes from the dwelling of God within us.

To be truly reborn is to live this new life in the radical power of the Holy Spirit and in the community of God, and we do not do it alone. Our commitment to do it all empowers us with the real rebirth proclaimed by Jesus and prefigured in the vision of the new city of Jerusalem—the city and yet not the city of which we have spoken. (Revelation 21.) The new Jerusalem is a city with no temple, no religious temptation; a city where the merchants have been conquered and the economic temptation terminated; a city restructured, where the political powers come under the authority of the Lamb. Thus the kingdom comes, but the holocaust of the principalities and powers which has ravished the world from its very beginning until now does not. But first the Lamb calls to us anew under the sign of Jonah: Are the Christian nations, like Nineveh, suffering the woes of cultural sin, ready to repent? Let the people turn away from their evil ways and from the violence which is in their hands (Jonah 3) and follow neither secular idols nor chaotic anarchism, but rather a "Gospel order"[73] which is indeed a new way, a new structuring of social life for all human beings.

CHAPTER FIVE

LIVING IN SIN: MODERN IDOLATRY

EARLY CHILDHOOD

Are the so-called Christian nations, suffering the woes of cultural sin, ready to repent like Nineveh? Are we living in a type of cultural, original sin in our modern idolatry of the nation-state? Must we now repent, turn around, before we can hope to change history? Must we be with John the Baptist before we can return to Jesus? I ask myself these questions, for my criticisms are only intellectual and analytical unless I am able to act upon them and repent of the sins which I was taught to commit by the church, the state, by my family and my schools. And so first the confession.

Simply put, the church taught me to avoid sin, and the state warned me to avoid law-breaking. My parents and church affirmed the admonition against sin, and my schools and government ratified the warning against law-breaking. Committing sin, for a Roman Catholic, was breaking the law of God and reinforced the idea of the broad authority of law. A type of civil religion is born in us very early. The distinction between church law and civil law was quite vague for a member of the pre-Vatican II Catholic Church, which found its strength in Old

146

Testament rewards and punishments. Only where one's church specifically held its law to be superior to that of the state or other churches did any distinction in law seem to appear. In my experience, this was usually limited to two areas: personal sin, and interference with church authority by the state. The church could do very little about interference with state authority by my time, but it claimed considerable authority over personal sin.

Of course, sin was anything the church (or often some cleric or nun) said was wrong. Although the church could not wield the sword, it wielded a power, perhaps not in the pristine manner enunciated by Jesus, but in a way which provided it with coercive force over individual members. The church's threats of punishment were all that remained of its temporal power, and those threats concerned a concept of after-life which could be made comfortable only if the individual sinner would cooperate with the church.

We were told that we were all born into a state of spiritual depravity called original sin which began with Adam and Eve's disobedience to God. We were born in sin which needed to be washed away for a clean start. Only the church could do something about this situation. So the church wielded a form of power in an area now completely removed from the state. Since it was a matter of abstract doctrine and belief and did not threaten the state directly, the state cared less; and the church was able to flex its spiritual muscle without interference. Even the Supreme Court of the United States ruled that where disputes involving internal church matters were in conflict, they were not to be litigated in state courts.[1] The state claims no jurisdiction over such matters because no threat to state sovereignty is at issue.

There was, however, a time and place when this was not so. In Europe after the first days of the Reformation, Anabaptists who did not baptize away the original sin of their infants within twelve days after birth were subject to the penalty of death by the civil authorities since the state enforced the views of the new reform groups.[2] It is well to remember that the Reformation really accomplished nothing insofar as a return to the life of the early church was concerned. Violence and coercive power were merely spread around, so not only Catholics used it but Lutherans and Calvinists as well; and they all used it against the Anabaptists who believed in nonviolence and adult baptism.

Today we see a more subtle complicity of church and state. The other side of reformer Zwingli's use of civil power to enforce church rule is the church's cooperation with civil power in return for tax exemption or other such privileges.

Zwingli's use of the violent power of the state is reminiscent of the early church's use of Caesar's power and leads to the same problem: dependence on the civil authority results in civil control. The same dependence results from the acceptance of civil privilege in the form of tax exemptions. Fear of losing the privilege becomes just another tool by which the state obliterates good, religious, corporate intent and practice.

Getting back to baptism—in my case: I was baptized a Catholic three times. My mother, a Roman Catholic, wanted to make sure that my father's Episcopalianism would not get to me, so she had a nurse sprinkle me at birth. As it turned out, my father was not anxious about such things, so I was subsequently baptized in his presence by a Catholic priest. My paternal grandfather, however, was anxious about such things. And since it was this grandfather who had the money and contributed to my family's prosperous lifestyle during the Depression, I got it a third time for grandfather's benefit. He'd missed the first two christenings, because my mother was sure he would not approve.

I won my first competition at age two when I was proclaimed "the most physically well-developed baby" in Kew Gardens, New York. That was to set me off on a long series of wins, both physical and intellectual, and a level of competition in my teens that was never tested against the Gospel at any time. By age five, I possessed a Royal Canadian Mounted Police uniform complete with toy gun, and I played cops and robbers and cowboys and Indians with three Roman Catholic children who lived next door and who went to the same church. I found myself, at the proper age, in the Cub Scouts. My parents made no mention of pacifist ideals (which I know now they knew nothing about) when we spent summers at Sabbath Day Lake in Maine, not far from the home of the Shakers.

At age seven, I was given the opportunity to receive another benefit which the state failed to possess—the body and blood of Jesus Christ in the form of the transubstantiated bread of holy communion. Wine was not offered in those days. The church tradition had been established long before: the blood of Jesus was contained in the bread, even though we could not see it. We could not see Jesus either, so that was at least consistent. I was taught that in receiving the bread I was receiving Jesus' body and his blood. And, I could not get Jesus anywhere else but in the Roman Catholic Church. Why would this spiritual privilege be so important? Why would one want to receive Jesus in this form? The answer is that it saved one from going to hell and cleaned one up so that one could go to heaven. These domains, heaven and hell, were beyond the visible grasp of the nation-state and so access to them was governed solely by the church. Finally, the church had found something to govern autocratically which was both inaccessible and irrelevant to the state.

The way to go to heaven and avoid hell was enunciated exclusively by the church. Assuming everyone came into this world with sin and it was washed away, one might think no further sin would remain; but of course, it did. First the power to wash away sin was a strong reason for membership in the church. Then the power to wash away the sins which replaced the sin which was washed away continued one's submission to the church.

Besides power over heaven and hell, a second power was offered in the form of sacraments. The sacrament of penance allowed for the reception of holy communion and offered time off from punishment in the afterlife. What sins could a seven-year-old child have on his soul? Actually, it was only the "big" ones that kept you from holy communion—murder (unless committed during wartime and excusable in the military), stealing, adultery. I certainly hadn't murdered anyone. I hadn't stolen anything except Walden Zittle's race car in retaliation for his stealing my toy gun. But that was later and was "justified." It was adultery which my mother decided I must reveal in my first confession. But how could a seven-year-old go about doing that, much less knowing about it? Apparently the nuns had told my mother that every sin was subsumed under the Ten Commandments and the "sin" that I had committed several years earlier could only fit under the commandment prohibiting adultery because it was a "sex sin." It seems that one of the boys next door and I, both age five, had spent a day under the sprinkler in our bathing trunks, two years prior to my first confession. When we were through with the sprinkler and bored with cops and robbers and cowboys and Indians, we pulled down our trunks and compared anatomies. We were amazed that we looked alike; our amazement lasted only a few seconds and we were then on to more cops and robbers. (Why is it either sex or violence?)

However, our parents found out about it and thus the conclusion that I had committed adultery and needed to confess it two years later to a priest in order to receive holy communion. I whispered to the priest this terrible deed in such a loud voice that those in the back of the church had smiles on their faces as I emerged from the confessional. I was embarrassed and for a long time I could not tell this story and certainly did not want my mother to reveal it to anyone. It illustrates to me, now that I can laugh at it, the ludicrousness of church power limited to this type of abstract coercion and control in matters dealing with speculation about one's life after death. But that power multiplied a million-fold was a great force indeed, and the modern locus of an ancient authority over people.

On December 7, 1941, when I was ten, the world changed again for me. The Japanese bombed Pearl Harbor and many old ships and young men and women were destroyed. I was terrified. Nothing in my religion made me secure from that terror. My survival was threatened. But Hobbes knew what would come to my aid. The nation-state! Both the church and the state came together in this time of attack to make me secure again. "Praise the Lord and pass the ammunition and we'll all stay free," went the popular song. "God Bless America" and other songs of civil religion helped restore my sense of security. Although church and state had told me things I was prohibited from doing, both church and state confirmed the need for young Christian citizens to shoot the guns of war in retaliation at the evil-doing foreigners, to kill the enemy for Christ!

My patriotic pleasure rose to its greatest height when I cheered our American violence at summer camp in Maine on August 6, 1945, as I read the headlines which reported the dropping of the atomic bomb on Hiroshima. The hundreds of thousands of people killed were not on my mind; only relief that the four-year war was over. That war had almost deprived me of a new bicycle. The bicycle was inconveniently obtained through the black market by my parents in 1944. That was not a sin to be confessed, but simply a business arrangement.

More than anything else the war showed me that most Christian churches thoroughly and completely supported killing in wars and mass destruction of innocent civilians; for war could not be waged without such casualties and perhaps never has been. Although the church would tell me about my personal sins, it never once made mention of any kind of "social sin" connected with the killing in war. It was far too late, wasn't it, for the church to expound upon this, having been complicitous at first with the Roman Empire and then taking on the killings themselves through the Inquisition. No one told me that Augustine's and Aquinas' just-war theories were in contradiction to the teachings and life of Jesus. Yet everyone told me that what the United States and its allies were doing was just and that what the Nazis and the Japanese and the Italians were doing was not only unjust but intrinsically evil. I learned that personal sin was essentially what I did with the boy next door and that social sin was generally committed by persons called criminals within the country, or foreigners called terrorists or aggressors who lived elsewhere and wanted to take what I had. As Lyndon Johnson was alleged to have said during the Vietnam War,

"They want what we've got and we're not going to give it to them."

We fought the war, I was told, for the Jews; and the enemy fought the war to eliminate the Jews and to take our possessions. Well, certainly this script is predictable. I joined the Boy Scouts during World War II and for many years on Memorial Day I marched with honor in a parade for "our boys" and our war dead, while sins of which I was completely unaware went completely unnoticed. "Our boys" were not the same as their boys whom we killed. I even spent the summer of my twelfth year in the Naval Reserve Officers Training Corps at Admiral Farragut Academy, with uniform, rank, and orders. Nothing challenged my set of values for over a quarter of a century.

I did have a little suspicion of authority, but what teen-ager doesn't? At college, I experienced a privilege, selectivity, and exclusivity in fraternity life and the edge of sinful sex. I also experienced some prejudice against Jews, Negroes (as Blacks were called then) and Roman Catholics, and began to identify myself with groups experiencing discrimination. I joined the NAACP.

My first identification with prejudice came somewhere between the ages of six and nine. I was told that my parents' friends, the Herberts, who had bought a new home near us in Scarsdale, New York, occupied their home in what was called a "restricted" area. It seems that Mr. Herbert had changed his name in order to live in this new, rich development where, otherwise, Jews could not live. He also spent some $35,000 in the Depression era to obtain his house. I asked my parents why, and they told me that he was Jewish, his wife was not, and to live in a restricted residential area he could not be Jewish. So he had changed his name to accommodate himself and his family to this cultural expectation—essentially to hide his Jewishness from North Americans who would fight a war to save the Jews! He masked his religious and ethnic background for the pleasure and security of our beautiful neighborhood. All I knew about Mr. Herbert was that he was a great guy and that on his way home from work he would always stop and throw a few baseballs with us kids. I liked him very much. I think others did too. I think we would have liked him whether he changed his name or not.

COLLEGE AND DRAFT

In 1949, I went off to college. I was surrounded by Jews in the New York City railroad station as we headed for Syracuse University. While I lived my freshman year in a college dormitory, not to move into a fraternity house until my second year, I was picked overwhelmingly by the eighty-percent Jewish population of the dormitory to be vice president of that little college community.

In college, I thought I had the best of all worlds, American and Roman Catholic, and I proceeded to idolize both. In reading one of my Roman Catholic books, I found out that Quakers (whom I knew nothing about) were "condemned" as heretics *because* they were pacifists.[3] I did not know much about pacifism and even less about heresy. After all, I was a Catholic and Catholics were neither. Certainly, I had no interest in becoming a heretic. The fact that Roman Catholics used to torture and burn heretics was of some concern to me.

After college I went to work for the U.S. Army as a civilian at the National Security Agency. I was given a top secret and cryptologic clearance in order to make the world safe for democracy, and when it came time for me to serve my country in military uniform, I did so without question, but with some internal reservations. My propagandized upbringing during four years of World War II probably adjusted me to military service more than anything else. In World War II we were fighting against an enemy that was committing racial sins, and I was indoctrinated to the belief that the United States of America was a bulwark against racism. My father stood out in my mind as a rare person who took a young Black boy home for lunch at the turn of the century. His parents were shocked, but I felt he was typical of our country, not his parents. I was free of any social sin of racism, I thought, either against Jews or

Blacks because of the example of my father and my country. I was later to find out that World War II was not fought on behalf of Jews, just as the Civil War was not fought on behalf of Blacks.

The day before I went to the induction center to spend a few years in military service, I remember telling my mother that I could not shoot anyone. But I did not tell anyone else, having no knowledge of the meaning of conscientious objection and no knowledge of the Christian Gospel requiring the love of enemies and avoidance of the "sword." I had no knowledge of pacifism as an acceptable, even central, Christian value. I did know that I could not kill anyone, but I could not justify that belief. I knew, in my heart, I was not a coward; but at the same time I thought others would think me so. I did not believe that my feelings should be universalized, or that all people should take this position. I believed that the United States government had a right to my services as killer, but that I simply could not do it. It was more an emotional, experiential feeling than anything that had been worked out systematically. I was ripe for the Army. Fortunately, for several reasons, the vast majority of my time was spent in the Medical Service Corps and not in the Infantry.

In 1954, on a car trip to report to Ft. Sam Houston, Texas, from New Jersey for medical service training, I entered a bus station to find a restroom. As I headed for the nearest one, a clerk stopped me and said I could not use that restroom because it was a "colored restroom." I guess this was my first experience with civil disobedience, but it was much more in self-interest than love of civil rights or love of humanity. I simply had to go and could not wait, and I was indignant that anyone would stop me from using any restroom. I was only secondarily concerned and sickened over the fact that Blacks were required to use segregated restrooms or no restrooms at all. But I was angry about that too.

Even at this time and with these experiences, the indoctrination of church and state was all-pervasive. I ask myself now, why, except in certain particulars, did the church so often support the state? Now I find it in shades of Revelation.[4] Having lost its temporal power, the church was virtually at the state's mercy. It lusted after the state's goodies in the form of tax exemptions and privileges. This is the modern trade-off, not unlike the relationship which the church entered into with Constantine, but in a much more subtle and a more limited manner. And so I prepared to go to war for the state, sanctified by the church's Just War Theory.

While I was in the military, I wrote a letter for a competition sponsored by the Armed Forces Radio Service at the Freedoms Foundation in Philadelphia. My interest in a competition with such politically conservative sponsorship and association is indicative of my conservative patriotic feelings at the time, as well as my emerging liberalism in the area of civil rights. The letter is dated November 10, 1954, and this is the way I summed up religious and political life as I saw it then:

Dear Sirs:

We who call ourselves Americans go through the process each day of living a comparatively free, just, and equal existence with our fellow citizens. Yet we, who are so fortunate, seem to be little concerned with the basic conceptions inherent in our nation's philosophical outlook. With this in mind, I submit the following as a brief picture of the many thoughts I've had on what America means to me.

We, in America, begin our day in the sanctity of our homes surrounded by our families. We spend our working hours at the occupation of our choice; or if we are not so fortunate to be employed where we wish, we still have the right to change our position, better ourselves, or even waste our time if we care to. Best of all, we are all rewarded in some way for our individual efforts. This state, America, which has through the years preserved our liberties continues to exist primarily for us. Finally we spend our evenings and leisure free to take advantage of any or all opportunities which this nation has to offer—to worship God in a multitude of churches or simply to visit the neighborhood theater of our choice. So each day we exercise

our free will. We may live a happy or unhappy life depending upon the actions we take. In other words, we may
create our heaven or our hell and no autocracy of the state
may subject us to its own desires. We have the right to be
religious or irreligious, notwithstanding the fact that this
nation has always in the writings of its famous personages
professed the profound belief in the Fatherhood of God
and the brotherhood of man.

America means justice. No matter what a person's race,
religion, or color, that person is entitled to reward for his
services, his "due" as Aristotle called it, for each and every
action or absence of action he performs.

America means liberty, the right to act freely with the
only qualification being that that act does not infringe upon
the rights of others.

America means freedom of opportunity. This does not
mean it should ever be construed that every man is entitled
to a like reward but only to the opportunity to receive like
rewards. If such were not guaranteed, the lazy would benefit with the talented and the incentive to progress would
be obliterated. America rightly calls all her flock equal to
begin with and lets each person freely undertake to better
himself and thus receive his just reward according to how
well he developed those talents God instilled within his
soul. Moreover, America does not forget its incapacitated
who, either at the beginning or somewhere down the line,
were unfortunate enough to continue along the competitive road. Lastly, America means the right to think, to grasp
for the truth, and put into practice these truths. A democratic nation is contingent upon the freedom of creativity.

Today, in this country we possess all of the above characteristics conducive to a true democracy. America gives
us the right to exercise these virtues.

I sincerely hope all of us never become so apathetic that
we lose our most precious of all political conceptions,
democracy; or else years from now we will find we may no

longer be able to write letters telling others what America means to me.

Sincerely,

William R. Durland, Private, Medical Service Corps, U.S. Army.

I didn't win. Apparently the letter wasn't patriotic enough, if that can be imagined! I spent three years in the military and was not required to shoot anyone.

LAW AND POLITICS

I received an honorable discharge and, being starved for intellectual activity, entered law school in 1957 and developed a legally trained mind. I took the values of Catholicism and Americanism into my legal practice in 1959 with a fairly well-developed concept of social justice. I had long before decided that capital punishment was unjust and that Black people should have their civil rights. It wasn't long after graduating from law school that these liberal propositions, growing out of my strong conservative, patriotic foundation, hinted of an emerging tolerance. Also, it wasn't long before my concern with the "public interest" found me active in public affairs and I was elected to the Virginia State Legislature in 1965.

Looking back, I see that I had often been one who stirred up the waters, as someone described my doing in state politics. I did it in our fraternity when I was discouraged by the way in which pledges were treated by brothers. And by the time I got to the legislature I had been working for the civil rights movement initiated by Martin Luther King, Jr., for seven years. So, by the mid-'60s my political legislation and my active life reflected a strong sense of social justice. That strong sense of social justice in my life as a citizen was fundamentally reinforced by the very best of Catholicism and Americanism.

Then the peace movement reared its startling head in the mid- to late '60s. I remember telling a political supporter of mine who was also supporting Eugene McCarthy's peace-movement candidacy that a peace administration could open the way for the Russians invading New Jersey the next day and all our accomplishments in human rights would be eliminated.

It wasn't till the very late '60s that what I would call a "religious experience" caused me to give up the civil religion of American Catholicism as I had known it for a commitment to the Gospel centered on the belief and practice of radical religious pacifism. One day shortly before Christmas 1969, I picked up a little book on Tolstoy's views of the Sermon on the Mount. I began to reread the Gospel without interpretation by Augustine or Aquinas. I was changed! As a result of this transformation the possibility of a new relationship to the world was revealed to me. My wealth would have to be diminished, my political power released, my religious beliefs and practices re-evaluated. I began my own journey toward pacifism, simplicity, equality and community.

CULTURAL SIN

It seems to me that somewhere our theological morality and philosophical ethics both have gone awry. What the churches call original sin is such an abstraction that few either accept the concept or believe in it, even though threatened with some heavenly judgment. What seems more real to me is cultural sin. I use the word sin advisedly because sin is usually associated with one's free will.

"Original sin" is said to be a state to which we are born and which seems to exclude the action of free will. My idea of cultural sin is much the same. It is not so much sin as a burden or yoke borne by virtue of having to grow up under the powerful influence of secular culture. Few of us have any real opportunity to challenge or question our culture before we have become completely indoctrinated and absorbed by that culture. We are born into paternalistic and hierarchical structures which condition us to adjust to a way of living and to adopt a cultural set of beliefs before we are able to analyze or reflect upon them or before we are conscientiously and freely able to accept or reject them. In this sense we are subject to a kind of determinist, original sin.

I call these cultural structures the powers and principalities. Our free choice with respect to this gradual acceptance of societal norms is severely limited. Our forebears acquiesced to the powers and principalities and we have no choice but to live with the resulting social constructs. We live in this sin or wrong without entirely "deserving" it. Rather, our "sin" is determined by the cultural practices of our ancestors or our parents, by our schools and our churches, in the sense that they established these structures and systems before we arrived upon the scene.

The ways of the world infect us with "original sin" long before we mature enough to discern for ourselves our proper relationship with the world. We have become acculturated by the ways of the world, the way of death described in the *Didache.* We suffer the penalties of Adam and Eve to live east of Eden and west of Oz. We experience physical death in a world captured by the powers and principalities before we were ever born.

But there is an alternative! To enter the Kingdom now and reject the surrounding culture means release from the heavy burden of cultural sin ("original" sin) by taking on the burden of Jesus alone, who claims his yoke is easy and his burden, light. (Matthew 4:30.) It is this alternative Kingdom we seek. We seek the content of the lifestyle which Jesus taught and which can be known from the Bible and by much prayer and reflection.

The fear of death colors the traditional idea of original sin and places too great an emphasis on doing good for a reward rather than for its own sake. Krister Stendahl writes that we miss the point. "The point is that the whole world which comes to us through the Bible, Old Testament and New, is not interested in the immortality of the soul. . . . The issue is not what happens to me but what happens to God's fight for His creation. . . . If God is God, I neither care for nor worry about the hereafter."[5]

The Garden of Eden temptation to eat of the tree of knowledge is a description of our cultural temptation to know with certainty all that God knows, while failing to follow the ways

God has revealed to us. Protestant fundamentalist Hal Lindsey, in his multitude of books, is the modern messiah of this temptation.[6] We need to have a certain answer for every religious question, for the date of the end times, for the number of the saved, the manner of salvation.

The Roman Catholic church, too, has embraced this lust for certain knowledge, this temptation of the Garden, by declaring dogmas of certainty. For example, believers are asked to accept, on pain of their loss of salvation, that Mary was bodily assumed into heaven. Another dogmatic formula affirms that Jesus was truly all God from the very beginning of creation. But does it really matter whether we know for certain about Mary's fate after death, or that Jesus was surely co-existent and co-identical with God from all eternity? The certifiability of certainty is not the issue. It is a distraction, not a help, in seeking the truth.

For a price Hal Lindsey will let us know the exact date and manner of the end times—how else will we know when our reward is to come, so that we can count on it and not be cheated? How else are we to know how long we have to pay for the reward? We must be certain that our soul is immortal and that we will receive a reward, if we just follow law one and not break law two. We must be certain we will be punished and burned for our failure to adhere to the doctrines and revealed dogmas of the institutional church. We also yearn to be certain that we will receive our reward and punishment immediately upon our death so that we will not have to wait any longer. The degree of egocentrism found in this kind of theology is appalling if not blasphemous.

According to Paul's theology, we shall rise and our bodies will disappear into nothingness as our free choice responds to God's call. But those who die now shall remain in the earth until the call. (1 Thessalonians 4:16.) There is nothing in the Bible about immediate afterlife gratification or eternal punishment, unless it would be Jesus' promise to the "good thief." (Luke 23:39-43.)[7] And yet we invent such "doctrines" to avoid waiting forever or dealing with uncertainty. Such invention is a prime example of the cultural sin we are talking about. It is a structure of the institutional churches, appearing in varying forms throughout history and in the several forms of the church.

There is nothing wrong in striving for some knowledge of God and ourselves. That is our lot and our responsibility. But the obsession for religious "knowledge" as enunciated in dogmas is the same obsession for certainty and security which causes us to empower secular institutions that are empty and illusory with coercive authority over our lives and our choices. The perverse pleasure afforded by thinking we are saved by the political state or the religious institution, and that others are not, is not in accord with the love Jesus expressed and the nature of his Parent, the God whose image and likeness we are called to emulate.

PHILOSOPHICAL MORALITY

Philosophical morality, as it is served up on the secular platter, tempts us as well to adopt ways of understanding knowledge that are at odds with Biblical morality. As we have noted before, faith is not a component of secular morality or humanism. Secular morality allows for no vertical connection with the Creator or the will of the Creator. Instead we take on kings and national idols, expecting salvation from them. Paul's explicit warnings against the philosophy of the Greeks and the law of the Jews indicates his understanding of this cultural problem.

Philosophy talks about morality in terms of deontology and utilitarianism. Deontology or ethics calls us to do rightness, as Kant says, with a good will.[8] Deontology places emphasis on the motive or intent, the will, more than on the act itself: we are not to determine what we are to do by weighing the consequences of our actions and then deciding the principle that we will follow. To do so makes the consequence itself the principle that we follow. This would make deontology just another utilitarian system. To follow the consequence tends to reduce what we will do to that which produces the greatest good, according to our prior calculation. The greatest good, however, remains at best a socialized hedonism (pleasure) or egoism (self-interest). Deontology, which avoids consequential reasoning, is devoid of any real, relational aspect, since it consists simply in standing on principle or duty.

In recent years, situational ethics, an adaptation of act-util-itarianism to Biblical morality, has become popular. Situation ethics uses "love" as the guide for determining the morality to be found in each situation. Fletcher comes close to an improve-ment of both utilitarianism and deontology, but Biblical mo-rality is *not* situational.[9] When Jesus forgave the woman caught in adultery and questioned her accusers, it was not the situation that made the ethic, but the relation of Jesus to the parties and of the parties to each other.

Superior to both deontological and utilitarian ethics is a re-lational ethic. Situational ethics and deontology both deal with abstract situations, but relational ethics deals with concrete, human relationships. Jesus' ethic of righteousness was one of faith in God and loving relationships with people in a given situation or better yet, in a given relation. It is an ethic with a faith stance that is subjective rationally, and objective spiritually. It is not simply situational because it is not rooted in the sit-uation. Principles and guidelines play a part; but the faithfulness of individuals in implementing the guidelines in relation to real people is of paramount importance. It is not simply "to love," as Fletcher says, but, as Jesus says, to "love one another as I have loved you." (John 15:12.) This kind of love cannot fall into the traps of hedonism or egoism because the norm upon which it is based is one of suffering and steadfastness.

This ethic does not allow judgment by appearances only as legal ethics requires. (John 7:24.) Legal ethics is capable only of judging conduct and not motives. Our motives, under the law, are usually deduced in the abstract from the consequences of our actions. The love of Jesus, however, is truly based on the greatest of all establishment antagonists—anarchy. The an-archy of Jesus is not political anarchy, but the "Gospel order" of a community which stands against the nations.[10] Emotion, intuition, imagination take an equal hand with the intellect, reason, and rationalization in the actualization of this faith ethic.

Jesus did not send us the exegete, but the Paraclete; not the philosopher, but the fool; not the lawyer, but the lover.

LAST-ACT ETHICS

One difference I see between the world of "living in sin" and the Way of Life is what I call, tongue in cheek, "last-act ethics." We have all noticed, especially as parents, that the child who is committing the dastardly deed just at the time the parent appears on the scene always gets the greater punishment. Brothers and sisters who may have incited the action invariably receive a lesser punishment, because at the time of the arrest and conviction, the one who fomented the deed is not the obvious one in the act that is taking place before the parent's eyes.

"Last-act ethics" simply means that we tend to hold the person who commits the last sinful act in a chain of sinful acts narrowly responsible for the entire progression of wrong-doing. We judge by appearances, and those appearances are more readily seen in the last act. It is easier to punish this way. The conduct is so stark, the sin is glaring before us. But does sin and wrong-doing happen this way?

When Jesus came upon the scene, it was said that the adulterous woman had been "caught in the act." (John 8.) She was clearly a guilty party. Her consort does not appear in the story, and there are only righteous people around to accuse her. But Jesus does not analyze the matter in that way. He develops a relationship with the woman and with the so-called righteous men who accuse her. The end result is that no punishment is forthcoming. Jesus knows that sin does not happen as the sole responsibility of one person. He also recognizes that we are all so embroiled in sin that we are not free to place all blame on another.

The Japanese bombing of Pearl Harbor was seen at the time as one of the greatest sins of the century. We were all off and running to do justice for ourselves after Pearl Harbor. Justice, by our definition, required that the Japanese pay for their act. Our leaders probably dropped the atomic bomb on the Japanese more to "get even" than for any other reason. But what was behind this "dastardly" act of the Japanese, as Roosevelt described it?

After World War II was over, I was shocked to learn about certain Japanese-American relationships before Pearl Harbor. There were many incitements for Japan's attack, including economic reprisals before World War II, political invasions of the Orient, restrictions of Asiatics to a small part of the earth despite their growing population.[11]

The last-act ethic is also traditionally applied in the personal, religious area. Divorce among Christians is a distressing and difficult problem. It seems to me it is so precisely because it is a problem particularly given to last-act judgments. The one who obtains the divorce, against which Jesus spoke, is seen as the sinful one. Acts, conduct, relational problems which took place in the history of the marriage prior to the divorce seem to fade in importance as soon as there is a "perpetrator" on whom to pin guilt. The wrong-doer is the one who takes the last step which "legally" declares that a divorce has taken place. In fact, divorces do not take place when the law courts say they do. Law courts simply recognize what exists in fact; and the sin does not take place by the last act itself, but by the relationship of all the parties involved in breakdown and alienation over a period of time. Can we judge by last acts any more than by external appearances? Is not the act of getting a divorce one that alone cannot be judged by external appearances? It is the plea of Jesus not to judge acts and appearances, much less the last ones. (John 7:24.) Rather, Jesus shows that a whole string of relationships matter in determining justice and fault, righteousness and folly. (Matthew 18.)

Was not the bombing of Pearl Harbor one act within a history of actions? Was not the rise of Hitler an event coerced by the sins of the righteous nations around him? Was not Britain at fault in destroying the budding relationship between France and Germany after World War I, which might have thwarted the apparent necessity for a figure such as Hitler? Did not Ho Chi Minh go to the Paris Peace Conference after World War I

with sweet images of Lincoln and American democracy, hoping
to find in Woodrow Wilson some kind of affirmation of his
dreams of democracy for Indo-China? Did not Wilson refuse
to see him?[12] The parameters of freedom and territorial rights
apparently did not extend to Vietnam. The last act of Ho Chi
Minh on behalf of his homeland is judged as an evil; whereas
Woodrow Wilson's refusal to see him is not so considered. Did
Wilson have a hand in what happened in Vietnam so many years
later?

We live in sin because of our false moralities. The culture
tells us that sin is failing to go to a church building for worship,
failing to defend our country in war, failing to keep our bodies
clean of drugs, tobacco, booze and sex, failing to perpetuate
"marriages" that are already dead, failing to support the so-
called stability of the state and the dogmas of the church. Did
not Jesus separate himself from the religious culture of his time?
Do not all truly radical movements constitute a breaking away
from stagnant institutional and cultural norms which have lost
their vitality and their morality? "I came to cast fire upon the
earth," says Jesus, "and to bring a division." (Luke 12:49-51;
Matthew 10:34.) He said these things because he knew the first
step is to say "NO," but after that come the "YESES"; without
the "fire" there is no change.

KARMA AND GRACE

Human affairs are governed by cause and effect, or karma, as
the Hindus have it. In the Bible, it is "what you sow you shall
reap." (Hosea 8:7; Galatians 6:7.) One of the great gifts of Jesus
is his breaking of the chain of cause and effect, the breaking of
karma through his grace and power. Karma is essentially
grounded in the idea of an eye for an eye, or justice and deserts.
It leaves the punishment or reward in one's own hands—what
one sows, one will reap. Grace is not based on deserts and
comes freely. It is a gift. (Matthew 6:26.) Sometimes it is said
to be irresistible.[13] One need only ask for it from the Holy

Spirit. Even that is not always necessary, for She blows where She wills.

If God acts through persons and history, and if prayer is efficacious, there is a way to override karma in our good works and bad. Mercy and steadfast love from Yahweh give us hints of the great gift which changes logical, evolutionary, and causal processes. It is an immense gift that God gives us to change the state of things before our very eyes and to revolutionize history. Grace breaks the chain of everlasting cause and effect and is, in a sense, an in-breaking of God into history. It means that God is everlastingly kind, even to those who do bad acts. It means that those bad actions do not necessarily culminate in bad deserts for those who create them, due to the everlasting and steadfast love of a God who seeks to save all of us for all time.

I believe the idea of "just deserts" is a human invention and is another primary example of cultural sin. We have become convinced by our religious and political institutions through the centuries that God's relations with humankind are based on deserts, on our getting what we deserve. We believe that we must earn God's grace, God's blessings, through attitudes and behavior of our own contriving. Equally, we believe that when disaster and misfortune overtake us, it is the result of our own misconduct or poor choice. The fundamental, revolutionary revelation about God which comes from Jesus in the Gospels is that God has given us a life in which we are chosen and called to be partners with God in the care of our sisters and brothers and of the earth, indeed, of all of life. Our lives and the lives of all people are filled with blessings and disasters, joys and misfortunes. These are not a matter of desert, but are simply the human condition in a world *culturally* estranged from God ("fallen"). Our calling is not to concern ourselves with who does or does not deserve what, but rather to be available to each other in succor and sharing, with the power of God's Holy Spirit, to support and augment our broken human efforts.

Philosophical and theological karma is much like the principle under which the institutional governments and religions work,

and it is certainly part of our social system. Jesus said prover-
bially that if you go to jail you will pay the last penny. (Matthew
5:26.) But this new radical in-breaking mechanism called grace,
spoken of in no other religion, no other isms, is here, a power
on earth for us to use. It is the activating power of Christian
pacifism and love that supplants the need for weapons and
defenses for those who live under the spell of karma; and it is
there for the asking.

CIVIL RELIGION

The underpinning for life in modern culture is called civil religion—the idea that through our patriotic institutions we spiritually justify our political ways as God's ways. Near David's
tomb in Jerusalem is a small Holocaust Museum. Outside is a
billboard advertising its presence and attracting attention to
historical events focusing on the world's hatred of the Jews. All
this is organized by the Zionist government of Israel as if the
Jews were the only ones experiencing hatred or the only ones
with a holocaust to remember. In the United States we forget
that the Native Americans suffered a similar fate, as did the
African Americans. The African Americans and Jews fortunately
got some of their rights back. The Native Americans are still
waiting.

North America is perhaps the leader in the institutionalization
of civil religion. Those who escaped George III's oppressive
religious actions were able to find freedom here. This country
became a religious sanctuary for Pilgrims, as separatists. Little
reflection is given to the manner in which Columbus and his
people overturned and dispossessed the innocent natives, so
"loving and peaceful," as Columbus described them.[14] Nor is
much thought given to the manner in which Quaker Mary Dyer
and others were persecuted here for their beliefs because they
fell outside the parameters of the developing civil religion.[15]

The civil-religion ideal tries to convince church-going North
Americans, and does so quite successfully, that Christians have
a duty to honor the state by killing its enemies whenever and

however asked. What a topsy-turvy, church-state relationship we have now compared with earlier ages. Here, in the United States, it is based on the deadly false notion that the United States is a *Christian* nation.

The state tempts us with the sin of security: to taste of the tree of the knowledge of good and evil, to know we are good and that "they" are evil, and finally, to commit even the sin that Adam did not—to take the tree of life and consume it. The state convinces us that it can secure our lives, give us immortality, and fulfill our wildest dreams of peace—that is, security from those who would take away our property, possessions, or prosperity. The state uses violence through war, law, and wealth, to attempt to reach this impossible end. Conservatives support violence to conserve the status quo; liberals justify violence to protect individual and social rights. The state mimics the Kingdom of God. As long as we worship the state and perpetuate it, we delay the millennium from coming at all. Ironically, it is the religious fundamentalists and charismatics who call for these end times, but also work for their delay by worshiping the state as the best protector of security and possessions. "Godless communism" must not get in the way of this kingdom on earth. Raising money for terrorists to blow up the Dome of the Rock of Jerusalem, thereby hastening the end times (at the expense of those living there), is yet another aspect of this mindset.[16]

There is no survival from physical death. The soldier dies young and even though the most successful and richest variety of the state apparently lives on, its days are numbered, as are the days of all nation-states. Only Jesus, not the state, can overcome death. He replaced law with love, for all law is used as dominative power for survival over enemies—those who adversely interfere with our own ends. There is no survival greater than love in action. So it is in our communities of radical caring and faithfulness rather than in our political communities of domination and exploitation that survival will be realized.

The state, which cannot love, as Niebuhr so rightly pointed out, must tempt us with other gifts within its grasp.[17] It tempts us with the illusion of survival and continuity. What a delusion! No state can honestly promise that, and yet we give it our total allegiance. Its device is war, and yet no war can be conducted in justice, and no war can ultimately guarantee security and survival for all.

Seventy percent of U. S. citizens own two percent of the land, while ten percent of U. S. citizens own sixty-five percent of the land.[18] Those who wage war and pass laws are usually the rich who have the greatest interest in protecting their property. That is why rich people usually become our presidents and generals.

War brings victory, but not peace, and seldom even temporary security. We have only to look at the modern state of Israel to learn this lesson anew.

Until governments follow the will of God, no government will survive. Friedlander, the Jewish philosopher, says that the principles of Jesus would destroy existing society, and he is right.[19] The corollary of this is that unless the political and religious institutions are redeemed and follow the teachings and principles of Jesus, they will destroy themselves.

Our choice, then, is agape, the willingness to suffer without the desire for retaliation; the willingness to serve without the desire for reciprocation.[20] All this was folly to the Greeks and scandal to the Jews. To suffer for your truth as a witness rather than to coerce others to your truth is not the way of nations but the way of God.

Consider the words of a Roman Catholic priest written on civil religion's number one holiday in this country, the 4th of July. The Rev. Rawley Myers wrote in a newspaper article: "Thank God for George Washington. Without him we never would be enjoying the freedom we have today. . . . The little colonial army would have collapsed in six months. . . . Washington miraculously held the men together. . . . At Valley Forge we see a painting of Washington on his knees praying to God. . . . Thank God for this great gift, liberty, and sending this country a man like Washington who won it for us."[21]

The justification of violence by the state is taken on by Christians at the price of hypocrisy. The subtle connections are begun for us very early in our lives. Little children see the seven dwarfs willing to commit murder to protect their property from an invader who fortunately turns out to be the harmless and sinless Snow White.[22] So Snow White does not have to be killed for the protection of their property. We have already seen how children learn why another sweet girl, Dorothy, accepts the "contract" to kill the wicked witch: Going home is worth the price.

SECULAR RELIGION

The Marines' Hymn says: "Heaven is guarded by the U.S. Marines."[23] In recent times, the queen of England, symbolic head of the Church of England, prayed for the navy in the Falklands War and provided a son as a fighter, while an Argentine chaplain blessed the Argentine flag and the Argentine government ordered sixty days' jail for those who refused to fight. Recently too, President Ronald Reagan was an adept at civil religion, outdoing even Jimmy Carter, who tried to move the state in the direction of Christianity but failed. It was said about Reagan that he was a fairly religious church-goer, but did not attend regularly because the Secret Service police said it would be too dangerous. He could have been a target.[24] Reagan pontificated nonetheless. He made the most blasphemous statements of any president yet, paying tribute to the nation's military personnel as "the ultimate guardians of our freedom . . . our final protection against those who wish us ill . . . they are prepared if need be to make the ultimate sacrifice for our nation."[25] But Jesus came preaching against sacrifice and for love. What Reagan and other like-minded officials throughout our history really meant is that those who make this kind of sacrifice, unlike Jesus, are killed in the process of killing others.

Living in sin, at its greatest depth, is found in the relationship of president and young soldier. The ultimate sacrifice that Reagan talked about is done in the process of trying to kill the enemy. The ultimate blasphemy of Reagan's statement is in finding "final protection" in a human army rather than in God's

providence. The ultimate love that Jesus talks about is the sacrificing of one's right to kill the enemy and to die oneself, if
need be. Killing the enemy is a sign of heroism in civil religion.

On Easter, 1983, Reagan delivered a message "expressing
confidence that faith will triumph over communism around the
world."[26] Reagan is not the first world leader in modern times
to co-opt Christianity. Winston Churchill is on record as saying:

> We believe that the most scientific view, the most up-
> to-date rationalistic conception, will find its fullest satis-
> faction by taking the Bible literally. . . . In the words of a
> forgotten Mr. Gladstone, we rest with assurance upon "the
> impregnable rock of the Holy Scripture."[27]

Churchill wrote that he was sure that everything recorded in
the Bible actually happened as "set in Holy Writ."[28] But how
could Churchill reconcile his literal use of the Bible and the
means he used in World War II to justify the bombing of
Dresden and other German cities in retaliation for Nazi bombings?

Reagan rallied his religious support from Evangelicals, many
of whom have made abortion a paramount moral issue. When
the legislative issue of abortion first came up in the mid-'60s
while I was a member of the Virginia State Legislature, Jerry
Falwell, living not far away in Lynchburg, was not public or
visible on "right to life."[29] Only a few Roman Catholic priests
were there, such as Bishop Walter Sullivan of Richmond, fighting against more liberal abortion legislation.[30] There were no
Falwellians present, but they now find issues such as abortion,
prayer in public schools, and tuition tax credits as their greatest
concerns. If we compare the stances on popular issues such as
abortion among Hitler, Reagan, and Jerry Falwell, we would
find each had been against abortion, all have been in favor of
capital punishment, all have been in favor of war, and all have
been against pacifism. Being against abortion does not tell us
much about a person or a politician. It may not even tell us if
that person has any real concern for unborn children.

In the final analysis, civil religion is simply an extrapolation of religious beliefs, which are then reduced to a moral code consistent with the principles and aims of the nation-state and used to support those aims. Civil religion has permeated every secular society. We find it in Hitler's Reich, enunciated by German bishops in sermons during World War II supporting Hitler and the fatherland.[31] And we find it today in our own country justifying economic growth and wealth, military violence, and religious and political cooperation toward the end of protecting what remains of a fallen religious institution's privileges and of the security of the nation-state.

"A soldier of civil authority must be taught not to kill men and to refuse to do so if he is commanded."[32] These are the words of an early church prelate. But today most bishops of most churches are intimidated by secular authorities and leave pacifism alone. For the western nation-state, the issue has been not how to stop nuclear war, but how to stop the communists. In 1983, North American Roman Catholic bishops took a stand on nuclear disarmament.[33] Seeing the draft of the pastoral letter as criticism of administrative policy, President Reagan delighted his audience described as "Evangelical Protestant Christians" by declaring that Christians should beware of the temptation of pride—the temptation of blithely declaring themselves above it all—and ignoring the facts of history and the aggressive impulses of an evil empire. He often quoted the Bible to support his military budget. (Luke 14:31, 16:8.)[34] Reagan also asked citizens to find peace through strength. (The word strength, when used by political people, is another way of saying violence.) Reagan described pacifism as simple-minded folly or wishful thinking.[35] "I would rather see my little girls die now, still believing in God, than have them grow up under communism, and one day die no longer believing in God," is a typically American summarization.[36] Reagan likened the antinuclear peace movement to "modern hype and theatrics."[37] In speaking to the American Legion in the summer of 1983, he said: "The members of the real peace movement, the real peacemakers, are people like you. You understand that peace must be bought by strength." But during Reagan's reign the standard of living of the poorest one-fifth of the populace dropped nine percent. The same standard for the richest one-fifth rose nineteen percent![38]

The other side of civil religion, the state side, is "religious secularism." When the pope, as a head of state, is saluted by twenty-one guns and greeted by a full military parade and all the glory that goes with that, when he does not refuse armed bodyguards, we see once again the similarities between pope and president.[39] The pope continues to support, by his actions, the military chaplaincy and R.O.T.C on Christian campuses, even though the inappropriateness of such institutions for Christians has been brought to his attention.[40]

Religious secularism is my name for church adjustment to political patriotism and power. It was only recently that I learned that every priest or minister in the United States officiates at marriages as a clerk of the state government. They proclaim people husband and wife even though they have no authority to do so, political or religious. Only the two can answer to God for their oneness, or the existence of a marriage between them. It cannot be declared by anyone else. It can only be announced by them in the presence of God and their community.[41]

The separation of church and state, which is an idol liberals worship in modern America, in fact does not exist. The myth of the separation of church and state is exposed when the priest works for the state and makes pronouncements beyond God's delegation of power to him or her. Religious institutionalism, itself divorced and broken, itself living in the sin of secularism, has no business making legally binding pronouncements about people's relationships, or condemning how people choose to live. Church secularized marriages are part of our cultural sin pattern and have little hope of succeeding in the manner in which they were intended by God. Some such marriages are for convenience, others for necessity, some out of fear, many in confusion, few out of love. Church secularized marriages have little hope of reaching a state of oneness because they are not founded upon a possibility of oneness.

The Roman church, unlike the Quakers, has been willing to compromise itself by performing secular marriages, but it has not been willing to have its priests subjected to clerical impurities through priestly marriage. It allows its lay people to be subjected to the impurities of pagan ritual, but will not allow its clergy to be tarnished by marriage.

During the first three centuries the church of Rome was closely allied with its Eastern counterpart. Many members of the clergy were married. It was a personal choice determined by the consciences of the persons involved. Believing that virginity, thanks to Paul, was the "proper" state, many opted for celibacy. The early hermits, monks, and nuns are examples of those at the celibate end of the continuum. A certain prestige flowed from this effort to be pure, then as now. Chastity was a means of representing purity through virtue and self-control. But in those days, pacifism, simplicity of lifestyle, and living in community were also understood as reflections of purity. Somehow, with the Roman Catholics, chastity in the form of virginity, and later celibacy, became the touchstone of purity, while the other elements, those which conflicted with Roman state interests, faded, and their purity was no longer recognized in church teachings or canons.[42]

The priest was set apart by ordination as an exclusive member of a club of celibates. By the end of the 4th century, marriage for clerics was frowned upon. The first canonical decision dealing with married and unmarried clergy was made by Basileious Justinianous in 528 AD.[43] He issued a decree that all men who had children would be excluded from the clergy. The law did not even then exclude married persons, but it demonstrated a preference for single males. Laws prohibiting clerical marriages were enacted primarily to prevent children of the clergy from inheriting church property.[44]

Earlier, the Council of Elvira in 300 AD ruled that priests "abstain from conjugal intercourse with their wives and the begetting of children, lest those who persist be degraded from the ranks of clergy."[45] Pope Leo, who did so much else for institutionalized Romanism, finalized the norm of celibacy in the 5th century. Not much has changed since then, as we continue to live in cultural sin.

A Vatican Declaration, made public in 1977, and approved by Pope Paul VI, describes the role of women in modern society and the church, and is entitled: "Declaration on the Question of the Admission of Women to the Ministerial Priesthood."[46] It says, among other things, that "the Catholic Church has never felt that priestly or episcopal ordination can be validly conferred on women."[47] The essential reason named in the document is that "by calling only men to the priestly order and ministry in its true sense, the Church intends to remain faithful to the type of ordained ministry willed by the Lord Jesus Christ and carefully maintained by the Apostles. . . . Jesus did not call any women to be part of the twelve. If he acted in this way, it was not in order to conform to the customs of his time, for His attitude toward women was quite different from that of His milieu, and He deliberately and courageously broke it."[48] The document goes on to say that within the apostolic church there was at no time a question of conferring ordination on women. It fails to note that at that time there was no ordination at all. The official position is that because the bishop or priest in the exercise of his ministry does not act in his own name but represents Christ, who acts through him, the priest truly acts in the place of Christ. The church concludes that being "in the place of Christ," i.e., taking on the role of Christ, means that the priest must be physically the image of Christ, or male. The church has thus deified the male anatomy of the man, Jesus, to a point which forever excludes women from the exercise of ministry in what is often a very real calling. In this case, the church has allowed secular patriarchy to be idolized.

Another attitude of secular religion is the inability of some Christian churches to preach love for criminals as they do for fetuses or unborn children. Catholic chaplains accompany the convicted to their executions and in no way rise up in witness against this killing.[49] When John Hinckley was judged not guilty by reason of insanity, one righteous person wrote the *Colorado Springs Sun:* "It is no time for the seventy times-seventy charity edict of Our Lord. Even He cleansed the Temple of the money changers. Their crime was as nothing compared to Hinckley's."[50] The writer further shrilled, "In the good old days a man would have hanged by his neck from the limb of a tree until his toes wiggled no more. It was considered good riddance to bad rubbish. . . . We should rise up in arms against the lawyers who defend such criminals, we should stampede against judges. . . . "[51] Why do Christians react so violently to justify secular punishment? How have the pastors been so neutralized?

Richard DeHaan, a much admired Protestant fundamentalist minister, writes: "All are benefited when law and order are in effect."[52] Years ago, a Christian couple being interviewed on TV, when asked for their comments concerning the murder of their daughter, said that the killer should be executed because "Jesus said 'an eye for an eye.' " According to DeHaan, God wants the state to punish, to deter crime, to protect the public, and to execute criminals for a morally uplifting atmosphere.[53] We literally fry our condemned victims. They sizzle, they catch on fire, they burn in the chair; and this, a Christian minister describes as an uplifting experience. It can only be uplifting if we accept religious secularism as our norm of spiritual depth and truth. In conclusion, DeHaan says, "Only in a society ruled by law can citizens live in a state of security assured that their property and persons will not be violated by evil men. . . . I am pleased to report . . . that the pendulum of public feeling is now swinging back towards stiffer penalties for crimes and executions for murder in the first degree . . . demanded by the Bible."[54] For DeHaan, what the pagan public demands is what the Bible calls for.

There should not be a case where an unborn child's life is taken, for the child is human and made in the image of God. But what sense is it to save the unborn child who, as an adult, takes to the field of battle with the duty and responsibility of either killing enemies or being killed for the preservation of a certain government and a particular way of life?

The Catholic Church has been for centuries a kept church, the chaplains and spiritual lackeys of the rich and powerful. It has not done its duty to proclaim to the wealthy as well as to the poor that they should sell all and give to the poor if they wish to enter the Kingdom of heaven.[55]

When John Paul II visited Palermo, he dropped a section from the prepared text in his speech in which he expressed support for the anti-Mafia campaign by Palermo's Roman Catholic bishops who were excommunicating Mafia members for committing murder and other violent crimes in Sicily. The Vatican officially explained that the pope "did not deliver part of his speech because he was running behind schedule."[56] Bishops in the United States who weakly tried to do something for peace did not receive papal excommunication, but neither did they receive enthusiastic papal applause. The official Vatican newspaper has made very little mention of the Bishops' Pastoral Letter of 1983.[57] A look at the whole history of Roman Catholic involvement in war-peace efforts in North America shows that war efforts have dominated.

At 9:15 on the morning of August 6, 1945, the Feast of the Transfiguration of Our Lord, the bomb was released that transfigured Hiroshima. One of the military persons involved in the atomic bombings of Japan wrote: "The Great Ariste piloted by Major Charles Sweeney dropped the bomb on Nagasaki that destroyed the major nunnery in the country. Why a second bomb? Simply to see how improved the second was over the first. *Time Magazine* at the time reported that it was so improved that the first one dropped only three days earlier was made obsolete."[58] Many of those who manned the planes and dropped the bombs were Christians. One thereafter committed suicide. Father George Zabelka was a military chaplain at that time. He has since become a dedicated pacifist and has called for an Ecumenical Peace Council.[59] His call goes unheeded.

We have tried to point out by our several examples that, although from time to time the church does speak out, it will not give up its ultimate and fundamental support for the principle of warmaking.[60] Churches, whether run by popes or preachers, continue to justify deterrence and treat pacifism only as a Christian option. But the civil religion of the secular nations is so ingrained in the religious secularism of modern churches that it is there to stay—at least until alternative life communities grow up in their midst as a witness to this folly.

THE BISHOP AND THE WAR MACHINES

I will draw this discussion of living in sin to a close with an example of what happened in a local parish concerning support for a warmaking mentality. One of the American bishops who signed the Pastoral Letter plays a role in this little vignette. In March of 1983, I was asked to speak on Christian pacifism and war-tax resistance at a local Roman Catholic church. The talk went well but an incident which occurred before the talk turned out to be of far greater moral import in the long run. My wife and young son came with me and we were ushered into the cafeteria of the parish school for coffee before the talk. As we were engaged in small talk, I noticed a group of children congregating around a machine. Just then some chairs which were stacked on a table near them fell because of the commotion they were making around the machine. I went over to the area and found that a video game was the object of all the attention. It was labeled "Tempest." Another machine called "Armored Attack" stood next to it. These machines dealt in the usual Christian temptation, warmaking. The directions on the first machine read: "After inserting 25¢, 1) Fire to start game, 2) Shoot the enemy, 3) Player loses a life when hit, 4) Hint: Hold fire button down for continuous fire, 5) Use the Super Zapper to Zap all the enemy, 6) Kill the enemy by shooting enemy."

I was shocked. So I got off a quick letter to the bishop who had local authority over this complex of churches and schools, and who is otherwise a good person and supporter of peace causes. I also sent letters to the pastor of the church and to the layperson who was the administrator of the program in which I was asked to speak. The letter said in part:

How can a school named after the Mother of Jesus and committed to the way of Jesus tolerate a game machine for her own children, even high school children, which teaches that the lust to kill is all right? What if the subject of that machine was sexual pornography or abortion? Would it be placed and tolerated in the school? If not, why does the lust for war receive such approval? Shouldn't you see to the removal of both machines forthwith?

I received no answers to my letters but instead got a phone call from the school's principal. So I wrote a second letter to the bishop expressing my concern over the telephone call from the principal, who was considerably angered by my criticism of the video games. The principal justified the machines' presence in the school and took credit for having introduced them there. He said that the machines were his business and not the pastor's or the bishop's. He said further that he assumed that the bishop and the pastor approved of his actions since they had raised no objections. I mentioned all this in my second letter to the bishop, and said further, "I was in the audience on the anniversary of the assassination of Archbishop Romero, when you said many glowing things about peace and justice and Christian love quoting Romero, who said, 'When you hear the word of a man telling you to kill, hear the word of God, thou shalt not kill.' Please let us hear each other. Let us talk. I ask to see you at your earliest convenience."

A week later the bishop wrote saying: "I don't agree with you on the magnitude of the impact of the game you are addressing might have on the students at the high school. I am . . . leaving [that situation] to the principal. If the principal we have hired does not find it offensive, I am going to trust his judgment."[61]

There was still no response to the offer to talk. Soon a letter came from the principal, saying: "The magnitude of your grossly overstated speculation regarding the harm and danger and morally destructive nature of these electronic games is unnecessarily rooted in an assumption that is unfounded, incomplete and perhaps reckless to even suggest."[62]

Having received no reply to my request for a talk, I wrote the bishop again. Upon his return from Chicago, where he had attended the gathering for the final writing of the Pastoral Letter on Peace, the bishop contacted me, suggesting I give his secretary a call to see when we might be able to arrange a meeting. I did so, but his secretary was on vacation till the end of the month, and no one could make appointments until she returned. As it turned out, I was leaving for San Francisco for a speaking engagement at the time his secretary would return. When I returned from San Francisco a week later, I found that the machines had been removed when the school closed for the summer. While all of this was going on, some members of the group before which I had originally spoken considered a petition asking that the machines be removed. But the group disbanded and the school closed before they took any action on circulating their petition. However, their spokesperson talked with both the bishop and the pastor. The bishop supported the Peace Pastoral Letter but apparently could not transfer those ideas to a situation so close to home.

A great teaching experience for both parents and children was lost. The church resolved the issue by quietly removing the machines between school sessions rather than facing an educational dialogue about the issue or by commenting upon its action, or taking any responsibility. It simply took them out when nobody was looking. Its resolution was thus political and not religious—another, and final, example of religious secularism and civil religion. Did they finally listen to a witness and to conscience, or was the equipment removed for other reasons? The bishop is now an archbishop.

OWE NOTHING TO THE KING BUT LOVE

There is a folk song that goes something like this: "What did you learn in school today? I learned George Washington never told a lie, that soldiers seldom die, that policemen are our friends."[63] There must be alternatives to our present political, religious, and economic institutions. If we say "NO," we must find the "YES" to take its place. We can't say "NO, that's all I've got to say." To those who say that no alternative exists, we need only remind them of the Sermon on the Mount, and the writing in Leviticus of the Jubilee and Sabbath Years, and the early Christian communities. We simply need to put these together in a radical, not reformative way. We need to seek diligently through these sources in a structural, systematic, not piecemeal way; for we already have the blueprint—this great historical revelation of God.

William Stringfellow calls us to have the mind of Christ, by not yielding to this world, and by freeing ourselves from the social, political, and economic principalities.[64] Stringfellow describes the Holy Spirit as the militant presence of the word of God in the life of creation, as agitator. He says there is no Biblical spirituality to be found in a vacuum, cut off from the remainder of humanity. It is living in the midst. We are in that midst. We are even in that which is ordained by the ruling powers as order, and it is chaotic. The politics of Biblical spirituality, Stringfellow says, involves the renunciation of worldly power and the conditions commonly associated with worldly power—wealth and control thereof, success, fame, applause, ambition, avarice, a competitive spirit. Biblical spirituality means powerlessness, living without embellishment or pretense, free to be faithful in the Gospel and free from the anxiety about effectiveness or similar illusions of success as the world defines it. We have chosen Camelot rather than community and we look for this imaginary and illusory return of King Arthur, who overcomes "might makes right" with "might *for* right." The mythology of the United States as a holy nation is the illusion of our present time. We have idolized the nation in place of the church theocracy of the Middle Ages. The appropriation of the Biblical tradition of the holy nation to a secular regime is a profound affront to Biblical faith. Stringfellow has said that the problem of America is repentance. I agree. Repentance, turning away from the sins of "living in sin" is what can serve to clear our hearts and minds and ready them to receive visions of what the alternative Kingdom would look like here on earth.

Some have said that the United States is the only nation founded on a creed. That creed is its civil religion. Our co-operation with civil religion influences church attitudes toward wealth. The majority position of churches on private wealth is to claim that it is consistent with Christian teaching to keep it and protect it—as long as about ten percent is contributed to the support of the institutional church! At best we may conclude that our wealth is a trust to be held in stewardship for the benefit of others. We refuse to look at wealth as something to be held in common. We cannot face, and our churches fail utterly to suggest, that such radical sharing might provide for a balanced community and do away with the temptation to want what others have. (James 4:2.) A voluntary poverty that calls us to live as poor, struggle for economic justice, and identify with the economically destitute is not popular in our civil religion. Rather than face our economic problems in this way, we attempt to cultivate a sense of interior detachment from material things, or to share our time (not our money) in counseling others on good stewardship and "bettering oneself." We need to end involuntary poverty, but we also need to end church-encour-aged, voluntary richness.

As we look around us in North America, do we see Christians suffering corporately for the sake of their beliefs and mandated lifestyle? The early church knew that persecution was not an accident but arose out of the nature of the faith of the church. Not so now. Rather than suffering persecution, many modern North American Christians stand by and do nothing when they are told by people like General Bernard Rogers, NATO's past supreme commander, that even without firing a shot, the Soviets "could try to force NATO into concessions by threats of a conventional attack that both sides would know could only be stopped by our first use of nuclear weapons."[65] The first use of nuclear weapons must remain a central element of NATO's "flexible response" strategy, the general said. The doctrine of flexible response clearly could not accommodate a NATO declaration of "no first use" of nuclear weapons.

The present archbishop of New York, Cardinal O'Connor, objects to what he calls "the growing implication that the only true virtue is in conscientious objection."[66] This takes away from the "honor" of military service. "Those who serve the country are to be lauded rather than indicted."[67] And a federal judge in Kansas City can say, "Only a moment's reflection should convince you that one's motive is not an excuse for intentionally violating the law."[68] But what if one's motive is a conscientious objection? It matters little in civil religion and religious secularism any more. Christians go to bed night after night with *The Imitation of Christ* by Thomas a' Kempis, in which it says, "God . . . judges all things according to the intent of the doer."[69] But Judge Bartlett tells us that the law of the nation is otherwise and must prevail.

Captain Gloria Orengo of the U.S. Air Force, a military officer and Protestant chaplain, says that "The military uniform makes the chaplain stand out in a civilian crowd; other than that, he/she is a minister, credentialed by a specific church organization to serve God in the military by bearing the Word to the men and women who work to protect America."[70] We are certainly dealing with two kingdoms when we hear these statements made by modern Christians in contrast with the words of Franz Jaeggerstatter, who was beheaded by Hitler on August 9, 1943, for refusing to fight in the war:

> Now anyone who is able to fight for both kingdoms and stay in good standing in both communities . . . such a man, in my opinion, would have to be a great magician. I, for one, cannot do so. . . . It is certainly unfortunate that one cannot spare his family this sorrow. But the sorrowings of this world are short-lived and soon pass away. . . . Is then the Kingdom of God of such slight value?[71]

In his time Jesus rose in the synagogue to tell us that he came to free the oppressed and to speak to the poor. (Luke

4:16-20.) Today the nuclear arms race is the clearest example of disregard for the value of life, as well as the principal source of the oppression of the poor.

Today, in our secular society our institutions are not informed by Christian values. They are secular institutions financed by the nation. The University of Colorado, for example, must become a world-class institution or the state may lose its high-tech industry, much of it the high-tech defense industry. The University of Colorado as of 1986 would not divest its funds in companies doing business in racially segregated South Africa.[72] The General Electric Corporation ("We bring good things to life") pleads guilty to defrauding the United States, but the government cannot afford to severely punish large defense contractors. The nation is dependent upon GE's defense contracts, "like a newborn baby is dependent on its mother."[73]

Three hundred years ago George Fox, founder of the Quakers, had a dialogue with a Jesuit priest which he reported in his *Journal* as follows:

> Then I asked him why they did put people to death and persecute them for religion. And he (a priest) said it was not the Church did it but the magistrates. Then I asked him whether those magistrates were not counted and called believers and Christians. And he said "Yes." "Why then," said I, "are they not members of the Church?" And he said, "Yes." "Why then dost thou say the Church does not persecute?" So I left it to the people to judge. . . . [74]

Fox added: "I owe nothing to the King but love, nor to any man, and love doth not kill but fulfill the law."[75] Obviously the University of Colorado, the General Electric Corporation, and many other institutions and corporations are full of Christians in high places, just as many of our presidents have claimed to be born-again Christians. But these Christians do not carry their values to the marketplace or the halls of government. If they did, society based on secular power might indeed be destroyed.

Jean Vanier says there are different ways of exercising authority and command. There is a military model, the industrial model, and a community model.[76] The general's goal is victory, the factory manager's goal is profit. The goal of the leader of the true Christian community is the growth of individuals in truth and love. We must now look to that community model. If we trust Gospel testimonies, the understanding of the community model will go through us like a shock, affecting the direction our lives are taking, our established systems of need, and even the very society we have helped to create. It will damage and disrupt our own self-interest and will point us toward a fundamental revision of our lives.

In the words of a prophet, Peter Dougherty, speaking out of the Oakland County Jail on Holy Thursday: "The resisting church will remain a minority. But a powerful minority, having an impact that will foster change while it also heightens conflict. That conflict will be within the churches and within the broader society."[77] It is now time for that conflict to reach within the churches and outside to the broader society. "The question of State-society relationships . . . is clearly *the* salient problem for the polity in the coming decades."[78]

In 1970 I helped to start the Community For Creative Non-Violence in Washington, D.C., and a new way of life began for me—radical religious community.

It was time for me to go out in the midst of wolves. It was time to brace myself for the deliverance and the dragging. It was time to give testimony before the nations. It was time to live in anxiety and practice endurance.

"Behold I send you out as sheep in the midst of wolves, so be wise as serpents and as innocent as doves. Beware of men; for they will deliver you up to councils and flog you in their 'holy places,' and you will be dragged before governors and kings for my sake to be a testimony before them and the nations. For when they deliver you up do not be anxious . . . she who endures to the end will be saved." (Matthew 10:16-18, 22.)

For in the end we will be saved, and that salvation will be, among other things, a new and eternal way of life. If we are to live as if the Kingdom has already come, we must give some thought to the manner in which it should and can be modeled.

CHAPTER SIX

FORMING COMMUNITY

RUPTURING THE RAPTURE

We come now to our attempt to identify specifically the structure of contemporary radical religious community.

Several years ago some members of our Colorado community were in a park in Colorado Springs beating a drum to commemorate the dead of Hiroshima and Nagasaki. We were approached by a friendly young woman who asked why we were doing this in the park. We told her we were Christians commemorating the tragedy of the nuclear holocaust of Hiroshima and Nagasaki. Each beat signified the death of one person caused by the American bombings. We told her we were pacifist Christians and did not believe in killing our enemies. She said she was also a Christian and did not believe in killing enemies and was overjoyed to find Christians on the street who felt the same way—such a rare occurrence!

This was not our usual experience during such street witnesses. Usually we are met with antagonism and hostility and comments like, "Why don't you go to Russia?" or "You're all communists, not Christians." The young woman, in this instance, said she was a member of a Pentecostal church and that the possibility of atomic war destroying the earth was of no concern to her as a Christian. She wondered why it was of concern to us.

Before hearing out our answer, she told us that to be so concerned was a humanist temptation. She, and all true Christians, she said, would be "raptured" before any such tribulation as atomic war would come about. She believed she would be safe, secure, and separated, and would meet her Lord in the heavens, as Paul predicted. (1 Thessalonians 4:17.) She would not suffer any pain or discomfort. So the Lord had promised her and her Christian friends.

I asked her if she intended, then, to avoid the tribulations to come; but she said none would come. I read to her from my Bible in Matthew 10 and 24 concerning Jesus' predictions of tribulations for Christians who truly practice the Gospel. There Jesus observes that for their stands against governors and kings his followers would be hated by the world and delivered up to tribulations. She said that was "the devil talking" and fled down the street. My immediate response was one of sorrow for this young woman and the many like her who are victims of popular theological writers like Hal Lindsey and mass-media preachers like Robert Shuller who preach only prosperity and comfort for God's approved Christians.[1] In the context of these teachings and influences, the young woman could not understand what we were about.

There are many who do not believe in a radical, alternative, religious community based on the life of Jesus, because they are not Christians. And there are many more who are Christians, who reject it in even stronger fashion. Oftentimes, behind this rejection is the belief in what some fundamentalist Christians call "the rapture." The idea of rapture does include tribulation, but not for Christians. There are numerous folders, pamphlets, and books in which fundamentalist teachers write about Christians being saved by the rapture, while awful tribulations befall those unfaithful ones and non-believers left behind. There is no rattle of Armageddon for the raptured ones. They are taken away from earth, safe and sound, to return with Christ when his Kingdom is established.

According to these teachings, the sins of the world do not include militarism, nationalist myopia, economic greed, and exploitation; they are instead homosexuality and use of drugs and alcohol. One writer, Leon Bates, pictures a sudden removal of the saved in the rapture causing a world crisis of confusion and panic. There will be airline crashes, bus and train wrecks, fires, looting, lawlessness, mobs without police control, rampant crime, families terrified and in shock.[2] While all this is going on, the saved will be swept up, clear of all the violence, which is, in fact, caused and exacerbated by their sudden disappearance. This violence is only for others. The true Christians are spared and protected.

This Bates pamphlet on the rapture says that it will be too late to prepare for the "rapture" when it finally comes. If you are left behind, you will be part of the tribulation and it will be horrible. The pamphlet continues: "If the rapture has occurred, you have NO ESCAPE from the Tribulation. *But* there may be *hope* depending on your response to the rest of this message."[3] This, again, is the other side of civil religion—religious secularism—a cultural religion which preys on fear and insecurity, causing people to believe and follow its principles of reward and punishment. The pamphlet ends by saying that for more details one can send for "Project for Survival" by Leon Bates at the Christian Bookstore. The similarities between the rapture message and civil religion are obvious: one will obtain survival, reward, punishment of evil-doers, and security, but only if one follows the rapture preachers' rules and believes the predictions.

But if one accepts the notion of the rapture, one must believe that it is possible to identify when these events will take place. This lust for certainty about the events of the end times is another cultural sin committed by followers of false Christianity, as we have already noted. Not even Jesus knew when the end would occur. But Hal Lindsey, in his book *The Late Great Planet Earth,* is certain that it will be "within 40 years or so of 1948."[4] (The date of the establishment of the state of Israel, 1948, becomes the point from which these predictions are figured.)

According to Jesus, "The Kingdom of God is not coming with signs to be observed." (Luke 17:20.) Yet Lindsey *et al.* believe that these signs may be observed. If we believe in this so-called rapture, then there is no reason, as the young woman on the street told us, to witness to the Gospel of Jesus or to provide service for those in need or to form intentional community. In sum, there is no reason to live a faithful life in the manner of the first Christians. There is no reason to have a social experience at all, because a select group will be saved and those remaining will be punished. Further, the pain and tribulation of social ills—even the catastrophe of nuclear war— are seen as part of the deserved punishment and therefore part of God's righteous plan. The formula for being saved has much more to do with a verbal declaration of belief in Jesus and a "ruptured" rapture than righteous relationships with each other and with creation.

For many Christians, the world is an eternal enterprise which will continue day in and day out exactly as it is today. For them the threat of nuclear holocaust is a fiction. That same day during the witness in the Colorado Springs park, we met ministers and militarists (Colorado Springs is the home of the major tourist attraction in Colorado, the U.S. Air Force Academy) who told us there is no threat to the world from nuclear weapons; the world will go on as it has, regardless of the existence of such weapons among us. They had no concern, as did the young woman, that there might ever be an end time. They were in agreement with her that we need not change our ways, for our ways are good. The world prospers—at least North America does—and is safe and secure—at least North America is—and our community, the North American community, is the best. So for many the quest for a new Christian community, with new structures and values, is of no consequence at all. We are not called to live *as if* the kingdom has come; we are to live as we have been living *until* the kingdom comes.

ALTERNATIVES TO THE RELIGIOUS TEMPTATION

The criticism that our mourning the deaths at Hiroshima and Nagasaki was simply an expression of secular humanism is challenged by Hans Küng. Küng sees Christianity as radical humanism, positing that Christianity and humanism cannot be antithetical opposites, but that Christianity must be humanist and humanists Christians.[5] Jesus, the paradigm humanist, is not a priest and rejects force as seen in the Lukan sword incident. In fact:

> Nowhere does he show any sign of acting with a political objective, to serve worldly power. On the contrary, there are no political hopes, no revolutionary strategy or tactics, no exploitation of his popularity for political ends, no tactfully shrewd coalition . . . no tendency to accumulate power. What we do find is quite the reverse (and this is socially relevant): renunciation of power, forbearance, grace, peace; liberation from the vicious cycle of violence and counterviolence, of guilt and reprisal. . . . The *story of temptations* [is] . . . the diabolic temptation of political messianism. . . . The obscure saying about the kingdom of heaven coming by violence and the violent trying to seize it by force may well be an explicit rejection of the Zealot revolutionary movement.[6]

What we are offered instead is community dedicated to nonviolent revolution. Jesus' entry into the Temple is a deliberate provocation, a symbolic act, an individual prophetic sign in action; it amounts to a judgment. For Jesus, politico-social revolution is not an alternative to the system. Love of enemies instead of their destruction, unconditional forgiveness instead of retaliation, readiness to suffer instead of using force, blessings for peacemakers instead of vengeance, these are the attributes of this alternative community.

The formation of community then is an imperative as long as the existing ecclesial institutions do not address this fundamental need with the methods taught and demonstrated by Jesus Christ. The two cities to which we belong can never coincide; the Christian must abandon one for the other. The opposition between the world and the Kingdom of God is total.

There are numerous, radical, religious communities all over
the world. They are basically lay communities, and almost always they are founded in egalitarian simplicity and nonviolence.
Why nonviolence? Gandhi said that nonviolence presupposes
the living presence and guidance of God. The leader depends
not on his or her own strength but on God's.[7] Such communities
live in voluntary poverty and simplicity. St. Basil said that the
bread we store belongs to the poor. The radical Christian community lives by the tenets of nonviolence and voluntary simplicity.
   Contrast this with existing, popular, political community:

> Essentially, for instance, . . . Communist society is based
> on the same facts as capitalist society: And at the bottom,
> the U.S.S.R. obeys the same rules as the U.S.A. Man is no
> more free on the one side than on the other, . . . only he
> belongs to a different section of mass civilization. Justice
> is just as much flouted on the Right as on the Left. . . .
> Whether we live under a dictatorship or in a democracy,
> the financial technique is always the same. . . .[8]

But for different reasons. The rejection of alternative community always seems to come from the same type of argument:
The need for institutional violence. The violence is the pre-
requisite of security.
   Russell Baker writes, "The United States' passion is security."[9] Baker traveled across beautiful, autumnal America. He
happened to pass through Beverly Hills, California, where
sumptuous houses contain vast riches. "Every other house
seemed to bear a large placard announcing the identity of its
private security guard service, and most of these carried a sup-
plemental placard which said 'Armed response.' Very little of
this professional search for security was evident in the country
20 years ago and now it is a national pastime. The irony is that
the more security we get the less secure we are. This is true
whether we are talking about so-called 'national security,' or
personal security against 'the criminal element.' "[10]

Ultimate security, survival, which is another way of describing what is at the heart of our domestic and international defenses, is not part of the Christian value system. There are two distinct value bases for ethics.[11] Secular living is primarily concerned with one's own survival in one form or another. John L. MacKenzie, the Bible scholar, says that all rational ethics have as their primary motivation, survival. When survival is threatened, all other values simply fall by the wayside. Actions ordinarily characterized as murder, arson, rape, lying, robbery, which usually are impermissible, become desirable, even noble, when done to ensure survival.

In the Christian ethic, on the other hand, the single highest value is not survival. The single highest value for Christians is agape or service—service to suffering humanity.

Survival and service are two totally different, fundamental approaches to human motivation and human existence. Survival is not in the Christian value system, nor is the brand of security that attempts to bring us survival part of that value system. However, security is part of institutional Christianity today because Christians have been taught that an enemy is one who can negatively affect one's survival or self-interest, or restrict one's freedom of worship.

The survival ethic is a fraud. "Perhaps the most insidious thing about the rational ethic is that the very thing that it promises, the very thing which it will turn virtue and vice upside down for (namely, survival) is the very thing that it simply cannot come across with. Survival is the one thing that the rational ethic cannot guarantee. All that it can guarantee is that something will endure for a little longer but survival is impossible. The rational ethic for all its claims is a fraud."[12]

The irony is: the more security we buy, the less secure we are. The more weapons we buy, the less secure we are.

The survival ethic is a type of demon, much more dangerous than any that are spoken of from the pulpits of our established churches. Because of this demon, we worship the idol nation-state as the guarantor of corporate and individual survival. It is this demon that Jesus experienced in his temptations. We, as modern Christians, have opted for this demon over Jesus. In so doing we not only preach apostasy, we practice idolatry.

Where then is our alternative security? I believe it is in alternative community. It is one thing for an individual to take on great risks, great suffering, great persecution alone. Only Jesus did this. He was the only one to go to the Cross in the manner in which he did. His followers all disappeared. The community had not yet been formed. Only with the coming of the Holy Spirit, who came for all times, and is found in that of God in each of us, only then did community begin.

Years ago, I was teaching about pacifism at the University of Notre Dame, and a young man said, "I could accept pacifism but not while living in a nuclear family. I could not give up so much without some kind of alternative community to become part of, to be nurtured by, and to live with." He was right. Pacifism is almost impossible to practice by oneself. So is witness and martyrdom. It is very hard to give up an adequate salary and to live with the poor as poor unless it is done corporately, in community. The first pillar of alternative life, the first pillar of our "YES" to the "NO" of existing society is community.

WHERE IS OUR SECURITY?

A few years ago David Janzen of Newton, Kansas, received a letter from a friend of ours, Ladon Sheats, who had been in prison for his Christian witness against the arms race. Ladon expressed the hope that the Mennonite World Conference, then meeting, would be called to confront the world-wide armaments build-up.

As David fasted and prayed over this letter, the Lord spoke the following message to him. He trembled as he wrote, wondering what temptations or persecutions this prophecy might bring on. But the Lord assured him that if he obeyed one step at a time, he could trust God with the future.

He shared the prophecy with his congregation, the New Creation Fellowship, and the congregation confirmed it. John Stoner, of the nuclear disarmament group of the Mennonite

Central Committee Peace Section in Akron, Pennsylvania, wrote
about the sharing of the prophesy with a group of seventy-five
persons at the World Conference. John felt led to share it with
as many World Conference participants as possible, and so it
came to me.

John said: "We do not presume to know how the Spirit of
Christ may lead individuals of the Conference to respond to
this Word, but we place it before you so that you might respond
as the Lord Jesus Christ leads you." The prophecy, in its en-
tirety, is as follows:

MY PEOPLE, I AM YOUR SECURITY

My people, proclaim to your governments and your neigh-
bors that you do not need armaments for your security.
   I am your security. I will give the peacemakers glory as
   I defended and glorified my own defenseless Son, Jesus.

My kingdom is international.
   I am pleased that my children gather all around the globe
   to give allegiance to One Kingdom. My kingdom is coming in power. No powers, not even the powers of nuclear
   warfare can destroy my kingdom.
   My kingdom is from beyond this earth.
   The world thought it had killed Jesus, Jesus through
   whom I have overcome the world. Therefore, Be Not
   Afraid.

You are a gathering of my kingdom;
   My kingdom will last forever.
   Taste the first fruits now;
   Embrace the international fellowship in Christ and
   praise me together.

Do not fear the nuclear holocaust.
   Do not panic or take unloving short-cuts to fight the
   armaments monster.
   I go before you to do battle.

This is a spiritual battle, the battle to destroy war.

Do not attempt to fight this battle on your own.
Fear, guilt and anger will make you spiritual prisoners
of the Enemy if you fight on your own authority.
Learn to hear my voice. Learn to be at unity with those
who love Me.
I will lead and protect My army.
I will co-ordinate the battle in many nations.
I want to show you where the idols of this age are hidden.
Learn where are the missile silos, the bomb factories,
the centers of military command, the prisons for dis-
senters.
Understand that those who bow down to Fear trust in
these idols for salvation.
Invite them to share your life in Me. Perfect love must
be your weapon, for perfect love casts out Fear.
If you obey My call, you will be persecuted, misunderstood,
powerless.
You will share in my suffering for the world,
But I will never abandon you. You belong to my inter-
national, eternal kingdom.
Do not say time is running out. Do not threaten or despair.
I am the Lord of time. There is not time to seek the
world's approval,
But there is time to do what I will lay before you.
By my mercy I have extended time.
I extended time for the perverse human race when I called
Noah.
I lengthened the time of repentance by sending my pro-
phets.
I have averted nuclear disaster many times for you.
Jesus offers you all time, time to repent and come to me.
Obey my call and there will be time to do what I am laying
before you.
Now is the time.
I want you to learn who around the world has refused to
bow down to the god of fear or worship weapons of terror.

Hold hands around the world with my soldiers, my pris-
oners.
Pray for each other and share my strength with them.
I love those who put their trust in me and will put joy
in their hearts.
There is time to build my kingdom.
There is time to protest armaments and to build a spir-
itual community for those who turn from the idols of
fear.
Call them to join you in the security that flows from
Father, Son and Spirit, My community, given to you.
My seed is planted in every one of my children;
It is waiting to break the husks of fear that it may grow
toward my Son's light. I did not plant my spirit in Rus-
sians, or Americans, Arabs or Israelis, Capitalists or
Communists . . . that they might destroy each other,
But that they might recognize my image in each other
and come together in praise of their creator's name.
My beloved children,
Share the burden of my heart,
Know my love so that you may learn to die for one
another.
There is time to do this.
Trust me and I will sustain you within my kingdom
forever.

July 1978[13]

This is truly a prophecy for our times. This is a call to community; a call to lay down the idols of weaponry; a call to live
simply and in trust and faith. It gives us a base for understanding
in what manner we can form this alternative community of peace
and service.

Those who go out to contend with the pro-military Christians
and their fear of Soviet communism might well remember this
prophecy, which contains the truth of Jesus that his seed is
planted in every one of his children. There is "that of God" in

Russians, Arabs, Israelis, Libyans, Nicaraguans, as well as in North Americans, capitalists, and communists. Christian militarists generally have two fears when confronted with the Gospel of peace: one about themselves and one about the enemy. About themselves they fear what it would mean to live this new life, the changes it would make in every aspect of their present lives. The second fear is from without, from the enemy—"What about the Russians, the "terrorists"? If I can't stop them, no one will!" And yet the prophecy says that Jesus has already acted. The message of the Gospel too is that Jesus has already died and been raised up and the victory has been given to him.

Ultimately, the denial of Christian pacifism and life is a denial of the efficacy and example of the atonement of Jesus Christ— of his life, death, and resurrection. Christianity is full of Evangelicals and Pentacostals and Charismatics and Fundamentalists who claim their avid support for the doctrine of Atonement. Yet they fail to witness to Christ's atonement. They witness to a false idol instead. Christ's atonement is in vain as long as we do not act upon it, as long as we still carry weapons of murder rather than the weapons of the spirit, as long as we still live in society rather than in community.

As we have seen, upon Jesus' death and the coming of the Spirit, a new community was formed in great power. That community was formed in contrast to existing communities. His disciples wrote that what is exalted among people is an abomination in the sight of God. Their community preached not to love the world or the things of the world. For if anyone loves the world, love for God is not in that person. (1 John 2:15.) The wisdom of the world is folly to God; and friendship with the world is enmity with God. Whoever wishes to be a friend of the world makes him or herself an enemy of God. The world hated Jesus because he testified to the evil of its works. He said that if the world hated his followers it was because it had hated him first. "If you were of the world, the world would love its own; but because you are not of this world, the world hates you." (John 15:13; Matthew 10:22.) He told them he said this to keep them from falling away. They will be put out of synagogues and they will be killed as an offering to God. But the hope he gave them was that the Kingdom of God was in the midst of them and that through many tribulations they could enter it. We enter the Kingdom *through* suffering, not by avoiding suffering. This is not so because a punitive God exacts a payment of suffering from us as our ticket of entry; but because the life of the Kingdom, lived in the world, provokes the wrath of the world.

God gave the earliest followers of Jesus the Spirit of Truth which the world could not receive because it neither sees her nor knows her. The same is true today. God gave them authority over all the powers of the enemy. Jesus told them he had overcome the world; and even through this tribulation, they should be of good cheer. Jesus' followers, then and now, can expect on his word that when his Kingdom comes fully, every rule and every authority will be destroyed and a new heaven and earth will emerge. God will dwell with them and they shall be his people. God will wipe every tear from their eyes and death shall be no more, for the former things shall pass away. (Revelation 7:17; 21:1.) What more beautiful blueprint could be imagined? Our task is only a small part of what will come to pass anyway. Our task is to live as if the Kingdom has already come, while we remain in the midst of nations.

LIVING IN COMMUNITY: ERIMIAS

There are many ways to live in community. We can live intensely and intentionally in community, or we can live in a more flexible form. We can live as hermits or as monastics. We can live as activists and prophets, as missionaries and apostles. But whatever mode we are called to, we do need to live in a corporate and sharing fashion so that we can most effectively support each other in bearing the tribulations we must experience. We need to live in a corporate and sharing way so that we may make visible to the world what the faithful life of the Kingdom looks like. We are *not* Jesus; but together in community we are called to be his body in the world. His Spirit is given to empower and encourage us. He would not ask the impossible of us. Together it can be done. I do not know of instances where it has been done perfectly. I do know of many faithful and worthy attempts. To illustrate my vision, I will describe some of the attempts with which I have the most experience, beginning with Erimias.

We formed the Erimias Community in 1983 in rural, southern Colorado. We came together to enunciate a statement of purpose; and in our preamble we recognized that "we walk upon hallowed ground, soil made holy through the joys and toils of others. This our wilderness home has sheltered and fed the bridled and unbridled, native and newcomer, hunter and miner. Each has walked this land and left marks of passage. We acknowledge the paths of those going before us and we pray that our footsteps be worthy of respect. May the land abide."

We described the vision of community which we were to put into practice as follows:

Our Calling: The Erimias Community seeks the kingdom of God; uniting to our consciousness God, the creation, and humanity through the ever greater knowledge and practice of peace. We are radically religious and pacifist, seeking to place our lives in conformance with the call to love God and love neighbor. Thus we are a family of families and of individuals seeking to discover and affirm the Divine aspects of all. In form and spirit we follow the Catholic Worker model. To this end, as stewards, we care for wilderness, farm, school, and house of hospitality. On matters of politics: we resist to the point of nonviolent disobedience the worldly powers and principalities which command us to render to Caesar that which is not his. Instead we strive to overwhelm enmity with love, using and supporting established political processes only to the extent that they conform to Kingdom principles.

Religion: We are committed to the life and teachings of Jesus of Nazareth as clear expressions of the highest spiritual truth for humanity. And we affirm those who discern his truth by other means than the Bible. We seek an al-

ternative to institutionalized worship through a House
Church which witnesses to kingdom living.

Education: We strive to grow in clarity of thought,
breadth and depth of vision and acuteness of skill in all
things pertaining to Kingdom living. To this end we employ observation, experience, contemplation, academic
study, round-table discussion, the arts, and prayer. We
promote dialogue in larger circles of society, using lectures, conferences, workshops, retreats, publications, public and private witness, and civil disobedience as
appropriate. We support the Center on Law and Pacifism
and its publication "Center Peace" as major aspects of our
ministry in the world.

Property: We consider all substance to be the creation
and rightful property of God. Our bodies and all that
sustains them are not our own but are manifest as gifts to
us by grace, in accordance to the Divine will. It is incumbent upon us to honor these gifts, use them in a spirit of
loving selflessness and to reverence their coming and
going. We seek neither to covet nor to demean that which
is not ours but rather to align our will with the Divine will
so that we might be a vehicle for the transmission of God's
gift to others. In this spirit and to this end we share with
each other both possession of and responsibility for our
material substance. We look to the Sabbatical and Jubilee
years as models for our economic activity. Finally we hum-
bly recognize that we are a Gandhian experiment in alternative living, and though resting on a Judeo-Christian base,
we aspire to remain open to the movement of the Holy
Spirit whenever, wherever, and in whomever she may
emerge.

Our day-to-day experiences of living in community at Erimias
bore out our understanding that Gospel requirements had led
us deeply into our search for community in the first place. The
previous ten years of our lives had been a pilgrimage into
radicalization, an awakening to the imperative for a lifestyle

which constantly seeks to model the way of the Kingdom in the midst of the nations.

Through our experiences we saw the spiritually communal life as the place where Christians can come together to share resources, skills, talents, and energies as the Body of Christ in the world. We saw the communal life as the place where Christians can begin to be more gentle and harmonious with the earth and its gifts. We saw the communal life as the place where Christians can dare to risk personal and family security, can risk assurances about future prosperity, can risk close associations with the people of the streets, undocumented refugees, prisoners, and all the marginalized people of our society. We saw the communal life as church.

Erimias consisted of Larry Woodward and Noreen Reavill and their son Jesse, and Bill and Genie Durland, and our son Christian. Also living in Erimias at the beginning were David Stallings, an artist and teacher, Genie's daughter Julia Halaby, and Bill's mother, Lillian. Larry and Noreen are farmers and builders. They brought to Erimias years of hard-gathered experience and knowledge about how to farm the reluctant land of southern Colorado. They brought to Erimias knowledge about nutrition and about how to maintain the natural harmonies between our bodies and our mother earth. They brought to Erimias knowledge about how to build and how to mend. Noreen is a nurse. She brought to Erimias knowledge of health and wholeness.

Genie and I are organizers, writers, teachers, activists. We brought to Erimias the work of the Center on Law and Pacifism and the refugee-sanctuary work of the established Irenaeus House Church of Colorado Springs. We also brought our experience with Catholic Worker hospitality and Quaker religious radicalism. We were open and expectant about others such as John Sousa who would come to add new members, talents, skills, visions to the living body of the community.

Our hopes for the future included an alternative school for our young children, supporting and feeding ourselves on the produce of our farm, providing hospitality for the homeless and the helpless, and sanctuary for refugees from Central America. Our vision was perhaps best articulated by Peter Maurin as he projected the idea of the Catholic Worker School consisting of farm, hospitality, and clarification of thought. The Catholic Worker model as immortalized in Peter Maurin's poetry and as incarnated in Dorothy Day's life and legacy, along with early Quaker witness, was the basis for our vision.

Above all, our hopes included being church. Worshiping, discerning, sharing together as one family and thereby being empowered to act in the world as if the Kingdom has come. Jesus said, "Be of good cheer, I have overcome the world." (John 16:33.) He did not say, "I will overcome the world," he said, "I *have* overcome the world." What does this mean in the face of the realities of violence, poverty, hate, and despair which are the world we live in? It means that we followers and disciples of Jesus must be his body in the world. We must make it happen anew in each generation. Jesus did overcome the world through his life and death. But he left it up to his followers to walk in his overcoming footsteps so that his triumph will be a continuing reality, judging, condemning, and negating the concurrent worldly realities of violence, poverty, hate, and despair.

Thus the house church or meeting became our implementation of religious community. We worshiped together at meals and at specific events. We planted strawberry plants by the tracks which the nuclear train followed. We gave strawberries from our farm to soldiers who brought the military presence to our town, and made signs which said, "Manure, not maneuvers!" We stood in front of the Post Office on tax day and prayed about money for bombs, advocating war-tax resistance and support for war-tax resisters. We worshiped in silence and song on our farm and in our house with our homeless guests and with each other. We experienced birth and death together. Each of us, in turn, or out of turn, would preside over our house-church liturgy and worship. Each of us would create from his or her own mind, experience, concern, the liturgy for the day.

The Erimias House Church—successor to the Irenaeus House Church in Colorado Springs which we had formed in August 1980—became an on-going base for the core of our religious community. This means that the community was organized on a religious and communal basis, with economic sharing and political witness, speaking truth to the powers and principalities outside our doors and farmland. The model of the early church's religious community nurtured us with its vision of no hierarchy, no paternalism, an ideal of egalitarianism, a real communal undertaking.

Another group of Christians called to form alternative community and say "NO" to the nations could very easily design a community in another way and still be true to the propositions that have been espoused here. The key to this, though, this new way of life, is found in some form of the focus on communal living. Such a community not only inwardly discovers itself, but reaches out with that discovery to affect the world. Communal living requires sharing of religious thoughts and beliefs and practices, sharing of economic goods, sharing of political witness. As the model community forms internally, the voluntary simplicity and pacifism and poverty practiced in the sharing of one's goods enunciates a social ministry of service to the secular world in hospitality, counseling, education, and human-rights advocacy. The prophetic aspects of the model community will extend into the larger community in preaching and teaching and in witness and resistance to the powers and principalities. The worship experience of the community can lead individuals into experiments in hermitage and monastic commitment. All of these will be spokes in the holistic wheel of the alternative "YES."

THE CATHOLIC WORKER MOVEMENT

There are several established examples of living in community. Perhaps the most eminent of all is the Catholic Worker Movement. The Catholic Worker Movement grew out of the coming together of Dorothy Day, a writer, and Peter Maurin, an itinerant theologian, to form the *Catholic Worker* newspaper, the houses of hospitality, and the round-table discussions. Most of all they sought to live within a communal movement that tried to illustrate in the life of the community the manner in which an alternative society could exist in the midst of the nation. From their own writings, the *Catholic Worker* has this to say about its movement:

The maldistribution of wealth is widespread: the fact that there are hungry and homeless people in the midst of plenty is unjust. Furthermore, we are struck by the spiritual destitution of our consumer society. Rich and poor suffer increasingly from isolation, madness, and growing individual violence side by side with a governmental emphasis on the implements of war instead of human well-being.

The rapid rise of technology, without a fitting development of morality, emphasizes progress based on profit rather than human needs. The triumvirate of military, business, and scientific priorities overwhelms the political process. "Democracy" is reduced to a choice between "brand names" in products and politicians. Bureaucratic structures make accountability, and therefore political change, close to impossible. As a result, there is no forum in which to express effectively different views of the events shaping our lives. The individual suffers as much from these transformations as does the whole social order.

On a scale unknown to previous generations, the poor throughout the world are systematically robbed of the goods necessary to life. Though we realize the United States is not the sole perpetrator of such immoral conduct, we are North Americans and must first acknowledge our own country's culpability. We deplore U.S. imperialism in its various expressions. Multinational corporations, economic "aid," military intervention have led to the disintegration of communities and the destruction of indigenous cultures—blatant violations of justice and charity.

The proliferation of nuclear power and weapons stands as a clear sign of the direction of our age. Both are a denial of the very right of people to life and, implicitly, a denial of God. There is a direct economic and moral connection between the arms race and destitution. In the words of Vatican II, "The arms race is an utterly treacherous trap for humanity and one which injures the poor to an intolerable degree."

To achieve a just society we advocate a complete rejection of the present system and a nonviolent revolution to establish a social order in accord with Christian truth—We see this as an era filled with anxiety and confusion. In response, we, as a lay movement, seek our strength and direction in the beauty of regular prayer and liturgy, in studying and applying the traditions of Scripture and the teachings of the Church to the modern condition. We believe that success as the world determines it is not a fit criterion for judgment. We must be prepared and ready to face seeming failure. The most important thing is that we adhere to these beliefs which transcend time, and for which we will be asked a personal accounting, not as to whether they succeeded . . . but as to whether we remain true to them.[14]

BARTIMAEUS COMMUNITY

The Catholic Worker community began in New York City in 1930. It still flourishes today. Some years later another community began in Berkeley, California, known as Bartimaeus Community. It was not traditionally Catholic but grew out of a Protestant background. Bartimaeus' call to discipleship stated that:

In the life and ministry of Jesus came the decisive announcement of the kingly rule and reign of God. This announcement is at one and the same time a summons and a promise. God wills to be present with us and will be with us all, to lift up the holy and bring down the mighty; to vindicate his righteousness in the earth. The particular recipients of this "now here, and not yet" (Küng) Kingdom of God are the little ones: those driven and hounded by people and structures of injustice. This Gospel is good news to all who will receive it: the poor who do not fit into the mold of the world system, and who are thereby rejected by it as "no-hopers;" the mourners, for whom the world holds no consolation; the humiliated, who no longer extract any recognition from the world; those hungry and thirsty ones, who cannot live without being caught up in the righteousness that God alone can promise and bring about in the world. Included also are those with gentle hearts, the merciful, who without asking about rights, become vulnerable to all sisters and brothers everywhere; the righteous, who are not equal to the rapacious and evil ways of the world order; those workers for peace, who overcome might and power by reconciliation; and finally, because of their striving for justice in the earth, the persecuted, who with torture and pains of death, are cast bodily out of the world. (Bornkamm.)

Via this Christocentric inauguration of God's reign, God, the provoking God, waits no longer, but rather comes to those who cry out to him. Thus the darkness of alienation and oppression is being dispelled and the dayspring streams in among us and we are forced to choose between allegiances. We are either born of God's new day or belong to the old order which is passing away. So, the Gospel becomes for us all a word of judgment as well as the word of salvation. This breaking in of God's new order means deliverance for the outcasts and liberation from the powers of sin and death for all who with joy receive it. God's call in Christ confronts us and the time is for choosing. God's intention is announced. . . !

Being "awake" in North America means choosing to struggle to live simply, collectively, nonviolently—thereby trying to allow these Kingdom values to transform our lives—which, conversely, seek to resist the darkness of consumptiveness, individualism, and violence and exploitation which are part of our social context. . . .

The "cross" of downward social mobility, marginalization, perhaps even political punishment may well be the result of our Christian struggle to live humanely in an increasingly a-human macro-society. But we know that this is a small price indeed to pay for solidarity with the special ones of God, the poor and voiceless throughout the world, who involuntarily bear the bitter cross of starvation, exploitation, oppression, and violence. . . . [15]

Each one of these proclamations concentrates on a religious overcoming of temptation in religious community, an economic overcoming of worldly temptation in simple living, a political overcoming of temptation in outward witness to powers and principalities, and a joining with those who are oppressed in freeing them from their oppression.

How do individuals live, specifically, on a daily basis within community under these guidelines? For some answers, let us look at Bartimaeus' statement of faith and lifestyle:

1. Commonality of Goods—Full members of the community participate in economic sharing or communality. We assume all the liabilities as well as assets of those who are members of the community. Common use does not abrogate individual stewardship. Stewardship of our common possessions is emphasized. All major financial decisions are made by our common agreement. Individual attentiveness to the financial decision-making process is emphasized. When a member leaves the community by a calling it will be provided that they will be equipped for the mission. . . .

2. Education—As a community of disciples we are committed to be learners. Three areas are affirmed: community teaching, outside learning of skills and theology, and personal study. . . .

3. Individual Spiritual Life—The need for each person to develop a "quiet time" is affirmed. Personal prayer is affirmed. We agree to each take two individual retreats a year, each for two days. We agree to each have interviews with the leadership group about our individual spiritual life.

4. Worship and Corporate Spiritual Life—We will have one yearly spiritual retreat as a community. . . . We will follow the church calendar. Community worship on Sunday will be called "lauds." Our midweek service will be called "vespers." Worship is facilitated by a worship committee. Preaching is facilitated by a preaching committee. A structure of worship that will enable children to participate in some way is affirmed. Mission groups are urged to take a spiritual retreat once yearly. . . .

5. Maintenance—We affirm the need to keep our common properties and possessions maintained.

6. Parenting and Child Rearing—When people join this community they are making a commitment to raising children. We want children to be able to participate in worship. For whatever structures we have for adults, we need to have parallel ones for our children. . . .[15]

Bartimaeus' *Statement of Faith and Lifestyle* speaks to other issues as well—issues such as pastoring, mission, leadership in the community, decision-making, bread-winning, and recreation. In like manner, each newly formed community seeking an alternative "YES" would follow some kind of basic statement of principle and some kind of daily process which will unfold as the community experiences itself.[16]

THE LAMB'S COMMUNITY

Complementing Catholic and Protestant versions of community is The Lamb's Community, a unique Quaker experiment. Its description pictures the life and activities of that community and states in part:

We have been called together to rediscover a revelation of the presence of the living Christ among us. We are Quakers because we are Christians, and we find at the center of Quakerism a true connection with original Christianity. . . .

As an intentional community gathered in gospel order under God "in the power and name of Jesus," we are committed to living our lives according to the way of Jesus and early Christians known to us through Scripture and by the continuing prompting of God as revealed to us in worship and in action. Our focus inwardly is on our personal commitment to God and to one another, and outwardly on serving people in need and publicly witnessing to the presence of the Commonwealth of God.

In this vision, our internal common life begins each day with worship. A common meal and family time draw us together in the evening. The Apostle Paul's advice, "Speak the truth with love," is our guide as we affirm a place for children, the elderly, the poor, and the infirm. We are stewards of what we possess, and use the land in trust, sharing all things in common as did the early Christians. Avoiding the excesses of secular culture, we seek to live simply and close to the earth. We take special care that our lives reflect our concern for the environment and the right sharing of the world's resources, and that our choice of food disturbs as little as possible the well-being of other living things. Common meals are vegetarian but with respect for individual differences in what constitutes right eating. We value laughter, music and artistic endeavor, find time for these and other leisure activities, and meet together for reconciliation and healing when needed. We honor a time for spiritual retreat in silence and contemplation.

As a non-hierarchical group, we reach decisions by striving to achieve unity with God and each other. Generally, in conducting community affairs, we follow Quaker practices as expressed in New England Yearly Meeting's *Faith and Practice.*

Our internal common life reaches out to those around us in varied ways. "Meetings for learning" to study the Bible and to seek "clarification of thought" on subjects related to the healing of creation are a weekly part of our community's practice in which others are encouraged to join.

Living in conformity with God's will as best we understand it often places us at variance with the practices of the institutions of society. We pray for strength to hold to what we believe is right without compromise, hoping to speak the truth and to act forthrightly without concern for possible risks. A primary focus of our outward witness is prayerful resistance to and transformation of violence in ourselves and in the structures of our society. Continuing the early Quaker practice of being Publishers of Truth, we strive to communicate broadly in a variety of ways, including a periodic newsletter and traveling in the ministry. . . .

The Lamb's Community was founded in 1988 by Paul Hood, Barr Swennerfelt, Eugenia and William Durland. It is presently located in two places, near Burlington, Vermont, and in Colorado at Erimias House, each part functioning autonomously and both parts committed to one statement of principles and to holding joint annual meetings and retreats. Numerous other intentional communities flourish around the country such as La Samartaine in Madison, Wisconsin, The Open Door in Atlanta, Koinonia in Americus, Georgia, and Bijou House in Colorado Springs, Colorado. Common Ground, now in Richmond, Indiana, Ground Zero in Bangor, Washington, and Brandywine Peace Community in the Philadelphia area are valuable, typical service and resistance communities. There are many other such communities all over the United States and indeed around the world.

The community, once organized internally, reaches out externally in many variations upon a common theme as these communities illustrate. The avowed pacifism and simplicity of the community reaches out to the secular, political world through resistance and witness, and to the economic world through hospitality and service. In our next chapters we will envision how this lifestyle and commitment can impact and overcome the economic and political temptations of the world and become the locus of the Christian alternative community answering the questions: how do we relate to society; how do we relate to existing government?

CHAPTER SEVEN

PRACTICING COMMUNITY

ALTERNATIVES TO THE POLITICAL TEMPTATION

Sometimes Christians experimenting with alternative community life experience the world's rejection. The witness of the community to the world can meet with hostility, fear, and denial fostered by the powers and principalities. An example is found in the experience my wife Genie and I had when we wrote the following letter to the editor of the *Trinidad Colorado Chronicle News*.

Since we returned from Japan on August 15, 1985, we have read with interest the comments and letters concerning the Army's take-over and encroachment upon Southeast Colorado—for that is what it is. Ever since America's indiscriminate bombing of Hiroshima and Nagasaki, where hundreds of thousands of Japanese, Korean, and American civilians there were killed in an attack without warning, this nation has suffered from an atheistic, macho-military complex. Isn't it time to stop? Sixty-four percent of our federal budget for the military necessarily results in thirteen percent unemployment in Trinidad [Colorado]. Militarism hurts all economies rather than helps them.

However, the Pinon Canyon take-over and the Trinidad city convoys are symbolic of an even greater than political-economic conflict. It is also a symbol of our moral-religious conflict. We are members of a Christian community. We believe that to be a Christian means to be loving and peaceful towards our enemies. Christians, unlike politicians and militarists, may not love their enemies and at the same time prepare to kill them. Most of our political leaders are Christians who refuse to recognize this simple Gospel imperative. If our trust is in Jesus, are we not called to reconcile rather than retaliate, lay our own lives down rather than take the lives of others? Is not our trust in God rather than in "chariots"? The only act which evidences that faith seems to us to be giving up our weapons of war and taking on the armor of the Holy Spirit.

This letter was greeted by a reply the following week, printed in the same newspaper, which went as follows:

The Durlands' joint and apparently parting shot from pacifist guns has a belligerent and insulting cowardly substance. The grapevine local tells us they have moved to Pennsylvania to teach. Their recent residence is for sale. No doubt my remarks will reach them. I hope so. Many of us who went to World War II did not have to, had opportunities to stay home and let other guys and gals go to hopefully keep our nation intact. Since then a lot of freaks with equal rights have come out of their closets to hold Bibles before them while telling us they don't appreciate the bloodshed to make it possible. However, there are more people who do appreciate it than freaks who don't, but are going out to teach noticeably somewhere else.[1]

Another letter said:

After reading your letter to the editor published August 29, 1985, *Chronicle News*, I can't help but wonder just how you could come to the conclusions that you stress in your letter. I was there with the 164th Inf. Reg. and may I say here, Thank the Good Lord we had no men with your opinion in the 164. Don't get me wrong, I am sure that men such as I have known and walked closer to Jesus and trust him more than you ever shall, or we would not walk in the Freedom that we know today. I for one really learned to pray in a fox hole. If you, with all your knowledge, could realize the millions of people that would have been killed with the invasion of Japan, you would find that Hiroshima and Nagasaki was a very small price to pay. If only you could have been there, to have seen 'he Rape of Nanking, the Bataan Death March, or been there to release some of the survivors from the Japanese Prison Camps, maybe you could talk with a little more authority of what you speak. If you could have held one of your best buddies while he died in your arms from a bullet fired from a gun held by an honorable Godfearing soldier of the Emperor's Army. You probably could speak as a man. In my line of thought your attitude is just the same as your relieving yourself on the graves of the many that gave it all, so that you might do what you do today.[2]

Unknown to the writer of this letter, I have a dear friend who was part of the Bataan death march, a Roman Catholic priest-pacifist named Father Richard McSorley, S.J., who has taught Christian pacifism at Georgetown University for many years. (About the time of this letter, our community was host to a Japanese guest from Osaka, Japan. That more than our letter may have set off this reaction.)

Those responses are typical of the responses we get when, out of religious community, we witness to the powers and principalities of our economic and political systems. It was quite a surprise when an editor of another newspaper, which also circulated in Trinidad, wrote the following in response to the controversy:

Let me begin by saying I'm not a pacifist. My candidate of choice during the 1984 presidential election before party fathers on both sides turned it into a two ring circus of extreme right and left, was Senator Ernest Hollings, a self-described hawk. This Democratic former South Carolina governor promised, among other things, to beef up conventional military forces and cut back on nuclear arms production. On a personal level I abhor violence but feel it is the sad but necessary right of every citizen to protect his life and property, with whatever it takes—even with a handgun. And I'm not ashamed to say I felt proud when I saw military convoys on the way to Pinon Canyon passing through Trinidad. The same soldiers subject to citizen concerns about downtown traffic flow would be on an airplane heading overseas within minutes should my right to vote or right for a non-censored newspaper be threatened. Surprisingly enough I find myself writing a column in defense of pacifists.

I've heard a lot of talk in Trinidad about the military, but what prompted these thoughts is the letter that appeared in a local newspaper about a Las Animas county Christian pacifist community. I have not had the honor of meeting any of its members but I understand their life and community philosophy is based on a literal interpretation of Jesus' command to love one's enemies. The gentleman who wrote the letter describing some community members and their protests against the Pinon Canyon maneuver site used the word "cowardly." Cowardly? On the contrary, I would say that such a stand requires more courage than most of us have. My decision against pacifism, I tell myself, was a rational decision. It was made in the face of ravings of certain world "leaders" as I watched old news footage of Jews being herded off to concentration camps. Like most "rational" decisions it was based on an emotion—in this case fear. The idea of disarming in the face of nations run by fanatics whose concept of justice extends no further than a Russian-made grenade launcher is frightening. For the most part, I feel good about my decision not to be a pacifist. But sometimes, after hearing of yet another nuclear warhead being added to the United States arsenal or reading of questionable covert C.I.A. activity, I wonder about my decision. Being the somewhat practical person I am, I probably will always be a non-pacifist. Yet I cannot help but wonder what would happen if the world population on a large scale had enough courage to adopt the philosophy espoused by that of the so called cowardly Christian pacifist community. More likely than not, they would be quickly quashed by the same tyrants that make the military a necessity. But maybe Biblical prophecy would be fulfilled. Maybe men would beat their swords into plowshares.[3]

We did go to Pennsylvania to teach, about just what we wrote to the Trinidad newspaper. There we also became part of a Quaker educational community—Pendle Hill. And, yes, our community house was up for sale for a time; but the community had moved, not to Pennsylvania but to a farm only seven miles away. The writers of both the hostile letters were aware of that. (We returned to Cokedale, Erimiais House and the Lamb's Community in 1989, and our overwhelmingly friendly neighbors there and in Trinidad.)

These letters however may illustrate what happens when pacifists living in community simply write a letter expressing the truth as they know it. There was no walking and public demonstrating in this case, no arrest or civil disobedience at a military site, no confrontations, simply a letter. Because of the power of our culture, these hostile reactions are typical. As we live in Christian community and go out to witness to the political temptations of the world, this, and much worse, can happen. The problem is not Japan or America or Russia. The problem is the fundamental nature of nation-states. In this exchange we would not have denied that Japan committed atrocities and inhumanities against U.S. prisoners. Just as we do not now deny the atrocities and inhumanities the United States is committing in Central America and elsewhere. Soldiers on both sides of every war hold their buddies in their arms while they die from the fire-power of those on the other side. As they do so, their human emotions are all very similar. (As it turned out, by the way, the Army presence near Trinidad has been only an economic and environmental detriment.)

Our witness is to an alternative power and ethic which liberates people and nations from the "need" to brutalize each other in order to protect themselves and perpetuate their way of life over against that of the "enemy." Our witness is never "*against* America" or "*for* Russia," as is so often the perception. Our witness is not political in the partisan sense; but it has profound political effect, which is what precipitates fearful responses from those who have placed their faith and reliance in political institutions. The degree to which we are seduced by this political temptation is poignantly expressed in an observation my friend George Zabelka once made.

Father George Zabelka was Catholic chaplain to the crew which dropped the A-bomb on Hiroshima. He is now a pacifist. He laments that what bothers him the most is why he did not come to his pacifist conclusions twenty or thirty years ago. He says, "I was so blinded, so caught up with all this patriotism that I wasn't even listening to what I was preaching—the Gospel of love, peace, and nonviolence."[4]

In addition to witnessing to nation-state violence, many Christian communities also witness about the state's treatment of criminals. There are those who witness before governors prior to state executions to bring the message that Jesus brought a totally different idea about prisons and punishment than that which the world practices. The best response to crime in ancient Israel was not the isolated punishment of an individual lawbreaker but the repentance of the entire nation, says Lee Griffith, in his seminal article, "Jesus and the Law-breakers."[5] Many Christian communities have witnessed to the legal institutions that prisons should not be reformed or rehabilitated, but should be abolished. It is not important on what specific issues various pacifist communities choose to focus. The point is that these witnesses arise from the pressure of the Holy Spirit on individual and collective consciences as they recognize the ultimate evil that is killing. These witnesses arise as gathered Christians perceive the sacredness of all life under God's parenthood. They arise from the recognition that if God is Lord of all creation, the hope for protection and sustenance can only, realistically, be placed in God. As such, these are not only faithful but most practical witnesses.

HOLY OBEDIENCE AND RESISTANCE

All the witnessing activities of alternative communities can lead to the community's disruption and separation through the imprisonment of community members. It is worth repeating here the words of Philip Berrigan, who says that imprisonment is a piece of realism, the moral counterbalance to the separations of war. When asked, "Is there a temporal order (this side of the Kingdom) which would not require resistance? If so, what would it look like?" Phil replied, "No. Evil flourishes side by side with good, as Christ's parable of the wheat and the tares illustrates. . . . There is no temporal order that would not require resistance. . . . One can get flashes of the 'Kingdom come' in communities of nonviolent resistance, but only because resistance is a way of life, a way of engaging evil personally and interpersonally as well as publicly. For example, observe how many members of a community hold one another accountable regarding prayer, mental discipline, use of time, sensitivity and consideration, sharing of shit work, etc. The fight against evil—injustice in its most crystallized expression—must be constant and vigilant."[6]

Civil disobedience is most often practiced by people living in community and community makes it possible. Those with children and families can find it possible to spend time in prison as long as they are members of a community that nurtures their families and supports them in prison. In this sense a primary purpose of community is to be extended family. Many people with this motivation and inspiration have gone to the locale of the idols of death, witnessing to the message of Jesus, and thereby breaking the laws of the state as Jesus did. The examples from my own experience and in my own acquaintance are numerous. A few of them follow.

Anti-abortion "right to life" demonstrators were arrested at a Pennsylvania medical center after they entered the building and approached women waiting for services. They sat down, sang songs, and offered counsel on alternatives to abortion.[7]

Twelve people of religious faith went on trial in Arizona, indicted for helping refugees fleeing from violence directed personally at themselves in their unhappy lands of Guatemala and El Salvador.[8] The refugees arrive wounded with the physical and mental effects of torture. The indicted sanctuary workers say that to return to their homelands would mean death for many of them. To give them sanctuary is to give them life.

In Missouri, a young man was arrested and charged with sabotage and willful destruction of government property. He had entered a Minuteman missile launch facility on launch-alert status and equipped with nuclear warheads. He carried with him a Bible, carpentry tools, and a banner declaring "Swords into Plowshares." On the silo he spray-painted the words, "Disarm or dig graves." Blood was splattered over the launch-facility lid. A leaflet expressed the young man's view that the United States was violating international law in deploying nuclear missiles in this way.[9]

Some people become only technically, civilly disobedient by breaking the existing law which they believe is unconstitutional. They do not necessarily have a Gospel-ordered motivation but do this in order to bring a case, based on their violation of the law, to show that it is, in fact, no violation at all. If the courts sustain a test case, then what had been a law-breaking action becomes a law-abiding one after the fact in conformity with the constitution and laws interpreted through the judicial process. Thus statutory law is made to conform to the higher constitutional law. Examples of this are found in the civil-rights cases of the '60s, and in later labor-law, particularly job-discrimination cases.

Another example of civil disobedience is as follows. The law may be broken time and time again without hope that a test case will change the law. People who do this believe that what they are doing resists law-breaking by the government at a higher level, or is a witness to their own alternative beliefs found in a set of values different from political or legal ones. This is exemplified by the Christian, resistance activity of those who witness to horrors perpetrated by government and business in the nuclear-arms race and "Star Wars" preparations. Such witnesses also dramatize their prophetic call for socially and humanly responsible government and business.

Gandhi attributed the expression "civil disobedience" to Thoreau. Thoreau's writing came to be identified with it when one of his essays was re-published after his death under that title.[10] For Martin Luther King, Jr., the word "civil" referred not so much to the type of offense committed as to the attitude of the offender—that he or she was civil in the sense of being motivated from a conscience-directed attitude and that he or she was willing to face the consequences of breaking an unjust law rather than flee or fight. Such civil disobediencee to Gandhi, Thoreau, and King recognizes the general legitimacy of government; but it also provides a witness to government's inhumanity through whatever sufferings might be incurred from that act.[11]

In a book on civil disobedience by Carl Cohen,[12] the author presents an analysis of what classical (not necessarily modern) civil disobedience is from the perspective of secular government. According to Cohen, "Making rules for the community, and enforcing them, is the job of government. No community can be truly civilized, therefore, without an effective and reasonably stable government. Civilized human life, therefore, requires that at least the vast majority of citizens recognize the authority of some law-making body."[13] Any act of civil disobedience, therefore, becomes suspect as an attack on the stability of the state."

The first characteristic of civil disobedience, therefore, is its *illegality*. The law-breaking character of civil disobedience "is at once its most notable feature and the source of much of the puzzlement it creates. Taken by itself, law-breaking is wrong."[14] So, for the courts, law-breaking is an action which is at least *prima facie* "wrong."

A second characteristic of civil disobedience is that the law-breaking is deliberate and intentional. Third, it is an expression of protest. Fourth, an act of civil disobedience is a public act. Fifth, civil disobedience is conscientious, that is, a disobedient does what he or she does in the honest belief that it is right in spite of its illegality. The act is seen as an expression of truth and as such is compelled by conscience. Sixth, it is an act of nonviolence. Violence presupposes the use of physical force in ways that are directly and willfully injurious to persons or property.[15]

There are at least two reasons for employing civil disobedience. The first is political in the sense that the motive is effectively to change conditions. If we look upon our government as based on the social-contract theories of Hobbes or Rousseau, and particularly of the "founding fathers" of our republic, we can say that when the government goes beyond the limits of justice, it is incumbent upon the citizens to re-institute a proper government by whatever nonviolent means are necessary. Jefferson called for means beyond nonviolence, but political pacifists refrain from violence. In this context, nonviolent direct action can be seen as a proper means for the reconstituting of the social contract. But this is not the primary motive of the Christian alternative community.

The second reason for practicing civil disobedience is a religious motive to witness to rightness. For the alternative Christian community this is the important one. Religious disobedients who are Christian use as their criteria the early Christian models of pacifism and nonviolence. These models inspire non-cooperation and nonviolent resistance wherever the government can be seen as acting contrary to the will of God. Civil disobedience then is really holy obedience. Christian pacifists identify the will of God as love of God and love of neighbor. Jesus taught that there are no commandments greater than these. Jesus also taught and demonstrated in his life that "neighbor" includes strangers and even enemies. For the Christian conscience, love of God and love of neighbor means that no Christian has a right, in love, to kill, or cause to be killed, or to prepare to kill any other person created by God.

HOLY OBEDIENCE IN THE BIBLE

There is a reasonable basis Biblically and historically for the legitimate use of holy obedience, i.e., breaking the law for a higher spiritual value. The Hebrew Scriptures, Exodus 1:15-22, tell the story of five women who frustrated the decree of an absolute monarch. The decree found in Exodus required midwives to kill the male children of the Hebrews at birth. The Egyptian Pharaoh was an absolute ruler; but the midwives rejected that understanding of his power because they had given their allegiance to another power. The Scripture goes on to state that, " . . . the midwives feared God and did not do as the King of Egypt commanded them, but let the male children live." A second decree of Pharaoh was directed to all "his" people, not just Hebrew midwives, that "Every son that is born to the Hebrews you shall cast into the Nile, but you shall let every daughter live." The women involved in frustrating this decree were the mother of Moses, his sister, and the daughter of Pharaoh with her maidens. Moses' mother hid her child for three months, then complied with Pharaoh's decree by placing her child among the reeds at the river's edge in a watertight basket. The baby was saved by a member of Pharaoh's own court, his daughter, the only one of the women to whom the decree applied, since it was directed not to the Hebrews but to Pharaoh's own people.

Exodus 2:11 through 4:17 describes the flight and call of Moses. Old Testament scholar Millard Lind points out that the fundamental point of the call of Moses, as with all prophetic calls, has to do with political legitimacy. Moses becomes, almost against his will, God's representative to Pharaoh. And for Pharaoh, the question of legitimacy, that of God or that of Pharaoh, must be resolved by display of force. The conflict between God and Pharaoh is a conflict which involves a competition for the allegiance of a people, allegiance to God or to the state. Against legal authority Moses leads the Hebrew people out of Egypt, followed by Pharaoh and his army. They reach the Reed (commonly referred to inaccurately as Red) Sea refusing to resubmit to Pharaoh. But the waters stop them. Moses tells the people, "Fear not, stand firm and see the salvation from the Lord, which he will work for you today; for the Egyptians whom you see today, you shall never see again. The Lord will fight for you, and you have only to be still." (Exodus 14:16, 13-14.) Quickly this new community is called upon to practice nonviolence in the midst of its own civil disobedience by relying solely on the weapons of their Lord and not on their own armaments.

The Hebrew Scriptures also record the trial of Jeremiah which took place centuries later. Jeremiah is the prototype, the forerunner of present-day symbolic protest. In the reign of Zedekiah, King of Judah, he is called by God to "Make yourself thongs and yoke-bars and put them on your neck," which Jeremiah does. (Jeremiah 27.) Jeremiah proclaims in the Temple precincts that if the people do not walk in God's law, Jerusalem will be destroyed. (Jeremiah 26ff.) The priests, prophets, and people declare that for these words Jeremiah is guilty and should die. The princes overhear this conflict in the palace precincts and set up court at the Temple's gates. The priests and prophets present their case, arguing that Jeremiah deserves the death sentence because he has prophesied against the well-being of Jerusalem. Jeremiah presents his defense, which is based not on a denial that he spoke as he did, but that his words are God's and not his own. The court recognized this plea as a valid one and declared him not guilty. Jeremiah's message in this court scene is directed to all the people, not just to the king and the political officials. This meant that all the people were held accountable before God for the illegalities of the kingdom under God's laws. Today, too, members of religious communities who practice civil disobedience present their message in court, not just to the judge and jury, but to all those who honor the established institutions of the judicial and political systems.

Finally, in the Hebrew Scriptures, the so-called Servant Songs of Isaiah (Isaiah 40-55.) provide the typology for the life (including "civil disobedience" or holy obedience) and the death of Jesus.

The life and teachings of Jesus, as known from the New Testament, provide the foundation for the lifestyle of the alternative Christian community. In the matter of civil disobedience and the relationship of the community to civil authority and religious institutions, Jesus' practices and teachings provide a wealth of example. All that is needed is for us to get behind the overlay of cultural interpretation which for centuries has masked their plain meaning. Jesus' idea of "nation" for his community was clearly that of the holy nation that was spoken of from the beginning. His prayer teaches us to ask our Parent "to forgive us our trespasses as we forgive those who trespass against us," making trespass a very personal and relational consideration.[16]

Trespass is relational in Biblical theology, as in Jesus' prayer. It has to do with the person, the motive, the intent, the goals, means and ends, the entire relationship of one to another. Trespass, under the positive law which supports the state, however, does not so much concern itself with persons but with things—land, property, facilities, weapons plants, or doomsday centers. This is easily demonstrated when an individual enters property claimed by a nuclear-weapons facility as a witness to the Christian Gospel, and finds that she or he has committed a trespass against the property. No personal relationship exists. The owners of the property, the judges, the prosecutor, all admit the individual may be sincere and innocent and is making a moral witness that they think could be done in another way. However, the other way always has to be the legal way. Why, when there is a choice not to break the law, would someone intentionally break it?

This example of the difference between the understanding of trespass in the teachings of Jesus and in the teachings of

Caesar points to Jesus' relationship to civil disobedience and to the law, and can help us to answer our question of how we live in relationship to the political powers.

An important account in the Gospels tells of a day on which Jesus and his followers went through a grain field on the Sabbath. His disciples were hungry and they began to pluck heads of grain to eat. When the Pharisees saw this they said, "Look, your disciples are doing what is not lawful to do on the Sabbath." (Matthew 12.) At that time the Jewish law was not separated, as our laws are today, into secular and religious jurisdictions. Priests practiced not only religious but secular law in the theocracy of the time; but they were themselves illegal under their own legal tradition, because they were no longer from the Zadokian line, having been appointed by the Roman political power. In this episode, Jesus was being accused of committing civil disobedience against the defenders of the nation as well as against the priestly caste. Jesus' response was to remind them that David and his men ate the Bread of the Presence illegally in the house of God when they were hungry, and that their act was unacceptable in the tradition.

In *Jesus*, Edward Schillibeeckx adds that there was no emergency here for Jesus to trespass and eat as there had been in the case of David. Jesus often answered the criticisms of his opponents by referring to the Hebrew Scriptures to explain and justify his own conduct. Here he cited two incidents: One, David and his companions fleeing from Saul ate the loaves of the Presence which were to be eaten only by the priests; and two, priests in the Temple worked on the Sabbath by offering prescribed sacrifices. So, if in the service of the Temple they broke the Sabbath laws, so could Jesus' disciples to serve the greater temple, namely the Kingdom of God. Jesus' response to his accusers continues: ". . . (H)ave you not read in the law how on the Sabbath the priests in the temple profane the Sabbath and are guiltless? I tell you, something greater than the temple is here. And if you had known what this means, 'I desire mercy and not sacrifice,' you would not have condemned the guiltless. . . . For the Son of man is lord of the Sabbath." (Matthew 12:5-8.) Jesus is pointing out that the very persons who use the law to their own ends are quite often the ones who have broken the law themselves.

Followers of Jesus who look to his life and practices as the fulfillment of his words see Jesus placing human needs over legal technicalities. They find Jesus locating ultimate values in radical religious precepts and not in conservative, political or legal doctrines. It is obvious that Jesus believed that the priests committed what otherwise would be wrongful acts but for the mere cover of law. Those with the cover and guise of institutional purity break the law, but their breaking of the law is called lawful, while Jesus' breaking of the law is called unlawful. This helps to explain why many modern followers of Jesus choose to "trespass" by entering a nuclear-holocaust arsenal or abortion clinic or by failing to pay taxes for war, thus incurring the legal guilt, penalties, and possible imprisonment for law-breaking which the nation wishes to impose upon them. Today, even the world's superpowers, Russia's state capitalism and North America's profit capitalism, violate their international-law agreements protecting human rights while at the same time they have condemned and imprisoned people who witnessed to their lawlessness or refused to cooperate with it.

Jesus asked for mercy, not sacrifice. (Matthew 12.) Our political leaders ask us to make more sacrifices to pay for war planning and preparedness, and they judge pacifists as cynics and appeasers for holding true to God's will. David broke the law because of the necessity of his hunger. Christian civil disobedients raise the argument of necessity in the courts of this land to justify their witness against the arms race. The hunger of the poor is multiplied each year that the military budget is raised as a sacrifice to our national greed. The first Christians were brave enough to break the law to preserve their morality. Some modern, institutional Christians break their morality to preserve the law.

There is another example in this same Biblical account. In the first episode Jesus committed an act of resistance—trespassing on land and picking grain on the wrong day, teaching that human need takes precedence over legal regulations. In the second example, Matthew relates that Jesus went out from there and entered into the synagogue.

> And behold, there was a man with a withered hand. And they asked him, "Is it lawful to heal on the Sabbath?" so that they might accuse him. He said to them, "What man of you, if he has one sheep and it falls into a pit on the sabbath, will not lay hold of it and lift it out? Of how much more value is a man than a sheep! So it is lawful to do good on the sabbath." Then he said to the man, "Stretch out your hand." And the man stretched it out, and it was restored, whole like the other. But the Pharisees went out and took council against him, how to destroy him. (Matthew 12:10-14.)

Schillibeeckx expresses the possibility that Jesus called to the man to "stretch out your hand" (or, in another instance, to pick up his mat) as an act of sheer provocation in a "gratuitous breach of" the Sabbath.[17] The act was certainly unnecessary to accomplish the healing, and it was also unnecessary to perform the healing on that particular day. But if the standard is that the infirm person might be liberated to begin taking responsibility for herself or himself and participate in the act of healing, then it can be argued that stretching out the hand or picking up the mat are most necessary acts.

This second example does not involve resistance so much as assistance. Yet the same charge is brought against Jesus—a legal violation of working on the Sabbath. The Jewish religion and its law was not then, nor is it now, capricious or arbitrary—quite the contrary. The Pharisees believed that if it were a matter of life and death, a healing could be performed on the Sabbath. But they held, and reasonably so, that to allow healing, if there was no immediate danger of death, was an unwarranted violation of the law. Jesus pointed out that the relevant question was not the life or death of a person, but whether love or law prevailed. Jesus' followers were not starving, they were hungry.

The man with the withered hand was not dying, he was infirm. But Jesus' compassion was so great that he could not wait till the Sabbath was over to feed the hungry and to heal the infirm. Furthermore, Jesus' optimistic love abounded with so much enthusiasm that he called upon the infirm ones to participate in the healing process. The necessity was broader than the Pharisees could see. Humans are not made for the Sabbath.

Today, in our law courts, necessity is broader than the judges can see and transcends any war-tax levied by any government against conscientious people or any restriction against trespassing on military bases where prayers must be said and witness must be made. We strive to feed the hungry and to heal the infirm, not to increase the numbers of the hungry and infirm in the world. Jesus broke the law quite readily, eating with sinners, talking with sinful people or Samaritans who were unclean. What he did illustrates the basic themes of this exploration of living in the Kingdom—community, simplicity, and pacifism. His community went through the grain fields. His pacifism was so powerful that it could be enunciated in lawbreaking. His law-breaking was necessary to be of service in economic hard times.

Finally, Jesus' action in cleansing the Temple was provocative and illegal and perhaps the primary cause of his arrest, along with the charge that he incited people not to pay their taxes. (Matthew 17:24.) He is not convicted on either count by the courts to which he is brought, but legal authorities frequently will not charge one with what they believe is the actual lawbreaking, but rather with a charge that can be more readily proved. Their utilitarian interest is simply to put away the unwanted one on whatever charge can bring conviction. The attitude of the high priests and Pilate in the story of Jesus' arrest and conviction seems to illustrate a universal mind-set of prosecutors.

Jesus' actions in the Temple were to witness to the traders in the house of God, and to remove them, at least for the moment, in a symbolic action (that is, an action that is not effective in secular terms). Zachariah 14 states that in the last days the Temple will be sanctified. The Temple was a strong-hold of police authority, and the police apparently supported the corruption that took place there. Obviously Jesus was infuriated with these abuses. His quoting of "I desire mercy, not sacrifice" was directed to the Temple practice in which one could substitute the sacrifice of an animal in the place of the real-life relationship of mercy toward people. (Matthew 12.) Furthermore, the necessity to exchange money meant that those sacrificing had spent their working hours dealing in foreign currency, an illegal act under Jewish law of the time. Finally, all of this happened in the place reserved for the gentiles who Jesus so compassionately wished to be a part of his healing of the nations.

The non-payment-of-taxes episode, which also took place shortly before Jesus' arrest, involved two groups hostile to him and to each other—the Herodians and the Pharisees. They asked him whether or not it was lawful to pay tribute to Caesar. This question was meant to be the perfect trap for Jesus in order to eliminate him as a religious, political, and economic trouble-maker. (Matthew 22:15-22.) The Herodians held that the tax was mandatory, and the Pharisees that it was not. If Jesus answered "NO," he would be crucified as an insurrectionist. If he answered "YES," he would lose his followers who saw him as the Messiah. Instead of answering directly, Jesus asked to see a coin the Pharisees were carrying. The coin provided was the Roman denarius, not the more common Tyrian sheckel. On one side was the face of Caesar with an idolatrous inscription about Caesar being divine. It is believed that the denarius was minted at the opposite end of the Mediterranean, and the few who possessed it were closely associated with the Roman government. It was used to pay the Roman legion and was also used by the wealthy who collaborated with the Romans. Religious Jews were prohibited from using this coinage, for it violated a principle of Judaism which forbade the worship of other gods than Yahweh. In other words, Jesus implied that the persons who confronted him were law-breakers themselves.[18]

Jesus simply responded that those who were loyal to Caesar, that is, those law-breakers who used Caesar's coinage when there was an opportunity to do otherwise, already demonstrated by their actions what their priorities were. So it was logical for them to contribute back to Caesar with his own money that which he demanded of them in tribute. But those whose lives are committed to God must bear in mind that submission to Caesar's violent demand is always a lower value than allegiance to God. Jesus broke the law or advocated law-breaking again and again. As a matter of fact, Jesus was a habitual criminal for conscience's sake.

WAR AND TAXES

Jesus' acts could be described as "civil disobedience," but are more accurately acts of "holy obedience." The first followers of Jesus, the early Christians, refused to pay tribute to the temple of Caesar in Rome, making them the first tax refusers for conscience, and they were put to death. Lactantius wrote in his *Divine Institutes*: (Chapter 18)

> When men command us to act in opposition to the law of God, and in opposition to justice, we should be deterred by no threats or punishments from preferring the command of God to the command of man. . . . When compelled to desert God and betray our faith, we should prefer to undergo death and should defend our liberty against the foolish and senseless violence of those who cannot govern themselves, and with fortitude of spirit we should challenge all the threats and terrors of the world.

The foremost historical record of early Christian belief and practice, C. J. Cadoux's *The Early Church in the World*, describes the common stance of active resistance and protest:

> The martyr-acts frequently speak of the prosecuting officials in terms of strong censure. . . . The words, "I am a

Christian," were persistently repeated, sometimes in reply
to questions from the magistrate perhaps on quite other
points, sometimes on the speaker's own initiative, and in
reply to no question at all. . . . It seems not to have been
uncommon for Christians attending the trials of their co-
religionists to protest boldly in open court against the
condemnation of innocent (men), and by thus disclosing
their own faith to draw the death sentence upon themselves
also.

  Christian disobedience under persecution was regularly
defended on the broad ground of the supremacy of God's
law to man's. . . . It is important to notice that *this doctrine
of disobedience is in principle perfectly general.* The Law of God,
which the Christians put over against the law of the state,
embraced a good deal more than the prohibition of idolatry and polytheism; it embraced the whole Christian
ethic. . . .[19]

Throughout history a remnant of Christians in each generation has understood their relationship to secular authorities
and cultural norms in essentially this way.

Colonial America experienced John Woolman's forceful presence against slavery and war. Woolman was a pacifist Quaker
who refused to pay taxes that were used to finance the French
and Indian War. His journal tells us, "I besought the Lord to
enable me to give up all, so that I might follow him wheresoever
he was pleased to lead me. Under this exercise I went to our
Yearly Meeting at Philadelphia in the year 1755."[20] There he
presented his scruple to other Friends who, at length, drew up
an epistle supporting his resistance. By 1795 many members
of the Religious Society of Friends had suffered for their civil
disobedience, and a letter from one of them, relative to the
conscientious scrupulousness of its members to bear arms, is
worth noting. It says, in respect to the reasons Quakers could
not bide with killing and war: "It is inconsistent with Christianity
to resort to arms—one crime will not justify another. The *Lex
Talionis* is not a part of the Christian religion; and the using of

arms, to resist an attack, is returning violence for violence, and opposing force with force, involving ourselves in the like criminality, and making ourselves as deserving of chastisement as they are on whom we inflict it. . . . "[21]

Since World War II we have entered the nuclear age, and the nature of history, and therefore of Christian responsibility, is radically changed. In 1952, A.J. Muste, a minister, labor leader, pacifist, and veteran Quaker peace crusader, evolved a position of absolute conscientious objection. His *Of Holy Disobedience* was published in 1952. It called for total non-cooperation with any preparation for war. Going to prison, Muste argued, is less damaging to the soul than participating in war or cooperating with war preparations.[22] The anti-war movement, however, was preceded by another movement, with more political and domestic immediacy.

KING AND GANDHI AND THE BERRIGANS

In 1957, a woman refused to obey a law that required her, simply because she was black, to move to the back of a public bus. From that moment the so-called civil rights movement took wing. Martin Luther King, Jr., was a leading voice of that movement and set up guidelines for the practice of nonviolent direct action to complement court proceedings by the National Association for the Advancement of Colored People. The movement was based on the proposition that every American should have the same equitable rights under the Constitution, regardless of race. King's famous "Letter from a Birmingham Jail" explained why civil disobedience was a legitimate part of the civil rights movement.[23] The civil rights effort, based on Gandhian techniques and the Gospels of Jesus, proved to be fundamentally successful through judicial and legislative means. It resulted in the repeal or revision of many racist policies restricting blacks from public accommodations, jobs, and voting and denying them other basic civil rights. The movement is still with us in its recognition of the essential need for the practice of resistance according to the King-Gandhi discipline.

Cesar Chavez brought nonviolence to the migrant workers and the labor movement.[24] And Dorothy Day's Catholic Workers practiced it in soup kitchens, in hospitality houses, and in resistance to war many years prior to the activity of Chavez and King. She may be the greatest heroine of the modern, American, religiously motivated, nonviolence-and-civil-disobedience movement. She transcended all varieties of resistance and had been herself—along with the Catholic Worker Movement—involved in the labor front, the civil rights front, and the war-resistance front. She inspired new variations of civil disobedience firmly based on Scripture; and at the age of seventy-three she was arrested for taking part in the illegal picketing of grape producers by migrant workers. This was by no means her first arrest.[25]

In 1965, draft cards were burned or mutilated and later, as the anti-war movement progressed, there were sit-ins, pray-ins, and die-ins. More directly there were blockings, chainings, and blood pourings—all of these performed as symbolic speech and actions to change death-centered events. This type of civil disobedience was and is addressed directly to the illegalities of the Vietnam War and the present nuclear build-up. Although this type of witness has its own vitality, and has been done for its own principles, it has also had an impact upon the constitutional laws of this land. For over twenty years Philip and Daniel Berrigan, and Phil's wife, Elizabeth McAlister, have provided fundamental leadership to this anti-war approach which they now properly refuse to call "civil disobedience."

Initiatory or direct, and indirect or reactive, are ways of describing the two basic types of civil disobedience. An example of initiatory or direct civil disobedience is the conspiring to trespass and the actual trespass itself of, say, a nuclear-missile site. Such trespass witnesses to a higher value than the "sacredness" of private or governmental property. An example of reactive or indirect civil disobedience is the refusal to pay military taxes. Some people refuse to pay all or part of their taxes because of their deeply held convictions that they cannot voluntarily give financial support to the Pentagon. We may also distinguish between moral and political civil disobedience, the former a lifestyle and the latter, often, a tactic.

In classic civil disobedience of the Gandhi-King style, one broke the law and rarely put on legal defense. The witness was made, the law broken, a guilty plea entered, the penalty accepted. More recently, in the American religious peace movement, as exemplified by the "plowshares" cases, a new action has emerged—the witness to state criminality. Evidence is presented to the effect that the government is the true law-breaker and as such has contrived the situation in which the defendant's law-breaking is secondary. In court, defendants argue that the government should be held responsible and not themselves.

Commonwealth of Pennsylvania v. Berrigan et al. illustrates this approach and the use of the necessity defense in a civil-disobedience action bringing international-law violations into play. The defendants described their own motives as follows, in a document entitled "The Plowshares Eight: the Crime, the Trial, the Issues:"

On September 9, 1980, in King of Prussia, Pennsylvania, eight people acted to stop the arms race. The Crime: Entering the General Electric Re-Entry Division Assembly site, the group destroyed two nuclear re-entry (warheads) cones with hammers and poured human blood on blueprints, damaged cones and tools. Their statement: The Prophets Isaiah and Micah summon us to beat swords into plowshares; therefore eight of us from Atlantic Life Community came to the King of Prussia G.E. Re-Entry Division plant to expose the criminality of nuclear weaponry and corporate piracy. We represent resistance communities along the eastern coast: each of us has a long history of nonviolent resistance to war. We commit civil disobedience at G.E. because this genocidal entity is the fifth leading producer of weaponry in the U.S. To maintain this position G.E. drains $3 million a day from the public treasury, an enormous larceny against the poor. We wish also to challenge the lethal lie, spun by G.E. through its motto "We bring good things to life." As manufacturer of the Mark 12A Re-entry vehicle, G.E. actually prepares to bring good things to death. Through the Mark 12A the threat of first-strike nuclear war grows more imminent. Thus G.E. advances the possible destruction of millions of innocent lives. In confronting G.E. we choose to obey God's law of life rather than the corporate summons to death. Our beating of swords into plowshares today is a way to enflesh this Biblical call. In our action we draw on a deep-rooted faith in Christ to change the course of history through his willingness to suffer rather than to kill. We are filled with hope for our world and for our children as we join this act of resistance.[26]

Today the greatest threat to law is war and particularly nuclear war. The danger is imminent and there are immediate attempts to abate the danger through civil disobedience. It is important to stress that this particular, imminent, world danger cannot be abated on the spur of the moment as might be the case where an individual sees a burning house with a crying baby inside and technically breaks the law of criminal trespass by entering the house without permission to rescue the baby. Minutes later the danger is over. This is the standard example of an instance when it is necessary to abate danger through an act which otherwise would be the commission of a crime. The imminence of nuclear war is such that acts of holy obedience aimed at preventing the occurrence of such war—acts which would otherwise be criminal—are necessary and justified from conscience, and from constitutional, international, and United States law. Here we have added to the traditional understanding of necessity an argument worthy of attention. Persons involved in this movement are not simply trying to abate danger and harm; they are trying to prevent a world holocaust and at the same time witness to an alternative way of life which is the only alternative to such holocaust.

Avoiding the political temptation calls us to resist the powers and principalities by a community witness which quite likely will result in tribulations and suffering; at the same time such acts will place us once again in the company of those earliest Christians—we will lead the life envisioned and practiced by their communities.

ALTERNATIVES TO THE ECONOMIC TEMPTATION

Christians in community are called not only to witness to the world's violence through resistance and holy obedience, but also to contend with the economic temptations by living in simplicity and voluntary poverty, serving and assisting in a variety of ways. A connecting link between these two kinds of outreach may be found in the attempt by Christians to break down the prison system at the same time they live out a willingness to go to prison for their own witness.

Christian activist Lee Griffith wrote:

> When we rely on the so-called "criminal justice system"—when we reach for the phone to call the police and someone is arrested as a result—we are at the same time declaring that the Gospel is irrelevant. Even though politicians like to score points talking about response to lawlessness and violence, our own response to crime is not a political issue, but a question of faith. Already much of American Christendom counts the Gospel as irrelevant internationally. There are not many among us who would call for turning the American cheek to the Russian first strike. . . . My proposition is this: Willful reliance on the power of the police, guns, and prisons is a renunciation of the incarnation of Jesus Christ—it is to say that the life, death, and resurrection of Jesus is valid only for some other world and not our own.[27]

In *U.S. v. Moylan*, a judge summed up as follows:

To encourage individuals to make their own determination as to which laws they will obey and which they will permit themselves as a matter of conscience to disobey, is to invite chaos. No legal system could long survive if it gave every individual the option of disregarding with impunity any law which by his personal standards was judged morally untenable. Toleration of such conduct would not be democratic, as appellant has claimed, but inevitably anarchic.[28]

Thus the world's great fear of the Christian conscience in action is translated into fear of anarchy. It is Christian anarchy. The Christian no longer adheres to the structures of society, but to the structures enunciated and exemplified by the life of Jesus. Indeed, we are Christian anarchists because we have a law of our own, and that law is the love of Jesus in community. John Adams rightly observed, "The Christian religion demands the crucifixion of self; a state religion demands the crucifixion of conscience." The consistent lesson from history is that political structures attempt to punish conscience; indeed, they see the suppression of conscience as a necessity for the survival of the state.

So much of this is interconnected. There are people in prison who are there because they tried to grasp a better economic life for themselves. They were simply sucked into the worldly, economic temptation. Every day the media display the luxuries that other people have. Anyone can walk through the suburbs and view the rich estates of the wealthy. The poor want a share of that, and many of them do not have the social conditioning in place that would enable them to pursue it through legal channels. As the Apostle James says, "You want that which you cannot have." The poor cannot have it because someone else has got it and someone else is going to keep it. The only way to come off this lust for acquisition, which causes some to live in jails and allows others to live in luxury, is a deliberate, downward mobility to voluntary poverty and simplicity.

The voluntary relinquishment of this lust may set an example for others who find themselves behind bars. Catholic Worker communities, which usually combine people who have been in prison for conscience's sake and people who are running soup kitchens and shelters for the homeless, find many of the people to whom they minister have also been in prison at one time or another. Usually such experience is connected with their own poverty and their need or want for something more. When these groups come together and share in a round-table discussion at a Catholic Worker house, the convict and the convicted of conscience often form a holistic community that is instructive for all.

VOLUNTARY POVERTY AND SIMPLICITY

The Catholic Worker philosophy holds that voluntary poverty is simply a means. We must avoid the danger of making poverty a Christian ideal in itself. A person made in the image of God was not made to starve. Destitution is not the poverty we seek. Voluntary poverty is good only because it is useful to remove the obstacles that stand in the way of spiritual perfection. Even though perfection is unattainable, we are all called to try to be perfect, so we are called to poverty. Once we begin not to worry about what kind of house we live in, Dorothy Day said, what kind of clothes we wear, once we give up the "stupid recreation" of the world, we have time which is priceless to remember that we are our brothers' and sisters' keepers, and that we must not only care for their needs as far as we are immediately able, but we must also try to build a better world.

In a classic article, "On Holy Poverty," Michael DeGregory wrote that we begin to create a new society within the shell of the old.

Voluntary poverty is a witness to this world and a vision of a new world. It is a call to share with the poor, to share both their suffering and the earth's fullness. It is a call to share in justice and to protest the injustice which divides humanity into rich and poor. As we live to love both God and neighbor, we might recall the words of John, the beloved disciple, "if anyone has the world's goods and sees his brother in need, yet closes his heart against him, how does God's love abide in him?" Let us not love in word or speech but in deed and in truth.[29]

And so, as an economic outreach to the temptations of the world, the Catholic Worker has devised houses of hospitality. Whether a house is large or small, structured or loose, efficient or in disarray, full-time or part-time, are not the main issues. Many families set aside a single room in their home to receive homeless guests. What is at stake is not an impersonal principle of organization; it is the principle of active love commanded in the Bible. Each Catholic Worker house has its special characteristics. In New York the workers live in or near three houses of hospitality, St. Joseph House, Mary House, and the farm that was at Tivoli and now is elsewhere. Primarily they see themselves as a family with many guests. Whatever families share in the way of joys and irritations, they can never be totally impersonal, and nobody can be more demanding and abrasive, more supporting and accepting than a family.

All Christians are called to hospitality and to be hospitable. But it is more than serving a meal or opening our door, it is to open ourselves and our hearts to the needs of others. Hospitality is not just providing a shelter but the quality of welcome within it. The only remorse Catholic Workers have is that they would like to be able to say that "we never turn anybody away," and indeed their soup lines and clothing rooms are open to all.

When it comes to shelter, however, limitations of space must be recognized. Traditionally, Catholic Workers have attempted to respond to need with a special sensitivity for those who do not fit into the system, and also without establishing rigid guidelines or principles of exclusion. At the same time, within the vision of personalism derived from Peter Maurin, Catholic Workers do recognize some limits, if only in the number of beds and space necessary to maintain some semblance of family living. A fundamental guideline for Christian communities practicing hospitality and seeking to define limitations is to say only that to delineate them too soon is the sin of despair; not to draw them at all is the sin of presumption. As Pascal noted, "When human beings seek to become angels, they end up as beasts." Catholic Workers heed his warning.

Catholic Workers and other radical Christians living in community and sharing their lives with the poor recognize that such a community will help them to understand and oppose the forces that create and tolerate the destitution we see around us. This life experience becomes the inspiration and motivation to resist degrading trends of militarism, centralization, class injustice, usury, and injustice. It is also the inspiration to challenge the ways of the world, to live with the poor as a family instead of doing things for the poor, to practice the corporal and spiritual works of mercy.

Catholic Worker communities have no illusions that they are counselors, psychologists, social workers, intake workers, mental hygienists, or consultants. They simply care for people where they are. They are not an organization but an organism.

How is this life and work of simplicity sustained without funds? This is the standard Catholic Worker answer:

> We do not solicit foundation grants, bank on interest, or accept stocks and bonds. We do not accept state assistance on the grounds that "he who pays the piper calls the tune." Even if we were willing to share a payroll with the Pentagon, we would rather be independent than try to conform to the state's definitions of what constitutes charity. We do not have a budget from the Church hierarchy or from Catholic Charities, for we are not an agency or organization but a community, and no one need bear responsibility for our positions and actions but ourselves.
>
> As a movement and a community we try to retain that same spirit of voluntary poverty that we practice as individuals. Aside from simplicity and not accumulating above our needs (and trying to keep those to a minimum), this

means avoiding the security (and dangers of complacency) that come from a regular source of income. We are constantly reminded that the continuation of our work relies on God's Providence which is revealed through the love and gifts of so many.

All our support comes from personal and private donations. Many people sustain us with their prayers. Many . . . send donations of money, clothing, and food. Many friends share their time and skills to keep the houses functioning. Many merchants give us free produce and reduced rates on necessary supplies.

We are convinced that, if this is the Lord's work, it will somehow continue. But we must remember that Christians are called to regard success and failure differently than the world. Poverty prevents us from forgetting that ultimately our success or failure will be judged not by the size of our budget or the number of our subscribers but our faithfulness to love.[30]

Some have asked what the Catholic Worker communities do about taxes. It is fairly well known that they do not pay federal taxes because approximately sixty percent of each tax dollar goes to the military. Their position is that: "Military spending has become symptomatic of a plague throughout the body politic, a plague fed on the unrestrained expansion of state power. We ask others therefore to join our refusal because of our anti-war convictions and because such evil squandering is an affront to the poor."[31]

On a related issue of tax exemption, they continue to decline classification as a charitable or non-profit organization. Part of the reason is identical with the refusal of state aid. In addition, they believe there is no reason for a Christian community to reap special benefits for doing what everybody ought to be doing anyway. "Finally we should not wear the mask of religiosity which exempts us from the moral dilemmas facing others. We are required not to evade political issues, but to engage in the clarification of thought about them and to develop a response that questions the givens."[32]

These principles of the Catholic Worker strongly influenced us when we formed the Erimias and the Lamb's communities. We worked at living according to the ideals expressed in them. If nothing else, it must be stressed that once community is formed and identified by principles of pacifism and simplicity, serious, profound consequences follow. A pacifist lifestyle includes witness that eventually results in holy obedience, or, as the state names it, civil disobedience, and arrest and imprisonment, possibly for years. Leading a life of voluntary poverty and simplicity with the homeless results in outward manifestations of that simplicity and poverty that have far-reaching economic and public impact. Taxes must be paid, but if war taxes are refused, the state will try to collect them by force. Some communities, including our own, have set up what they call land trusts to help them reap a harvest of peace. "Land must not be sold in perpetuity, for the land belongs to me and to me you are only strangers and guests. You will allow a right of redemption on all your land and property." (Leviticus 25:23.) Based on this Biblical precept, some communities have given up the secular presumption of ownership rights to the land they use.

Those communities which place their land in land trusts hope that taking land entirely out of speculation will encourage others to see land as a heritage and common resource. Because land is a common resource, the trust recognizes the rights of individuals to use the land in ecologically sound, energy- and matter-conserving ways.[33]

Some groups such as one formed in Ft. Wayne, Indiana, called "Matthew 25" reach out to the poor in the form of medical services.[34] Others have served by forming centers such as the Center on Law and Pacifism to counsel those who develop problems of conscience in witnessing to the powers and principalities on the abuses of religious, political, and economic structures—systems and institutions that seek to restrict alternative lifestyles. Draft registration resisters, war-tax resisters, people who trespass on military bases to hammer swords into plowshares are some of those who receive service and counseling from those who live in such communities.

THE SABBATH AND JUBILEE YEARS

It is beyond my ability and experience to describe systematically what living economically in the Kingdom would look like, primarily because it has never been done perfectly. However, a blueprint is available. It is found in the historical records of the Israelites and early Christians.

We know what we wish to avoid economically: growth for its own sake, upward mobility, taking more than we need, feeding our greed. A positive start toward radical economic alternatives would certainly embrace the Israelite conception and practice of Sabbath and Jubilee Year as fulfilled in the life of Jesus. "Think not that I have come to abolish the law or the prophets. I have come not to abolish them but to fulfill them." (Matthew 5:17.) So he did in respect to the Sabbath and Jubilee laws as he preached in the Nazareth synagogue:

> The Spirit of the Lord is upon me, because he has anointed me to preach good news to the poor. He has sent me to proclaim release to the captives, and recovery of sight to the blind. To set at liberty those who are oppressed, to proclaim the acceptable Year of the Lord. (Luke 4:18-19.)

Throughout his ministry Jesus equated the blind with those who could not comprehend his Gospel. The fulfillment of the Jubilee and Sabbath years was part of that Gospel to which those around him were blinded. The Jubilee and Sabbath years spoke of the practice of releasing the oppressed, freeing the prisoners and the slaves, proclaiming freedom, preaching joy for the poor who would be saved. (Leviticus 25ff.) It is not a year of judgment, but a year of favor.

Jesus was not welcome in his home town when he made this prophetic claim. Some say the ultimate crime with which he was charged was that of false prophecy. In Nazareth he was convicted from the start as the locals rose up to drive him away. This must be a false prophecy. How could one Jew fulfill the Jubilee and Sabbath years that all Jews were unwilling or unable to practice over many centuries? Their fear is not hard to understand. After 2000 years we still live in a way which essentially denies this most revolutionary challenge of Jesus. It is thought that the Jubilee Year (seven Sabbath years, or 49 years) is numerically also based on the 50 days between Passover and Pentecost. It has been questioned whether Jubilee year was ever really practiced, because the writings describing it were considered post-exilic (700-600 BC). Recent scholarship indicates it is an early phenomenon and a practical one as well.[35]

Specifically, the Jubilee year called for the following: A proclamation of "liberty throughout the land to all its inhabitants" (Leviticus 25:9-10.) causing: first, emancipation or release of Jews who had become enslaved to their Jewish masters; second, return or release of property to its original owners or their families, including fields and homes in unwalled country towns, when such property was held by fellow Jews.

Earlier legislation (Exodus 21:26.) called for liberation of slaves at the Sabbatical year. The Sabbatical year provided first for all agricultural labor to be stopped, that is, fields were to remain uncultivated, and second, the cancellation of debts. In the North, agriculture was the predominant way of life. This provision of the Sabbatical year pertained to the use of the untilled fruits of the field, orchard, or vineyard for the poor who were not property owners. It also provided a humbling reminder to the landowner to rely upon God's grace for all sustenance.

The Priestly Code, which appeared even later in the last years of the 5th century, and was enforced during the ensuing five centuries until the time of Jesus, did not include the Sabbatical year at all. With Judaism institutionally centered in a Temple amid an urbanized population, the priesthood apparently could

not stomach economic liberation, nor could their commercial-
ized flock.

The Jubilee and Sabbatical years were tied to a life apart
from the city. The cancellation of debts would be impractical,
unrealistic, perhaps not even just in secular terms. The priests
and the merchants combined to end this radical, rural, economic, religious innovation. As far as we know, only the Qumran
sect followed the practices of the Sabbatical year for the last
four centuries of the pre-Christian era. John Howard Yoder
aptly points out that Jesus spoke to each of the four precepts
of the Jubilee and Sabbatical years: leaving the soil fallow; the
remission of debts; the liberation of slaves; and the return of
property.[36] In order to practice these precepts, the religious
community, it seems, must be freed of priestly dominance and
commercial greed and must live apart from the city. This echoes
the call heard from Jeremiah and Hosea to return to the time
of the bride and live in nomadic simplicity. (Jeremiah 2; Hosea
6.)

URBAN OR RURAL?

Must the religous community be rural in order to be faithful?
Must the model, modern community, like the ancient Essenes,
flee the city? To live with the poor as poor is another calling
and it will pull us to the city, where North America's poverty
is concentrated at its most lethal level. How is this seeming
contradiction to be resolved? The work of the city is assistance,
mission; and the work of the country is community, monastery—
today both need each other. The crucial point for the urban
community is not to become dependent upon urban structures;
for rural community, not to become isolated. Each must remain
radically unassimilated.

Writing about the monastic lifestyle, Thomas Merton said:
"The monastic flight from the world into the desert is not a
mere refusal to know anything about the world, but a total
rejection of all standards of judgment which imply attachment
to a history of delusion, egoism, and sin. Not of course a vain

denial that the monk too is a sinner (this would be an even worse delusion), but a definitive refusal to participate in those activities which have no other fruit than to prolong the reign of untruth, greed, cruelty, and arrogance in the world. . . . "[37] The point is exactly the same for the radical Christian community, whether rural or urban. The point is to be divorced from the ways of nations! Merton goes on to observe the fundamental political nature of this kind of stance. He sees the primary obligation of Christians as not to try to influence the secular state to be governed by the ethics of God's Kingdom, but rather to dissent, to object, to testify, to witness against the ways of nations, to witness for another way while living in their midst.

My hope here is to cause imaginations to run free. Therefore, I am not about filling in the gaps, I am about nudging for a beginning. What would a Jubilee economics look like? How can modern Christians implement an Israelite blueprint? What has Jesus given us as a fulfillment of this law? It is in tune with the Sabbatical and Jubilee years to follow the inward attitudes provided by Jesus—do not be anxious but rather look to the lilies of the field—and the outward manifestation of that is to be liberated. (Matthew 6.) This year may be your Sabbath or Jubilee year. The Spirit of the Lord may be upon you. Look for your anointing. Preach good news to the poor, rub shoulders with them, send yourselves to proclaim freedom to the prisoners; they are often found in prisons as physical prisoners, or in rich country clubs as spiritual prisoners. Help the blind to recover sight—the blind of our fearful military installations, the blind who have been wounded by our nuclear experiments. Release the oppressed, open the doors. You know where they are. Proclaim the Year of the Lord's favor to both sets of blind and oppressed, the prisoners, the poor. There is so much in the Old and New Testaments upon which to build an economic community. The early Christians all shared, they lived in community, they assisted their neighbors, they resisted the powers and principalities. At least, we are called to live in some kind of community, in some authentic, intentional, and accountable

way. In some way we must incarnate servanthood. In some way
we must share the pain of the poor and the burden of the
spiritually deprived. In some way we must nonviolently resist
the powers and principalities, and not passively acquiesce to
their tax dollars and war-making.

The plan for community does not have to be monolithic, but
it should be cohesive. The community must have an identity;
it must be a body, a living body, Christ's body, our body.

How do we live together? In community. How do we relate
to the existing government? In pacifism undergirding resistance
and holy obedience. How do we relate to society? With voluntary simplicity and poverty expanded to assistance and hospitality and service to the oppressed.

How, then, may we face the oppressed where human rights
have been sorely abridged without recourse to violent revolution or legal reform? This question brings us to another form
of service the alternative Christian community is called to provide: being advocates for the oppressed and witnessing to the
needs of people deprived of human rights. The sanctuary movement and base-ecclesial-community movement are current examples of the way radical Christian communities may combine
prophetic resistance with helping the oppressed.[38] We are called
not to live in complacent, internalized community, but to reach
out and become involved in the structures of society so that
the oppression of those structures can be felt and radical responses can be made.[39] It is to this obligation that we now turn
our attention.

CHAPTER EIGHT

CHRISTIAN ADVOCACY FOR THE OPPRESSED

HUMAN RIGHTS AND LAW

How is the Christian to witness as advocate for the oppressed? A starting point is to understand human rights in the context of law. An examination of human rights and the law brings to light several descriptions of such rights: Divine rights, natural rights, relative rights, constitutional rights, civil rights. Along the way we define these rights and find that different writers describe them in different terms. The best place to begin is *Black's Law Dictionary:*

> [Right:] As a *noun,* and taken in a *concrete* sense, a power, privilege, faculty, or demand, inherent in one person and incident upon another. Rights are defined generally as "powers of free action." And the primal rights pertaining to man are enjoyed by human beings purely as such, being grounded in personality, and existing antecedently to their recognition by positive law. But leaving the abstract moral sphere, and giving to the term a juristic content, a "right" is well defined as "a capacity residing in one man of con-

trolling, with the assent and assistance of the state, the action of others."[1]

Black's adds the following concerning absolute and relative rights:

> . . . *absolute,* which are such as pertain and belong to particular men merely as individuals or single persons; *relative,* which are incident to them as members of society, and standing in various relations to each other.[2]

Natural rights are discussed by *Black's* in the following way:

> *Natural* rights are those which grow out of the nature of man and depend upon personality, as distinguished from such as are created by law and depend upon all civil society; or they are those which are plainly assured by natural law; or those which, by fair deduction from the present, physical, moral, social, and religious characteristics of man, he must be invested with, and which he ought to have realized for him in a jural society, in order to fulfill the ends for which his nature calls him. Such are the rights of life, liberty, privacy, and good reputation.
> *Civil rights* are such as belong to every citizen of the state or country, or, in a wider sense, to all inhabitants, and are not connected with the organization or administration of government. They include the rights of property, marriage, protection of the laws, freedom of contract, trial by jury, etc. Or, as otherwise defined, civil rights are rights appertaining to a person by virtue of his citizenship in a state or community.[3]

Constitutional rights are those rights which attach to an individual by virtue of the *highest* positive law. From time to time, in constitutional law cases and in the writings of the philosophers of law, the phrases "fundamental rights" and "inalienable rights" appear. A fundamental right is short of what some writers describe as "absolute," but it is a right held by all people (perhaps under a constitution), a *prima facie* absolute, until it runs into conflict with another fundamental right. "Inalienable rights" are those which generally cannot be taken away; but in particular situations these rights are always in jeopardy when they run counter to other rights or powers.

John Stuart Mill states:

> To have a right, then, is, I conceive, to have something which society ought to defend me in the possession of. If the objector goes on to ask, why it ought?, I can give him no other reason than general utility. . . . The interest involved is that of security, to everyone's feelings the most vital of all interests. . . . When we call anything a person's right, we mean that he has a valid claim on Society to protect him in the possession of it, either by the force of law, or by that of education and opinion.[4]

Mill goes on to examine security as the most vital of all "interests" and says, "All other earthly benefits are needed by one person, not needed by another; and many of them can, if necessary, be cheerfully forgone, or replaced by something else; but security no human being can possibly do without. . . . Now this most indispensable of all necessaries, after physical nutriment, cannot be had, unless the machinery for providing it is kept unintermittedly in active play."[5]

It happens that John Stuart Mill's thought proceeds from an ethical philosophy of utilitarianism. However, whether utilitarians or not, the political, social contractarians all essentially agree that when one enters a state of society, one gives up absolute freedom as a trade-off for some semblance of security; otherwise there is no incentive to take on the duties and restrictions of political institutions. It is hoped that a substantial amount of freedom remains within a political institution and only that portion of one's freedom is divested which is replaced by this guarantee of security. So the right to security within the commonwealth becomes an essential, absolute right. Providing security from within against criminals and from without against "enemies" becomes a fundamental duty of the state. Security becomes a fundamental right of the individual whom the state protects with justified institutional violence. Thus, in the end, great expenditures for prisons, for the enforcement of capital punishment, and for "defense" preparations and war-making itself are deemed necessary to serve these rights.

When persons enter into society and assume rights and duties under the umbrella of society, the question immediately arises: Do they retain any rights that are inherent to the individual, natural to the person, perhaps even absolute, which cannot be divested upon entering such society? Or, upon people's entering such society, do all rights and the law—the method for the enforcement of society's goals—merge?

Jeremy Bentham's position, one which has been influential in the development of western political institutions, was that the "law was instituted to protect" persons in the enjoyment of their rights. He saw natural rights as "sacred and indefeasible" and held that insofar as law protects that condition it conforms to what he called "natural justice;" but that when law deprives persons of their natural rights it is "repugnant to natural justice."[6] Indeed Bentham clearly held that only laws conformable to natural justice are valid, and that laws contrary to natural justice are *ipso facto* void and instead of being observed, ought to be resisted. His position provided a clearly stated philosophical ground for the classical forms and motivations of civil disobedience in western democracy. He claimed unequivocally that those who make unjust laws are tyrants and those who attempt to enforce them are the tools of tyrants. The hallmark of Bentham's position was his refusal to distinguish between natural and positive law.

Hans Kelsen saw the relationship between law and rights differently. He held that validity of laws cannot be judged or questioned on the ground that their contents are somehow incompatible with some moral or political value. Kelsen drew a clear distinction between law and morals and saw them as independent of each other. In so doing, he designated positive law as a system "created and annulled by acts of human beings," and natural law and morality as expressions of the "will of nature" or of "pure reason."[7] Kelsen was not a theist, but had he been, he surely would have included "Divine will" in this area.

Kelsen's brand of legal reasoning is generally described as "positivism," which gets us ultimately into two camps of philosophy of law: the positivist camp and the natural law or rights camp. In the positive-law camp, we see law and morality merged, or morality non-existent, so that any claim to a right beyond the positive law is considered to be fictional.

HUMAN RIGHTS AND MORALITY

One of the natural-law philosophers, Immanuel Kant, had this to say about rights: "*Right*, therefore, comprehends the whole of the conditions under which the voluntary actions of any one Person can be harmonized in reality with the voluntary actions of every other Person, according to a universal Law of Freedom. . . . The universal Law of Right may then be expressed thus: 'Act externally in such a manner that the free exercise of thy will may be able to co-exist with the freedom of all others, according to a universal Law.'. . . . All Right is accompanied with an implied Title or warrant to bring compulsion to bear on anyone who may violate it in fact."[8]

Commenting on natural rights, he says: "Innate Right is that Right which belongs to everyone by Nature, independent of all juridical acts of experience. *Acquired Right* is that Right which is founded upon such juridical acts."[9] For Kant, there is only one innate or natural right, the birthright of freedom—that is, the right of the individual to be his or her own "master."

Thomas Hobbes considered that a person's only natural right was self-preservation. More "liberal" theorists add to life and security, liberty, the pursuit of happiness, and sometimes property or equality.[10] Maritain enumerates a list of nine natural rights which include, besides the rights of life, liberty, and property of the older formulations, the right to pursue a religious vocation, the right to marry and raise a family, and finally the right of every human being to be treated as a person and not as a thing.[11]

Whether from the Kelsean positive-law approach, the Kantian deontological, natural-law approach, or the Millian utilitarian, natural-rights approach, all agree with Hugo Grotius that "rights do not attain their external end, except they have force to back them."[12] Ezra Pound states, "A legal right is a capacity of influencing the action of others through the force of politically organized society." That force includes the use of institutional violence to that end.[13]

Civil, constitutional rights, part of the positive law in its highest form, must be enforced in the U.S.A through the process of appeal and decision-making, ultimately by the U.S. Supreme Court, as we saw in the civil-rights movement. The Supreme Court attempted to secure the civil rights of minority groups such as blacks. Those rights might have been natural, inherent, inviolable, inalienable, fundamental, but in the last instance they were secured because of constitutional amendments that were interpreted by the Supreme Court to apply in a way beneficial to the civil-rights movement against the states in which those rights' violations were instituted. Later we saw the reverse process happening in the same Court using the same constitutional formulations as conscientious objectors were stripped of their fundamental, natural and inherent rights.[14]

Much of the province for human rights, particularly that of advocating the rights of the oppressed, involves natural rights which, although recognized by legal and political philosophers, are frequently unenforceable in the courts of any particular country. The essential distinction between legal right and moral right hangs on the question of enforcement. "No person has a legal right which cannot be claimed from some other person and which the law will not enforce."[15]

The common theme of natural rights is their political character, so that they constitute moral rights which are political in thrust. For example, is there a natural right not to be forced to kill another human being against one's will? There are nu-

merous laws in every country which compel human beings
against their will to follow orders which result in killing other
human beings. This legal duty, this law, is justified, even by
moralists and theologians. But the consequences of such enforcement for an individual who otherwise would refrain from
such actions are immeasurable. Let us assume that such a position is based on moral values. We then have a specific conflict
between legal duties and moral or natural rights. The positive
law compels what the moral and natural law prohibits, regardless of the consequences.

In summary, then, a legal right, as well as a legal duty, is
what the positive law says it is. Under the Dred Scott decision
of the last century, an American citizen could hold a Black
person as a slave, a chattel, and this was a right of the white,
American citizen. The Black person possessed no legal rights
whatsoever. Fortunately, this is a famous instance where the
natural rights of the slave to freedom eventually became the
slave's positive-law right as well. But, by law such rights could
again be divested. The rights of the unborn child, near perfection in the 19th century in American law, do not find the same
level of perfection in the 20th century; this because of a conflicting right of the woman to be free to determine what to do
with her own body apart from the compulsion of law. When all
is said and done, a legal right is nothing more than a tautology.
A legal right is a right enforced by law. For example, in international law, "Everyone has the right to liberty and security of
person. No one shall be subject to arbitrary arrest. No one shall
be deprived of his liberty *except* . . . by law."[16] (Emphasis added.)
All expectations beyond positive law are the subject of moral
or religious values.

We have said much already about the relationship of moral
and legal rights, but a further clarification is needed on the
specific subject of human rights and morality. According to
Wasserstrom:

If any right is a *human* right it must, I believe, have at least
four very general characteristics. First, it must be possessed

by all human beings, as well as only by human beings. Second, because it is the same right that all human beings possess, it must be possessed equally by all human beings. Third, because human rights are possessed by all human beings, we can rule out as possible candidates any of those rights which one might have in virtue of occupying any particular status or relationship, such as that of parent, president, or promisee. And fourth, if there are any human rights, they have the additional characteristic of being assertable, in a manner of speaking, "against the world." That is to say, because they are rights that are not possessed in virtue of any contingent status or relationship, they are rights that can be claimed equally against any and every other human being.[17]

A moral right is commonly explained as being some sort of claim or power which ought to be recognized. D. G. Ritchie, for instance, observed that a moral right may be defined as "*the claim* of an individual upon others recognized by society, irrespective of its recognition by the State."[18] Ryan and Boland, explaining the Catholic (Thomist) view of rights, state, "A right in the moral sense of the term may be defined as an inviolable moral *claim* to some personal good. When this claim is created as it sometimes is, by civil authority, it is a positive or legal right; when it is derived from man's rational nature it is a natural right."[19]

The word "claim" is the key here, because morality, except through the pressures of cultural mores and society, does not have the power of enforcement by law. (This is not always the case. Attempts have been made to enforce morality in many societies.) Morality should not be forced, however, because the very essence of moral value—free choice—is obliterated by the use of compulsion, coercion, or violence. So, in this particular sense, morality is quite different from law. Yet we have moral rights. The key to the rights here is the claim, not the enforceability. This makes moral rights very much like natural rights in their essence—rights which exist whether law recognizes

them or not, or whether one is able to have those rights per-
fected or not. These rights exist apart from positive law and
apart from their enforcement. They exist in nature, they exist
self-evidently in the relationship of all human beings to each
other. John Rawls says of rights in the moral sense: "A conception of right is a set of principles, general in form and
universal in application, that is to be publicly recognized as a
final court of appeals for ordering the conflicting claims of moral
persons."[20]

For a religious moralist, such as John Locke, the fundamental
principle of morals is that: "If one person is created by another
(in the theological sense), then that person has a duty to comply
with the precepts set to him by his creator."[21] It is in this way
the Locke identifies God as that legitimate moral authority.

In summary, in distinguishing between legal and moral rights,
the claim to rights exists in both instances; but the apparatus
of enforcement is not found in the concept of moral rights,
even though the justification of enforcement (even by violence)
may be. Finally, we must examine the question of rights in the
theological or religious perspective, if we are to reach a theology
of rights from a Christian perspective.

HUMAN RIGHTS AND RELIGION

Are there such things as rights in the context of the Christian
religion? Richard McCormick says, "It is a basic principle . . .
that every man possesses his right to life from God—not from
man or society. . . . There is thus no man, no human authority,
no science, no indication (whether medical, eugenic, social,
economic, or moral) that can justify deliberate and direct destruction of innocent life. The life of an innocent human being
is simply inviolable, altogether immune from direct acts of
suppression."[22] McCormick finds human rights (at least the
basic right to life) grounded in religious principle. But the right
to life as presented here is limited. It sounds like an *absolute*
right but it is qualified by the phrase: "Innocent human life"
leaves out the right to life as an absolute right for criminals or

combatants in war, or anyone whom society may judge as "guilty" by whatever standard society wishes to apply. A further qualification is the word "direct" which apparently is meant to exclude acts which result in the death of a fetus, but which are not intended to do so, such as the removal of a cancerous uterus when the uterus contains a fetus. Does this, then, represent a giant step toward distinguishing religious values from legal/moral ones? No. I think we have here a so-called religious right couched in less than religious terms, certainly in moral and legal terms and heavily influenced by secular judgments. Does the Bible call for a right to life for other than "innocent" people? May a fetus be killed by the application of a Catholic theology of "double effect?" What does the Bible say about other so-called human rights—that is, rights other than the right to life?

Any quest for religious rights must begin in the first books of the Bible, the Hebrew Scriptures of the Old Testament. In Genesis 1:28, God gives dominion over animals and plants (a right) to people, but does not extend that dominion over other human beings (a right to freedom from oppression). In Exodus 21, it is said that if a man takes a woman to be his wife, he shall not diminish her food or her clothing or her marital rights. Further, a man will have no right to sell a woman slave to foreign people. The economic rights of the Sabbath and Jubilee years are promulgated in Leviticus 25. In Proverbs 29:7 it is said, "A righteous man knows the rights of the poor, a wicked man does not understand such knowledge." Proverbs 31:4-9 states, "It is not for kings to . . . pervert the rights of all the afflicted. . . . Open your mouth for the dumb, for the rights of all who are left desolate. . . . Maintain the rights of the poor and needy." The same from Amos, Hosea, and especially Jeremiah: "They do not defend the rights of the needy" (Jeremiah 5:28.) becomes the harshest of judgments upon the people, one that ancient Israel could readily understand because of their tradition.

Proceeding from that tradition, Jesus and the New Testament speak a similar, if more radical language: The hungry have a right to good things. The rich have no such right and will be sent empty away. Those of low degree have been exalted and the mighty have been put down from their thrones. The proud have been scattered in the imagination of their hearts. These visions of a radical conception of human rights are from the Magnificat of Mary. (Luke 1:47-56.) Jesus preached good news to the poor. He said he was sent to proclaim release for captives and recovery of sight for the blind, to set at liberty those who are oppressed. (Luke 4:16-20.) He said the hungry have the right to be fed and the thirsty the right to drink. The stranger has the right to be made welcome; the naked, the right to be clothed; the sick, the right to be visited; the prisoner, the right to be comforted. (Matthew 25.) These are the rights of the oppressed, not enforced by law, but guaranteed ultimately by God. They are commandments of duty for the Christian disciple.

Paul talks of rights in the relationship of husband and wife, "The husband should give to his wife her conjugal rights, and likewise the wife to her husband." (1 Corinthians 7:3.) Further, in the Epistles we find a right to freedom from slavery in 1 Corinthians 17; a right to food and drink, to work, to marry, in 1 Corinthians 9; rights of the poor in 1 Corinthians 16; a right to equality in 2 Corinthians 8:14; rights and duties between parents and children in Colossians; rights of orphans and widows in James 1:26; the rights of the poor in James 2:5. Even in Acts we find mention of the right of state protection (Acts 25:10-11.) and the rights of Roman citizenry. (Acts 16:35; 22:25.)

In spite of all this, the word "right" seldom appears in the Bible or in Biblical theology. According to Kittel, the closest we come to it is *exousia*, the "ability to perform an action to the extent that there are no hindrances in the way."[23] *Exousia* literally means authority. And Kittel's first definition of authority sounds more like a definition of power than of rights. His second definition: "The right to do something or the right over something," his third definition: "freedom," and his fourth definition: "legal permission or freedom," come close to what we have been talking about in our discussion of legal and moral rights. Kittel finds *exousia* in the context of parents to children, masters to slaves, owners to property, individuals to personal liberty. The right to do something or the right over something, in Biblical perspective, seems to follow from a covenant relationship with God in which God, in mercy and grace, does things for human beings and human beings in return fear God and follow God's commandments. Flowing from the duties of human beings to God, there emerge certain rights, rights to act in behalf of others, certain power, not controlled by law or secular or philosophical morality, and not defined in terms of enforcement or order. The "right" of Jesus and his followers was and is based on the Lordship of God. (Luke 12:5.)

Much of Biblical literature depicts human rights, especially the rights of the poor and the oppressed, in such a way that they can be seen as being commensurate with the best of secular and humanist descriptions of such rights. The Bible is not necessarily unique in its many calls for freedom, liberation, relief, and justice for those who are in any way victimized by cultural, economic, even religious exploitation and oppression. What is unique about a Biblical discussion of rights is the way in which the right and the duty of the faithful merge and become one. The duty or obligation which accrues to the faithful in response to God's love and saving grace becomes that person's right to act (in a God-like manner) in behalf of another. Jesus' life was and is the paradigm of how this works.

Take, for example, Jesus' tendency to transgress the religious laws and usages of his time (to which we have already referred) in the service of his Gospel. Certainly the existing religious structure at that time did not accord the right to cure illness on the Sabbath unless it was immediately life-threatening. But Jesus' duty to God to personify God's love became his right to act accordingly. He acted in a way that appeared as disobedience to the existing legal structure.

CHRISTIANITY AND THE FORBEARANCE OF RIGHTS

This brings us to that which is ultimately unique about any Biblical picture of human rights, and that is that the individual

Christian has the freedom, even the duty to forbear his or her own rights of reciprocal justice. "You have heard that it was said, 'An eye for an eye and a tooth for a tooth.' But I say to you, Do not resist one who is evil. But if any one strikes you on the right cheek, turn to that one the other also; and if any one would sue you and take your coat, let that one have your cloak as well; and if any one forces you to go one mile, go with that one two miles. Give to the one who begs from you, and do not refuse the one who would borrow from you. . . . Love your enemies and pray for those who persecute you. . . . " (Matthew 5:38-43.) Christians are admonished to forbear their own rights of justice, reciprocity, even perhaps of compensation. An eye for an eye and a tooth for a tooth is a traditional statement of reciprocal justice. But Jesus tells the Christians to forbear their justice, forbear their rights, not to resist one who is evil but, as Paul says, to overcome evil with good. Mechanisms of violence, even though justified, ultimately destroy the rights of others, innocent or not. One cannot love one's enemy and kill that enemy at the same time.

Christians have a duty to give up certain human rights. In 1 Corinthians 9 Paul asks, "Am I not free?" and goes on to enumerate the human rights of free people. In verse 15, however, he says "But I have made no use of any of these rights . . . ." because he recognizes that the exercise of his own human rights can possibly compromise the Gospel he preaches. In order to be sure of exemplifying the Ways of the Kingdom, "Why not rather suffer wrong? Why not rather be defrauded?" (1 Corinthians 6:7.) than to go about securing one's own rights? A Christian, as Luther said, may be called to abdicate natural rights and take on suffering.[24] But may the Christian disregard the rights of others?

How does a Christian advocate human rights for the needy or the poor or the oppressed and at the same time remain true to the demands of Scripture and to the Spirit of God to honor free choice and to refrain from the means of violence in so doing?[25] How does a Christian advocate human rights for the powerless, the needy, the oppressed, after deliberately subjecting himself or herself to the same condition through the forbearance of his or her rights to justice and reciprocity? Probably the most seductive idea alive in the church today is the notion that Christians have an *obligation* to acquire and maintain both personal and institutional wealth, status, and political power (seen as rights in our culture) in order to use those as tools effectively to advocate and perfect the rights of those who are oppressed.

Hugh Koop writes the following:

> Since the Christian ethic is obviously an ethic of obligation or duty, how can human rights play any role of significance? The Christian life finds its paradigm in the sacrificial life of Christ. Can there be any room for agapic love where rights prevail? Here again the problem is illusory. The most fundamental duties arise because of the rights of others. Only when we respond to their rights are we responsive to our duties. Agapic love never denies but persistently transforms human rights.
>
> A series of possible situations can demonstrate this apology. When we are faced with the competing claims between two or more parties we cannot ignore their rights. Along with an analysis of the facts comes a determination of their respective rights. The loving thing to do may well be more than the determination of the right thing to do. It will never be less. Love's concerns are not attained apart from the concerns of justice. The situation becomes more difficult, however, when the competing claims emerge between oneself and others. Is it not, in this situation, more loving to abandon one's own rights as well as one's own interests, to serve the claims of the other? Before the hasty response, note first that the rights one claims may well be representative of the rights of others. To give up one's own rights may thus be doing an injustice to the other one represents as well. Proceeding to more difficult ground the situation may involve competing claims between oneself and the other with no additional involvements. By elimi-

nating the representation of others we are clearly in a different situation. Here too, the abandonment of rights may include the abandonment of duties. The maintenance of one's rights may be the necessary means of serving the other, for example by instructing him in his duties as well as his rights, by presenting the realities of human existence to the other.[26]

The forbearance of our own rights is entirely a higher concept of love over justice as enunciated in the Sermon on the Mount. But Koop feels that in some instances the forbearance of one's rights may do harm to others and certainly in the area that we are most concerned with here—advocating the rights of the oppressed. The abandonment of one's rights can be devastating to those who would remain in a position of oppression presumably as a result of that abandonment. Does not the sinner under God possess certain rights? Can we abandon the criminal to the death penalty simply by saying that the state operates under a different set of ethics or laws and that the Christian can separate, retreat, and abandon the state and its values to those who choose that kingdom? But if we decide that, as Christians, we have a duty and obligation to perfect the rights of others, when these rights are within the legal realm, where most often they are, may the Christian simply adopt the means of established law or lawlessness to garner these rights for the oppressed? The Christian is called to a theology of liberation, but this does not assume that the means must be secular; and by secular, I mean the tools of force and violence. Jesus, the liberator, liberated us with nonviolence, but also with violence done to himself on the Cross. It would appear to the secular mind that he abandoned his right to justice and self-defense at a time when his advocacy was desperately needed. We can do no other. Whether the oppressed call on us for violence or not, Jesus calls us to be nonviolent and at the same time to be involved; not to be of the kingdom of the world but at the same time to be in the midst of it.

The cutting edge of an investigation, from a Christian perspective, is the *means* by which we claim the rights of others. This means must be nonviolent. Even in response to institutional violence against the oppressed (who are usually not powerful enough to do violence) violence cannot be used for their benefit. As Tolstoy wrote, "if once we admit the right of any man to resist by violence what he regards as evil, every other man has equally the right to resist by violence what he regards as evil."[27] For every time violence is used, a violation takes place. And a violation is an abridgment of the rights of someone, somewhere. There is much good in the law, but institutional violence to enforce the law is not part of that good. There is much good in morality and ethics, but the absence of faith and the grace of Jesus makes them incomplete. We do find a complete and holistic theology of justice and rights in the Christian principle of agapic love. We are always free to give that love. No institution, legal, political, or ethical, can in any way prevent us from giving love.

ADVOCATES FOR THE OPPRESSED

The Christian Declaration on Human Rights states that: "We understand the basic theological contribution of the Christian faith to be the grounding of fundamental human rights and God's rights on God's claim on human beings."[28] God's claim on human beings requires us, makes it our duty, to become advocates for the rights of the oppressed. But God's claim on us also requires us to be advocates using the means that God has exemplified for Christians: the principles of the Sermon on the Mount as the method toward the goals of the Magnificat of Mary, Matthew 25, and Luke 4. Human beings have rights; but there are those human beings who are so oppressed that they are powerless. As Christians, we have a duty to overcome that oppression through the power of God, through the means God has given us. The minimum we can return for God's grace is justice without violence, love unto suffering and persecution, and witness without fear of consequences.

We should not be tempted, however, by a desire for immediate results, for success, for winning. The perfection of human rights from a Christian perspective must always take into consideration, unlike legal and moral counterparts, that perfection may not come in the way we envision, or may not come at all in our lifetime. The perfection of human rights from a Christian perspective is fundamentally God's business, and the outcome of faithful human effort is always, finally, in God's hands. So, essentially, what we look forward to is not effectiveness but significance, not winning but witnessing, hoping the while that the power of the witness will overcome in a manner which God desires.

We began this investigation by looking into ways of speaking about rights, how such language functions in the discipline of ethics and in our society. Often we are co-opted by institutional thinking into positing a theology of justice and human rights rather than a theology of righteousness and relationships.

Righteousness is a thoroughly religious concept, never mentioned in the courts or in the secular, political forum. Justice, however, is one of those cultural terms that transcend law, politics, and religion. Unless we are very careful with its use, our language may get us into trouble.[29] The same is true of the quest for rights. "Rights" is often an adversary term. Someone has a right, someone has a duty, someone has a claim, someone has an obligation. The next step is enforcement and enforcement leads to violence. Rights and duties quite often divide people. Labor unions have rights against employers and vice versa. Labor unions should not be needed in a Christian community. It is only when community breaks down that rights need to be defended. In a true Christian community or Christian society there would be no necessity for rights, because what we would be dealing with is sharing—with living with trusting relationships and not with adversarial relationships. "Justice" has much to do with adversarial dealings in the secular world and its narrow meaning has been taken over by the religious world because some religious people feel they must go into the secular world accepting its language and concepts before they can practice justice or affect that world in any way. It is possible to be in that world but not of it.

THE RELATIONSHIP OF RIGHTEOUSNESS TO RIGHTS

Righteousness in the Old Testament is the fulfillment of the demands of a relationship, whether that relationship be with persons or with God. "Righteousness as a forensic concept is not an impartial decision between two parties, based on a legal norm such as is known in Western law."[30] The constant plea of the prophets is for righteousness, for restoration of the foundations of communal life, that is, relational life. Obedience to a law does not make any person righteous. The relationship of Yahweh, the relationship of faith is primary. Were righteousness to depend solely on the fulfillment of the law, any sin would shut off the sinner from God's grace. But such is not the case. Yahweh's righteousness is never solely an act of condemnation or punishment. There is no verse in the Old Testament in which Yahweh's righteousness is equated with Yahweh's vengeance toward the sinner. Not even Isaiah 5:16 or 10:22 should be understood in such a manner. Because Yahweh's righteousness is the restoration of a right to the one from whom it has been taken, it at the same time includes punishment of the evil-doer; but the punishment is an integral part of the restoration. Discipline and salvation go hand in hand for Yahweh. Yahweh's righteousness is first and foremost saving. What gives oppressed Israel, or the afflicted person within Israel, ground for hope in Yahweh's deliverance is not his or her own sinlessness. Human righteousness consists not in ethical or moral blamelessness. Righteousness, rather, is based upon faith, the fulfillment of one's relationship with Yahweh.

For Christians the test of any relationship is compassion. God compassionately upheld the covenant, even when legally broken by the Israelites, by sending Jesus, not in justice but to restore the relationships. Whoever heard of such a foolish or risky kind of relationship, then, as that enunciated by Jesus! "When you give a feast, invite the poor, the maimed, the lame, the blind, and you will be blessed, because they cannot repay you." (Luke 14:13ff.)

The question of rights comes up only when righteousness breaks down on the part of one party or in the case of communities, on the part of one community against another community. We should be very careful when people come to us complaining about the violation of rights, careful that we do not jump to the secular gun and adopt the mechanisms of the political world in order to respond. We may seek out the protection and restoration of rights and forget that deep down, before the question of rights and duties and secular justice, is the necessity first to restore the relationship. This means to deal with people on the basis of a relational theology that recognizes that not any one person or group is totally wrong or totally right. What is needed more than the enforcement of rights is the mediation, arbitration, and resolution of disputes aimed at the restoration of the relationship. And if there was no relationship to begin with, then the relationship must be created. Only religion, in part, ethics, and hardly ever law or politics can accomplish this. Law and politics cannot restore broken relationships because those institutions are based inherently on institutional violence. Ethics cannot because ethics is totally philosophical and has no faith concept. Religion, yes, because in its original, charismatic, and non-institutional form, it is complete, holistic, and it can look at a conflict of rights and duties and proceed to a restoration of the relationship, not just the restoration of a particular right of a given person or group. It is only in the radical ethic of Christian faith that the foolishness of voluntary poverty and pacifism may be seen as part of God's plan of righteousness.

Is there a difference between righteousness and justice? Is there a difference between justice and love?[31] Or are we just playing semantic games? In my twenty years of legal practice I have heard the word "justice" over and over again in courtrooms. I have never heard the word "righteousness" mentioned once. I am not saying that justice is a totally irrelevant concept, nor is a theology based upon it. I am saying that justice, whether you call it secular or theological, is not a holistic concept. It is a moral value of very high note. But it is also the moral value that gave birth to the just-war theory. It is the moral value that creates paranoia over rights, those rights quite often being my rights over against your duties rather than my duties respecting your rights. The concept of justice, if not completed through a marriage with religious righteousness, becomes ego-centered, nation-centered, even thing-centered.

Consider the years of the civil-rights movement spent gaining rights for Black minorities. Those rights consisted in being able to live in the mainstream of American society. Today we know what it is like to have the right to live in the mainstream of America. It means having a good job, living in a fairly rich environment separated from the oppressed, and being obligated to pay inflated federal taxes for the purpose of building horrendous weapons of war. Were those rights worth it all? It was worthwhile obtaining the right, the freedom. But the obtaining of a civil right is not complete. We need to investigate further, beyond rights to relationships, beyond justice to agapic love.

Consider in closing this dilemma: A friend of mine was a bombardier in World War II; in justice (and I don't argue the justice of his attitude and acts) he dropped bombs on Japan. How could he do it? He couldn't see the Japanese—no relationship, just a concept of justice. Would a relationship have made it more difficult for my friend to drop those bombs? He says so: "I couldn't drop it if I had seen what devastation it had done. But I wanted to drop it because I knew it was *just*. I did it for others, not myself." If the "others" he knew and loved included Japanese as well as Americans, he would have acted differently. Righteousness, the theology of relationships, breaks down the justice of violence. We must pursue a theology of righteousness in human relationships because in the end a theology of justice and rights can never alone be the answer—the agapic love of Jesus alone is the answer because it makes all else whole. "But seek first his kingdom and his righteousness, and all these things shall be yours as well." (Matthew 6:33.)

Around the world, largely caused by the superpowers' own economic and political domination of it, there are people in great misery, there are people calling for liberation and finding their liberation in the same old way, in the same old political revolution. There must be another conquering hero than the conquering hero of political revolution. It is to this other conquering hero that we now turn as we conclude our study and reflection upon the alternative community that must be ours if we are to overcome the political, economic, and religious temptations of this world, as we live among the nations as if the Kingdom has come.

CHAPTER NINE

"SEE THE CONQUERING HERO COMES"

See, the conquering hero comes!
Sound the trumpets, beat the drums:
Sports prepare, the laurel bring,
Songs of triumph to him sing.
See the god like youth advance.
Breathe the flutes, and lead the dance:
Myrtle-wreaths and roses twine.
To deck the hero's brow divine.
Sing unto God and high affections raise
To crown this conquest in unmeasured praise.
Sweet flow the strains that strike my feasted ear:
Angels might stoop from Heaven to hear
The comely songs ye sing to Israel's Lord and King.
. . .
Rejoice, O Judah, and in songs divine,
With Cherubim and Seraphim harmonious join.
Hallelujah! Amen!

I have a weakness for triumphal music. Handel's oratorio *Judas Maccabaeus* is one of my favorites and the chorale quoted above never fails to stir my blood and conjure images in my head of the most blatant and glorious and decadent kind of triumphal parade! Perhaps I suffer some guilt about these feelings, given the beliefs I have expressed throughout these pages. At any rate, it has occurred to me lately to deomythologize this chorus and these words and to take them back for my own purposes. Upon investigation I uncovered the following history.

Handel used these words supplied to him by his friend, the Rev. Thomas Morell, in 1745 as part of an oratorio entitled *Joshua* and later translated for the 1746 oratorio, *Judas Maccabeas.* George II was king of England in 1745 when the last attempt of the Stuarts to regain the throne occurred. The young pretender, Charles Stuart, landed on the Scottish mainland and joined his rebel army. After some victories, he was finally vanquished on April 16, 1746, near Inverness by an army led by George II's youngest son, William, Duke of Cumberland. The Duke's elder brother, Frederick, Prince of Wales, requested that Handel write an oratorio to honor William's victorious return to London. So, under the triumphal veil, Cumberland becomes Judas Maccabeas defeating Antiochus Epiphanes.

Antiochus IV came from the line of Antiochus I, the Syrian Seleucid ruler. Antiochus called himself Epiphanes, that is, "god manifest." In mocking hatred the Jews dubbed him "Epimanes"—madman. Antiochus thought himself to be a manifestation of the Greek god Zeus, and had himself pictured on a 5th century BC coin. He ordered Zeus' statue to be erected in a place of honor in the Jerusalem Temple. The Jews condemned the act, calling it the "abomination of desolation" or the "terrible sin" from Daniel 8. To my mind, the words and triumphal music commemorating any warrior hero may equally be appreciated for the powerful entry of the world's foremost nonviolent prevailer—Joshua, or more accurately, Yeshua, the anointed one of God—or as we know him better in our western language, Jesus, the Christ. Obviously the conquering hero comes to undo those who would pose as god manifest. As the nations put forth their idols of economic, political, and religious temptations, Jesus, the God manifest, overcomes Antiochus Epiphanes and all other such pretenders.

This oratorio, ironically, was originally entitled *Joshua*. Handel's hero was a bloody one, like the first Joshua. The Duke was nicknamed "Billy the Butcher" for the violent reprisals initiated after his victory. Yeshua does not come in that way. But this story of the ways of nations may point us to the manner in which he comes, for come he does. The nations of the world, which Jesus said would hate his followers, were on a collision course toward mutual self-destruction then as now. The world has not learned over the 2000 years since the time of Jesus how to practice his teachings. Instead it has distorted both what he said and what he meant. That is, it both rewrote and reinterpreted his call to us to truly love our neighbor, even our enemies, and without qualification; to live simply, and to witness to the powers and principalities which obstruct this way of life. From the time of the Assyrians, Babylonians, Persians, Greeks, Romans, Egyptians, to the modern Arabs, Israelis, Britons, North Americans and Russians, secular culture has accepted the world religious, economic, and political systems as normative, and thus has given in to the political, economic, and religious temptations of Satan.

THE RADICAL CHURCH

The Romans looked upon the first Christians as atheists belonging to an illegal sect. Atheist, because they did not worship the gods of Rome, and illegal because the Christians denounced as demons the gods who protected the fortunes of the Roman state. Today, North American governments look upon Christianity as the broad base upon which it can rely for support in thwarting the communist threat. The North American governments view Christians as God-worshipers, not atheists. But have we, in this Constantinian trade-off, contracted long ago, sold our souls to a demon we do not even recognize?

In a recent interview, Philip Berrigan said, "Something has happened to Americans . . . a high point in demonism—a form of possession by the bomb, which seemingly slammed every door except one, slavish complicity in the lockstep towards nuclear doom."[1] The beast that died but rose again has become our god. (Revelation 13.) Its prophet, in different guises over the centuries, has urged Christians to feed it with their tax dollars and their unquestioning cooperation. The religious resistance movement, as part of the larger peace movement in the United States, is a response to this deception.

In the face of violations of international law and human rights, there is an urgency now felt by people of religious conscience who recognize that the nation-state is out of control. People of conscience believe that the danger of the destruction of the world by nuclear missile and first-strike weaponry may be dramatically exposed by the use of nonviolent, direct action. People across the land are risking arrest, trial, conviction, and imprisonment in the face of always more sophisticated weaponry, human rights' eradications, and military anarchy. Before us may very well be tragic Armageddon, brought about not only by the devil incarnate, but also by our own dark side taking control because good people refuse to act.

Religious as well as political institutions, church and state, have been slow to recognize the courage of these modern-day crusaders who take up the cross of holy obedience. We make heros and heroines of our past holy law-breakers like Gandhi, King, and Dorothy Day, but the Berrigan brothers, Liz McAlister, the Douglasses, and Cesar Chavez, and countless more in a growing swell of resistance, are alive and well and still anathema in most church circles. Churches cling to their dependence upon civil religion through tax status, exemptions, and property privileges. The greatest effect on church-state relations is precisely the ineffectiveness of the church. Will the churches free themselves from this unholy grasp? Are they willing to give up corporate status and government "benefits" for Christian community?

The church community is called to be radical. That is a call to give up tax exemptions and land privileges voluntarily, and to be weaned from these advantages which the state has given the churches. The church of Jesus knows no such status. Its witness is religious, not political, although its actions have a profoundly political effect on the nation-state when it exercises its liberationist nonviolence for all to see and feel. The church is called to be radical, religious, and pacifist. Only through this call may it truly witness to the powers and principalities that have persisted as a temptation for us ever since Jesus in the wilderness thwarted those culturally religious, political, and economic temptations. He was tempted to give up his radical ministry and we are tempted to do the same. A church community is called to be radical; it must go to its roots, back to the Bible, back to the early Christians, back to the Holy Spirit, back to those historical heros and heroines who have given it its true meaning.

A church community must be religious and not merely "worship as usual." The alternative includes worship, thanksgiving, Eucharist, witness, and martyrdom. The church community must also be pacifist—it has to be pacifist. We can no longer injure. There is no such thing as a just war. We are *all* the children of one parent, God, making us true sisters and brothers; there is part of God in each of us, so how is it that we can contemplate harming or killing each other? The *culture* tells us that such killing is justified by such excuses as "godless communism" or "terrorism." Under God's spirit such claims have no power and no reality; certainly, they do not justify killing.

The roots of the church that we strive to recapture look like this:

Nonviolent, not violent, not even justly violent; but rather justly pacifist.

Justice, not just secular justice, but justice including active love; justice that is righteous. The state's highest constitutional value is justice, yet the church is called to more. The roots are not legalistic but relational.

Attitudes, intent, motive are as important as our actions, notwithstanding the judges' cries of "irrelevance and inadmissability" in our North American courts today.[2] We do not live by the consequences of our actions, but by the rightness of our attitude in action, and the trust that the consequences are in God's hands.

Faith, not proof or evidence, is our empowerment. We act unilaterally, not bi-laterally or multi-laterally. Translated from political to religious language, this means we risk harm and suffering up front as an example for others to see and then to follow. We walk the extra mile. Survival and security are very low on our list of priorities.[5] We are rather called in powerlessness and worldly insecurity to risk our survival and to be a presence in a world that is countercultural, a light to the nations, a community of Christians, rather than a corporation of capitalists or a collective of socialists. The Gospel of Jesus knows of no profits, and no boundaries of land, property, or money protected by computerized war machines. The land is not Caesar's in fee simple absolute, but is a trusteeship given by God for our common earthly use. When that trust is violated, as it is when warheads become more valuable than refugees, then the land reverts to its rightful Owner, its Creator.

The call has gone out. We live in times of necessity and emergency. Necessity is laid upon us. There is precious little time for us to witness to these powers and principalities and to disarm them with the power of God's Holy Spirit. Empowered in our weakness we seek not peace through strength—the way of the nations—but strength through peace—the way of Our Lord.

One of the most insightful writers of our day on the systems of the world is Jacques Ellul. *In Season, Out of Season* outlines Jacques Ellul's life and activism. He describes his own personal quest to overcome the worldly powers:

> ... it is certain that the failure of almost all the efforts I was able to make in what I consider a revolutionary direction gave me a very strong feeling that this world is powerful, rigid and cunning, and that radical political change is impossible in this world. . . . I thought that the world is separated from God and therefore evil. I still believe it. But whereas I used to believe that God's judgment separated the lost, the condemned (to show God's justice) from others who were saved (to show God's love),

I am now convinced that there is universal salvation, and
I firmly believe that human history is leading to the new
creation and the resurrection.[4]

This idea is nowhere more clearly enunciated than at the end
of the New Testament, Chapter 21 of the Book of Revelation,
where a new earth and a new heaven come together.

Philip Berrigan comments: "The Bible teaches that the seat
of the Kingdom is to be this world. When Christ conversed
with Pilate he asserted 'my Kingdom is not (derived) of this
world,' i.e., it does not draw on the violent means of this world.
The Beatitudes of Matthew maintain 'Blessed are the meek
because they will possess the earth.' (Matthew 5:5.) Revelation
speaks in the same vein: 'You have made of them for our God
a Kingdom of priests and they will reign *on earth*.' "[5]

I believe that in spite of any threat of nuclear holocaust, if
we do not by our own faithful witness help to avert the destruction of the world, it cannot finally be destroyed because
God has willed a new heaven and new earth. Or, better said,
it may be destroyed by our madness but it will rise again with
God's power to form the new heaven and new earth. How much
better though for us to live now as if the Kingdom has come;
to be witnesses and prophets of the impending destruction, and
the possibilities of its avoidance, and the bringing of a new
Kingdom of heaven and earth out of our own trials by God's
grace. Do not mistake me. As Ellul says, "There is no possible
continuity between man's actions on earth and God's establishment of his Kingdom. Or in another way, that one can't
obtain salvation ... by an accumulation of works or by a successful spiritual life, and that man can't achieve good on his
own. . . . The good of which Scripture speaks is not the equivalent of moral goodness but a condition of conformity to God's
will."[6] This is what is called for—a conformity to God's will in
witness and martyrdom and simplicity and nonviolence is all
that we can offer. Any significance and eventful effectiveness
that comes of that, any redeeming of this earth, is in God's
hands.

Ellul has said over and over again that if Christians were awake, they would understand that society absolutely must be changed. It is actually within their faith that a revolutionary movement should take seed, a movement that has nothing in common with either the revolutionary bluff of leftists or conservation of the status quo by rightists:

> We cannot be satisfied with changing just a constitution or a few structures. We must carry out a fundamental transformation of beliefs, of prejudices and of presuppositions. We must do an iconoclastic work, destroying the false gods of our society. For I believe it is on this deep level that the revolution is decided, and not just in modification of economic organization. But at the same time we must have the courage and lucidity for this questioning. All this seemed to me to be an inevitable consequence of the Gospel and the prophets, but not limited to an intellectual or an ideological change; it necessarily implies a resulting socio-political revolution.[7]

As we undertake to greet the conquering hero with our own energies and witness, how might Christian theologies of politics be understood and applied to this activity?

THREE THEOLOGIES OF POLITICS

There are at least three theologies of politics dominating the political scene today in predominantly Christian countries. The first and most familiar is a conservative or traditional theology of politics—the electoral or legal approach. Under this view, Christians are told that it is their duty to register to vote, follow the example of John Kennedy, Pat Robertson, George Bush, Jesse Jackson, or whomever, to seek political office and thus bring religious and Christian motivation to the forefront of the secular scene. This position assumes the basic goodness and rightness of secular law and legal institutions (and is often justified by "Romans 13" or "giving to Caeser."). This approach is conservative vis a vis the two other approaches. On issues of abortion, capital punishment or "National Defense," the major party adherents, whether Republican (conservative) or Democrat (liberal), push the American Dream—wealth, weapons and waste—to a greater or lesser degree.

The second, I call the liberal approach. It is primarily expressed in liberationist revolutionary movements which seek, with Christian motivation, to overthrow or replace oppressive governments and institute in their stead governments with Christian-Marxist variations. An example of this motif is the Nicaraguan experiment where Ernesto Cardenal, a Catholic priest, holds a secular position in the government along with Marxists.

This approach, like the conservative electoral approach, depends ultimately upon violence as a means of social change. In the first conservative, electoral mode, law is defended by violence; in the second liberal revolutionary mode, violence is seen as the means to overthrow conservative legalists for a more humane regime. More recently some liberationist theological movements have moved toward pacifism, i.e., base communities.

The third Christian theology of politics may be described as radical and structural, and is enunciated today by those theologians who are developing what is called political theology as opposed to liberation theology. Academic political theology comes primarily out of Western Europe and liberation theology out of South and Central America. The African-American, feminist, and pacifist movements all have identifications with both liberation and political theology.

Openings for Marxist-Christian Dialogue, written in 1968, and edited by Thomas W. Ogletree, quotes Engels from his "Preface to Marxist Analysis of the Civil War in France" (1871):

> According to the philosophical conception, the state is "the realization of the idea" or the Kingdom of God on earth, translated into philosophical terms, the sphere in which eternal truth and justice is or should be realized. And from

this follows a superstitious reverence for the state and everything connected with it. . . . People think that they have taken quite an extraordinarily bold step forward when they have rid themselves of the belief in hereditary monarchy and swear by the democratic republic. In reality, however, the state is nothing but a machine for the oppression of one class by another, in the democratic republic no less than in the monarchy. At best the state is an evil inherited by the proletariat after its victorious struggle for class supremacy, . . . until such time as a generation reared in new, free, social conditions is able to throw the entire lumber of the state on the scrap heap.[8]

Apparently Engels was no less idealistic than was Leo Tolstoy, who saw the state as structurally wedded to violence. More than 100 years ago Tolstoy wrote:

My spiritual instructors taught me that the law of Jesus was divine, but, because of human weakness, impossible of practice, and that the grace of Jesus Christ alone could aid us to follow its precepts. And this instruction agreed with what I received in secular institutions and from the social organizations about me. I was so thoroughly possessed with this idea of the impracticability of the divine doctrine, the idea conformed so well with my desires, that not till the time of awakening did I realize its falsity. I did not see how impossible it was to confess Jesus and his doctrine *"Resist not evil" and at the same time deliberately assist in the organization of property, of tribunals, of governments, of armies; to contribute to the establishment of a polity entirely contrary to the doctrine of Jesus, and at the same time pray to Jesus . . . that we resist not evil. I did not see, what is very clear to me now, how much more simple it would be to organize a method of living conformable to the law of Jesus. . . .*[9]

Both Engels and Tolstoy indicate that the nation-state will fall from the weight of evil and violence inherent in its own structures. Tolstoy differs from Engels and the Marxists in his opinion on the use of violence to destroy or change the nation-state. Tolstoy believed that the rule of Jesus would never allow the use of violence for any end, good or bad.

Political theology, as a reaction to the consequences of the Enlightenment and secularization, tries to overcome the relegation of faith to personal, private, and individualistic aspects of life. It is primarily ecumenical and seeks to respond to secularization without using a recognition of God's presence in society as the justification for society's evils and injustices.

The base of political theology is the assumption that the modern world is secularized and that a new structure of government in a religious sense needs to be found to communalize and humanize our social endeavors. The church is seen as a non-worldly phenomenon, diametrically and definitionally opposed to the state. A disengagement of church from state is needed. At the same time, this disengagement is recognized as being highly political, just as Jesus was highly political in his disengagement from Caesar and the Pharisees.

Classical liberation theology, on the other hand, has responded to the oppression and injustices of an existing state and attempts to establish a new state that will be more just, less oppressive, and motivated by Christian principles adapted to an existing secular structure. Some liberation theologians point out the need to deal with an exploitative state *now*, and not to wait until some ideal system is discovered or evolved. They feel that secularization is not an absence of God but a commitment of the church to that order. They concentrate on the end, the need for social change, and they will adopt, at least in parts of Latin America, such means as will bring that end about as soon as possible.

The alternatives advocated by both the political theologians in Western Europe and the liberation theologians in Latin America have met with some resistance from the Vatican, which still espouses the conservative theology of politics. It seems that institutional churches, for the most part, accept the conservative electoral approach to politics as the only acceptable one because it is the only one of the three that refuses to admit lawbreaking for a higher conscience. Put another way, the conservative approach usually sees no apparent conflict between secular law and God's requirements.

The Vatican seems to be seriously concerned about liberation theology because it derives some motivation from Marxism. In a statement on liberation theology, the Vatican said that, "the overthrow by means of revolutionary violence of structures . . . is not ipso facto the beginning of a just regime."[10] This is true. However, the Vatican has also had a hard time dealing with liberation theology because the Roman Catholic Church's traditional "just-war" theory has sanctioned the use of violence only *by those in authority* as a proper moral means to a good end. Liberation theologians often justify the use of violence but from a revolutionary perspective and also as a means to a good end. The Roman Catholic just-war theory has never been extended to support revolutionary or rebellious violence as opposed to violence instituted by those in legal authority, whether kings or presidents. However, in 1986 a Vatican document approved of armed revolution in some limited cases.

It also seems to be the Vatican's view that "in the logic of Marxist thought, the analysis is inseparable from the practice and from the conception of history to which this practice is linked. . . . Consequently for the Marxist, only those who engage in the struggle can work out the analysis correctly. The only true consciousness, then, is a partisan consciousness. . . . There is no truth, they pretend, except in and through the partisan practice."[11] This may or may not be peculiar to Marxism. It is certainly a concept shared by Christian liberation theologians and political theologians, and by people who have worked in the civil-rights movement, in the Gandhian movement, and even in Jesus' own movement. One cannot analyze an event in a vacuum.[12] One needs to participate. One cannot truly understand what it means to live in intentional community unless one lives in intentional community. One cannot truly understand what it means to suffer unless one suffers.

Another Vatican criticism is the impatience and "desire for results" which has led some Christians, despairing of every other method, to turn to what they call Marxist analysis: "An intolerable and explosive situation requires effective action that cannot be put off. Effective action presupposes a scientific analysis of the structural causes of poverty. Marxism now provides us with the means to make such an analysis, they [liberation theologians] say. Then one simply has to apply the analysis to the third world situation, especially in Latin America."[13]

All this Marxist logic is a deviation from Christian faith and living, according to the Vatican. But is there that much deviation? Some Marxists espouse violence, the Vatican espouses just violence, some liberation theologians espouse violence—all from a vision of justice. Cicero espoused violence (providing the basis adopted by the church for the just-war theory), and American presidents and Russian presidiums espouse violence. Violence seems to be the common denominator of religious, political, and economic institutions, both on the conservative right and the liberal left.

The "political theologians" are on the edge of something radically new. Many of them are not pacifists but are emerging pacifists. That is, they are willing to concede that new structures cannot be created or originated in violence because violence simply begets violence. True liberation cannot be born in blood—not even that of the oppressor.

We must abandon "effectiveness." We must follow the cross, the footsteps of Jesus, even in abject failure, refusing to use violence against the Pharisees and against the Romans. The future placed in God's hands will then be assured of God's effectiveness. A nonviolent new heaven and earth will emerge through the impact of God's grace and power as women and men make themselves subject to God as a result of their forbearance of violence and their affirmation of social love.

One difference between some liberation theologians and the political theologians is aptly illustrated in the continuing dialogue between Daniel Berrigan, S.J., and Ernesto Cardenal. When asked, Berrigan said that his problem with Cardenal "is the assumption on his part, more or less overtly expressed, that the revolution is the Kingdom of God. I have difficulty with this casting a religious aura around a secular and violent conflict."[14]

The grass-roots movement of nonviolent resistance in rich North America leads to military bases, to nuclear weapons manufacturers, to jails. It offers the alternative that we nonviolently follow Jesus as lawbreakers to an end which incarnates now the inbreaking of the Kingdom of God upon political institutions and into the hearts and souls of people in this world. Although we "fail" by the world's standards—spending seemingly wasted efforts on hospitality for guests who come and go with no worldly "improvement" in their lot—the message and authority of the God of the Jews and the Christians is that at the end of this journey of faith there will be a new heaven and earth brought about through the cooperation of God and his followers creating his Kingdom action by action and jail sentence by jail sentence.

It seems to me that to undergird the radical church community, we need a social theology that takes the best of Marxism, liberation theology, political theology, and traditional theology. Marxism's recognition that nation-state structures are a major cause of oppression and alienation among people is valid. From liberation theology we gain the assurance that oppressed and exploited people need to be liberated and that the Gospel provides the motivation for that liberation. Political theology points out that secularization is the problem, and that reformation or revolution of secularized structures creates nothing but temporarily enlightened secular structures. And traditional theology reminds us that in grace, prayer, and fasting is found the power for the new revolution. This combination leads to a *radical* theology of pacifism, equality, simplicity, and community.

The Kingdom of God and not the nation-state of Russia, the United States, or Nicaragua, or any other country is the answer. I think this alternative, for Christians, the radical structural one, which takes the best from Marxism and liberation and political theology, as well as from traditional Christian teaching and

Biblical understanding, will pave the way, ultimately, for an experiment in Kingdom living which has heretofore been an unexperienced adventure by most Christians in this world. The call is not for a model of failed theocracy, but rather for an innovative new "mission" serving each other, and restoring the meaning of "neighbor" to a sick world.

In *Against the Nations: War and Survival in a Liberal Society*, Stanley Hauerwas says: "Within a world of violence and injustice Christians can take the risk of being forgiven and forgiving. They are able to break the circle of violence as they refuse to become part of those institutions of fear that promise safety by the destruction of others. As a result some space, both psychological and physical, is created where we can be at rest in world that knows not who is its king."[15] Hauerwas' dictum is not a doctrine, though, that calls us to quietly wait for the end of time. According to Ron Perrin, professor of political theory at the University of Montana, Hauerwas' insistence, on the contrary, that no human enterprise has value if it is not placed in contrast with ultimate and final goals, carries the conviction of the radical activist. "No state," Hauerwas declares, "will keep itself limited, no constitution or idealogy is significant to that task unless there is a body of people separated from the nation that is willing to say no to the state's claim on their loyalties. . . . Demons are released whenever human power is divinized."[16] Hauerwas has clearly enunciated once again the imperative of saying NO to the nation-state and of being against the nation. Jeremiah long ago warned us about the ways of the nations. The history of the world has given us repeated, sad experience of the idols of the nations. And it is the vision of Revelation that leaves us at the end of the Bible with the optimism that the nations may be healed.

HEALING THE NATIONS

Our call is to live as if the Kingdom has come, to pray that the Kingdom will fully come soon, as it has been coming in power since the time of Christ, even as the nations continue to live with their idols. In so doing, we may very well be the witnesses who will bring on the conquering hero who will redeem the nations and make them holy once more.

Christians are a people whose imagination has been challenged by a God who has invited us into an otherwise unimaginable reality.[17] We have heard of this Kingdom, we have read about it, and yet we have lived in another kingdom our entire lives. We are a people whose imagination has been challenged with an invitation. How else will we find our way into that Kingdom except through our imagination? As we imagine that Kingdom, our imagination will be empowered with the grace that will direct us to it.

We are thus faced with not only changing our institutions but also with changing ourselves. The difficulty with changing our institutions is immense and can become very discouraging, but there is no excuse for not beginning with ourselves and our personal relations to those institutions.

Each great political leader started at that point alone. Jesus, in the wilderness, Fox at the steeplehouse, King, Gandhi, Day, and more. When Jesus gave his first sermon at the home synagogue, he had no followers. Yet he chose to read Isaiah's great call to radicalize the institution to those present:

> The Spirit of the Lord is upon me
> because he has anointed me to preach good news to the
> poor.
> He has sent me to proclaim release to the captives
> and recovery of sight to the blind,
> to set at liberty those who are oppressed,
> to proclaim the acceptable year of the Lord. (Luke 4:18-
> 19.)

To proclaim the acceptable year of the Lord is a direct reference to the Jubilee Year. In a sense he was calling for its reinstitution while at the same time his own lifestyle was committed to one of voluntary poverty and simplicity. He was, in fact, saying that his life would henceforth incarnate the Jubilee.

Before he was through there, his listeners rose up to drive him out of town.

A catholic (universal) community developed among Jesus' early followers. That community aligned itself more with the poor than the rich, more with the prisoner than the prosecutor, more with the physically blind than the intellectually blind, more with the oppressed than the oppressor. That community dedicated itself to a simple life and to restructuring institutions. It did this to restore and reconcile the poor and the rich, not to alienate them from each other. Truly the ancient church was then our mother! Clearly we are not that community now. But we could become such once again: a community *of* the poor, the prisoner, the oppressed, the lame. We must meet the challenge of our own ecclesiastical roots and not only work for the rights of people within the existing economic, political, and religious institutions, but also act as a catalyst for the nation-state to be true to its own moral values. Even beyond that, we must work for an alternative self grounded in a nurturing community with a lifestyle of voluntary poverty and simplicity, radical pacifism and resistance, and egalitarian and communal, religious sharing—an outpouring of ancient Catholicism, Anabaptist Protestantism, and historic Quakerism.

> *See, the conquering hero comes!*
> *Sound the trumpets, beat the drums:*
> *Sports prepare, the laurel bring,*
> *Songs of triumph to him sing.*

When the conquering hero comes at a time we know not— would we rather he find us living as if the Kingdom has come in the midst of nations, or living as if the nations have overcome the Kingdom? If "the Way" is now clearer how we may attempt to live in community, how we may witness to the existing nations round about us, how we may serve humankind, then we have begun our triumph over the religious, political, and economic temptations, and cooperated in the healing of nations and the emergence of a new heaven and earth.

The conquering hero surely comes—prepare the Way of the Lord!

Notes

Introduction

1. Baum, Bobbs-Merrill Co., Indianapolis, Ind., 1903. My criticism is one of the play and not specifically of the book itself, which has been interpreted as a whole in other than violent themes.
2. Nickalls (ed.), *Journal of George Fox*, Religious Society of Friends, London, 1975, p. 65.
3. *Ibid.*, p. 357.
4. Rosenzweig (ed.), *The Wisdom of Tolstoy*, Philosophical Library, New York, 1968, pp. 20-21.
5. See Durland, *No King But Caesar?*, Herald Press, Scottsdale, Pa., 1975, pp. 30-49. Justice in the Hebrew Scriptures is first described as "the way of the Lord (Yahweh)," Genesis 18:19.
6. Verses 1-3, the *Didache* (c. 100 AD) or *The Teaching of the Twelve Apostles*. This writing is thought to be the earliest handbook of Church rules. Its author is unknown.
7. Jeremiah, Ch. 10ff. The imagery pictures well our modern manifestation of rockets and missiles.
8. See Chapter 2, "Moses and Violence" for a detailed explanation.
9. *The Book of Revelation*, Ch. 13 and elsewhere images religious and political beasts.
10. Kittel (ed.), Vol. II, Eerdmans Pub. Co., Grand Rapids, Mich., 1974, p. 364.
11. *Ibid.*, p. 368. e.g., Isaiah 8:9.
12. Harnack, *What is Christianity?*, Harper Torchbooks, New York, 1957; Brandon, *Jesus and the Zealots*, Charles Scribners Sons, New York, 1967. For a treatment of various images of the historical Jesus, see Durland, *No King But Jesus! Matthew 25 and the Biblical Basis of Christian Nonviolent Assistance* (doctoral dissertation), University Microfilms International, Ann Arbor, Mich., 1977, Chapter 3, "The Historical Jesus: Violent or Nonviolent?"
13. McGill, *Suffering: A Test of Theological Method*, Geneva Press, Philadelphia, Pa., 1968, p. 23.
14. The author served in the U.S. Army from 1954 to 1957 as a private and corporal and in the reserve in 1966-67 as a captain.
15. McGill, *op. cit.*, p. 21.
16. Comblin, *The Church and the National Security State*, Orbis Books, Maryknoll, New York, 1979, pp. 3-4.
17. *Ibid.*, p. 4-5.
18. *Ibid.*, p. 6.

19. *Ibid.*, p. 4.
20. Yoder, *The Politics of Jesus,* Eerdmans Pub. Co., Grand Rapids, Mich., 1972, p.14.
21. *Ibid.*
22. The phrase is suggested by its use in a book by Stanley Hauerwas, *Against the Nations: War and Survival in a Liberal Society,* Winston, New York, 1985, pp. 57-58.

Chapter One: YAHWEH AND THE PEOPLE OF GOD

1. Lind, *Yahweh is a Warrior: The Theology of Warfare in Ancient Israel,* Herald Press, Scottsdale, Pa., 1980, p. 44.
2. Brown, Fitzmeyer and Murphy (eds.) *Jerome Biblical Commentary,* Prentice-Hall, Englewood Cliffs, N.J., 1968, p. 19.
3. *Ibid.*, pp. 18-19.
4. *Harper Study Bible* (R.S.V.), Zondervan Pub. Co., Grand Rapids, Mich., 1971, p. 225, Note 20. 8.
5. Bruce, *Israel and the Nations,* Eerdmans Pub. Co., Grand Rapids, Mich., 1969, pp. 23-24.
6. David was politically a victim of kingship, economically of urban wealth and technology, religiously of a geographically confined "god." The example of the Rechabites to obey God's covenant emphasizing equality rather than Canaanite pyramidic feudalism was not followed. It might be added that with kingship came also an active prophetic witness which kings were called to obey.
7. Ellul, *The Politics of God and the Politics of Man,* Eerdmans Pub. Co., Grand Rapids, Mich., 1972, p. 17.
8. *Ibid.*, pp. 18-19.
9. I am indebted to Adolph Holl and his little book, *Jesus in Bad Company,* Holt, Rinehart and Winston, New York, 1972, for this understanding.
10. Montifiore and Loewe, *A Rabbinic Anthology,* Shocken, New York, 1974, p. 446.
11. *The Koran,* Penguin Books, Baltimore, Md., 1974, pp. 24, 28, 68, 185, 193, for some examples.
12. References concerning wealth and poverty are numerous: Genesis 1:28, 22, 26; Exodus 23:6; Leviticus 25:13, 25; Deuteronomy 8:18, 24:10-19, 28:11; Amos 2:6, 5:11; Job 21, 31:24, 47; Psalms 37:14, 37:25, 41:1, 49, 52:7, 62:10, 73:3, 107:9, 112, 113:7, 146:7, etc.
13. Ellul, *The Meaning of the City,* Eerdmans Pub. Co., Grand Rapids, Mich., 1970, pp. 1-9.
14. Bruce, *op. cit.*, p. 81.

290   William Durland

15. Bright, *The Kingdom of God: The Biblical Concept and Its Meaning for the Church*, Abingdon Press, Nashville, Tenn., 1953, p. 9.
16. *Ibid.*, p. 10.
17. *Ibid.*, p. 18.
18. *Ibid.*, p. 43.
19. *Ibid.*, p. 68.
20. Ricoeur, *The Symbolism of Evil*, Beacon Press, Boston, 1969, p. 57.
21. *Ibid.*, p. 62.

Chapter Two: JESUS AND HIS COMMUNITY

1. Mateos, "The Message of Jesus," *Sojourners*, Washington, D.C., July 1977, pp. 8-16.
2. Nolan, *Jesus Before Christianity*, Orbis Books, Maryknoll, New York, 1978.
3. Mateos, *op. cit.*, p. 9.
4. *Ibid.*, p. 10.
5. Berkhof, *Christ and the Powers*, Herald Press, Scottsdale, Pa., 1977.
6. Ellul, *The Meaning of the City, op. cit.*, pp 122-23, 125, 131.
7. Friedlander, *The Jewish Sources of the Sermon on the Mount*, DJAV Publishing House, New York, 1969, pp. 65-67.
8. Schnackenburg, *The Moral Teaching of the New Testament*, Herder and Herder, New York, 1966, pp. 83-84.
9. One of the theories concerning the original meaning of Matthew 25 is this: that Jesus is referring to his own group—in prison, as strangers, thirsty, hungry, sick, poor, from their persecutions for witnessing to his Gospel.
10. Chandler, *The Trial of Jesus From a Lawyer's Standpoint*, The Harrison Co., Atlanta, Ga., 1956.
11. Cassidy, *Jesus, Politics and Society: A Study of Luke's Gospel*, Orbis Books, Maryknoll, New York, 1978.
12. *Ibid.*, p. 77.
13. *Ibid.*
14. *Ibid.*, p. 77-78.
15. *Ibid.*, p. 79.
16. Moltmann, *The Crucified God*, Harper & Row, New York, 1980, p. 130.
17. *Ibid.*, p. 131.
18. *Ibid.*, p. 131-132.
19. He was crucified in a manner reserved for the political rebel and was clearly a seditious threat to Rome. His "holy obedience" in breaking the theocratic laws is well documented (Matthew 12, etc.). Insofar as the priests received their appointments from the

Romans and engaged in the secular practice of law, i.e., matters considered today as strictly civil law such as estates, wills, misdemeanors, it is obvious that Jesus broke secular law as well.

20. Berrigan, Philip, "We Are One Family," *The Catholic Agitator*, Los Angeles, Calif., Jan. 1982, p. 3.
21. Jesus teaches us not to judge lest we be judged in like manner. (Matthew 7.) There is an absolute prohibition against condemnation and a relative one concerning judgment. (John 7:24.)
22. See Durland, *No King But Caesar?, op. cit.,* pp. 40-49.
23. McSorley, "The Gospel of Peace," *On the Edge*, p. 5; reprinted in McSorley, *The New Testament Basis of Peacemaking,* Georgetown Center for Peace Studies, Washington, D.C., 1979.
24. Kazantzakis, *The Last Temptation of Christ,* Simon & Schuster, New York, 1960.
25. Cadoux, *The Early Christian Attitude to War,* Seabury, New York, 1982, p. 211.
26. See Father Charles McCarthy's splendid videotape series *A Nonviolent Theology of Peace and Justice,* Brockton, Mass.
27. Ellul, *The Politics of God and the Politics of Man, op. cit.,* p. 190.
28. Nolan, *op. cit.,* p. 17.
29. See Introduction, Note 22.

Chapter Three: CHRISTIANITY AND EMPIRE

1. "Strength through force" is a favorite phrase of modern nation-state leaders as well.
2. Tacitus, *Annals*, 15:44.
3. The language used by the U.S. Supreme Court is "compelling state interests." It is not found in the U.S. Constitution and takes precedence over the First Amendment. See *U.S. v. American Friends Service Committee*, 419 U.S. 7, 15.
4. Tax exempt status is granted by the Internal Revenue Service if the applicant organization can demonstrate that its charitable work "relieves the burdens of government." The I.R.S. also takes to itself the defining of what love (charity) is!
5. O'Connor, *The New Community,* Harper & Row, New York, 1978, p. 58.
6. Yoder, *op. cit.,* p. 238.
7. Phillips, *Ancient Israel's Criminal Law,* Basil Blackwell, Oxford, Eng., 1970, p. 83.
8. *Ibid.,* p. 84.
9. McKenzie, "Violence and Kingdom," *Source*, No. 1, Thomas More Assoc. (no date), p. 13. (from a hand-transposed copy).

10. *Ibid.*, p. 23.
11. The judge in *Moylan v. U.S.*, 417 F.2d, 1002, 1009 (4th Circ.), 1969; cert. den. 397 U.S. 910 (1970), equated conscience with chaos.
12. Cotone, "The Apostolic Tradition of Hippolytus of Rome," *The American Benedictine Review*, Vol. 19, 1968, p. 501.
13. Ferguson, *The Politics of Love*, Clarke Pub. Co., Cambridge, Eng., p. 64.
14. Durland, *No King But Caesar?*, *op. cit.*, p. 27.
15. Schillebeeckx, *Ministry: Leadership in the Community of Jesus Christ*, Crossroad Pub. Co., New York, 1981, p. 32.
16. Gorman, *Abortion and the Early Church*, Intervarsity Press, Downers Grove, Ill., 1982, p. 87.
17. Durland, *No King But Caesar?*, *op. cit.*, p. 73.
18. Cadoux, *The Early Church and the World*, T.&T. Clark, Edinburgh, Scotland, 1925, pp. 103, 128-29.
19. *Ibid.*, p. 613.
20. *Ibid.*, p. 615.
21. *Ibid.*, p. 251; Durland, *op. cit.*, p. 73.
22. *Ibid.*, p. 351.
23. *Ibid.*
24. Corbett, Fitsimons and Smith (eds.), *World History* (The Catholic High School Social Studies Series), W. H. Sadlier, New York, 1957, pp. 115-16.
25. Durland, *op. cit.*, p. 87.
26. Cochrane, *Christianity and Classical Culture*, Oxford University Press, London, 1977, vi.
27. *Ibid.*, p. 45.
28. *Ibid.*, p. 48.
29. *Ibid.*, p. 54.
30. *Ibid.*, p. 177.
31. *Ibid.*, p. 184.
32. *Ibid.*, p. 185.
33. *Ibid.*, pp. 213-14.
34. *Ibid.*, pp. 219-20.
35. *Ibid.*, p. 227.
36. Küng, *The Church*, Doubleday, New York, 1976, p. 25.
37. *Ibid.*
38. *Ibid.*, p. 522.
39. *Ibid.*, p. 467.
40. *Ibid.*, p. 285.
41. *Ibid.*, p. 534.
42. Schillebeeckx, *op. cit.*, p. 30.

43. Küng, *op. cit., p. 569.*
44. Schillebeeckx, *op. cit.,* p. 30.
45. Gager, *Kingdom and Community: The Social World of Early Christianity,* Prentice-Hall, Englewood Cliffs, N.J., 1975, p. 107, referring to Max Weber.
46. *Ibid.,* p. 124, quoting "The Letter to Diognetus."
47. Brown, *Augustine of Hippo,* University of California Press, Berkeley,, 1967, p. 161.
48. *Ibid.,* p. 213.
49. *Ibid.,* p. 214.
50. *Ibid.*
51. *Ibid.*
52. *Ibid.,* p. 224.
53. *Ibid.,* p. 238.
54. *Ibid.,* p. 239.
55. *Ibid.*
56. *Ibid.,* p. 251.
57. *Ibid.,* p. 291.
58. *Ibid.,* p. 315.
59. *Ibid.,* p. 323.
60. *Ibid.,* p. 421.
61. *Ibid.,* p. 422.

Chapter Four: CHRISTENDOM AND THE NATIONS

1. These phrases were adopted by the author from the events of the "Watergate Scandal" of 1973. Constantine took over the church from the inside and Augustine, in his writings, never refers to the older writings of disciples who espoused and practiced pacifism, simplicity and community. See Durland *op. cit.,* for a synopsis of such writings.
2. Percival, *Seven Ecumenical Councils: Nicene and Antinicene Fathers,* Vol. XIV, Eerdmans Pub. Co., Grand Rapids, Mich., 1929, p. 27.
3. *Ibid.,* pp. 74, 605-7.
4. *Ibid.,* pp. 47, 93, 114.
5. See Schillebeeckx and Küng, Chapter 3 and early church canons.
6. Percival, *op. cit.,* p. 153.
7. Noel, *The Anatomy of the Catholic Church,* Doubleday, New York, 1980, p. 13.
8. Ullmann, *The Growth of Papal Government in the Middle Ages: A Study in the Ideological Relations of Clerical and Lay Power,* Methuen & Co., London, 3rd ed., 1970, pp. 1-2.
9. *Ibid.,* pp. 3-4.

10. *Ibid.,* p. 4.
11. Ullmann, *A Short History of the Papacy in the Middle Ages,* Harper & Row, New York, 1972, p. 8.
12. *Ibid.,* p. 7.
13. Matheson, *The Third Reich and the Christian Churches,* Eerdmans Pub. Co., Grand Rapids, Mich., 1981, p. 31.
14. Tuchman, *A Distant Mirror: The Calamitous 14th Century,* Knopf, New York, 1973, p. 4.
15. Durland, *op. cit.,* p. 87.
16. Ullmann, *op. cit.,* p. 11.
17. Percival, *op. cit.,* p. 396.
18. Ullmann, *op. cit.,* p. 16.
19. *Ibid.,* p. 17.
20. *Ibid.,* p. 18.
21. *Ibid.,* p. 22.
22. Ullmann, *Growth of Papal Government, op. cit.,* p. 10.
23. *Ibid.,* p. 34.
24. Tuchman, *op. cit.,* p. 37.
25. Bettenson (ed.), *Documents of the Christian Church,* 2nd ed., Oxford University Press, London, 1982, pp. 98-101.
26. Ullmann, *Growth of Papal Government, op. cit.,* p. 120.
27. *Ibid.,* p. 132.
28. *Ibid.,* p. 158.
29. *Ibid.,* p. 320.
30. *Ibid.,* p. 333.
31. Power-Waters, *The Crusader: The Story of Richard the Lionheart,* Turret Books, New York, 1963, p. 1.
32. *Ibid.,* pp. 36, 47, 55.
33. Ullmann, *Growth of Papal Government, op. cit.,* p. 430.
34. *Ibid.,* p. 278.
35. See Knowles, *Thomas Becket,* Stanford University Press, Stanford, Calif,. 1971; Winston, *Thomas Becket,* A.A. Knopf, New York, 1967; Eliot, *Murder in the Cathedral,* Harcourt, Brace & Co., New York, 1935.
36. Winston, *op. cit.,* p. 153.
37. Knowles, *op. cit.,* p. 170.
38. *Ibid.,* p. 171.
39. The Bull of "Unam Sanctam," Bettenson, *op. cit.,* p. 115.
40. Moorman, *A History of the Franciscan Order,* Oxford University Press, London, 1968, p. 404.
41. Tuchman, *op. cit.,* p. 31.
42. *Ibid.*

43. Todd, "Luther's Hints for Future Church," Address: Tantur Lectures, Jerusalem, Oct. 27, 1983.

44. Wormser, *The Story of Law*, Simon & Schuster, New York, 1982, p. 145, quoting from the "Institutes of Justinian."

45. Durland, *No King But Jesus!, op. cit.*, p. 245.

46. Morris (ed.), *The Great Legal Philosophers*, University of Pennsylvania Press, Philadelphia, Pa., 1954, pp. 15-39.

47. Somerville and Santoni, *Social and Political Philosophy*, Anchor Books, New York, 1963, p. 8ff.

48. Schwartz, *Freedom and Authority*, Dickenson Pub. Co., Encino, Calif., 1963, p.21.

49. Nisbet, *The Social Philosophers*, Washington Square Press, New York, 1982, p. 3 (paperback abridged updated edition).

50. *Ibid.*

51. Schwartz, *op. cit.*, p. 32.

52. *Ibid.*, pp. 35-36.

53. Nisbet, *The Social Philosophers*, Thomas Y. Crowell Co., New York, 1973, pp. 59-60.

54. Somerville and Santoni, *op. cit.*, p. 120.

55. Nisbet, *op. cit.*, p. 60.

56. Schwartz, *op. cit.*, p. 189.

57. *Ibid.*

58. *Ibid.*, p. 190.

59. *Ibid.*

60. *Ibid.*

61. In *U.S. v. Moylan*, 417 F.2d 1002, 1009 (1969) cert. den., 397 U.S. 910 (1970), the court said that: "to encourage individuals to make their own determinations as to which laws they will obey and which they will permit themselves as a matter of conscience to disobey is to invite chaos." See Durland, *People Pay for Peace*, Center Peace Publishers, Cokedale, Colo., 1984, p. 64.

62. This is also a fact of our own times.

63. Augustine, *City of God*, Book IV, Modern Library, New York, 1950, p.123.

64. Thielicke, *Theological Ethics*, Vol. 2, Eerdmans Pub. Co., Grand Rapids, Mich., 1969, p. 179.

65. *Ibid.*, p. 542. See also Aquinas, *Summa Theologica*, Part 1, Question 96, Article 4.

66. Durland, *No King But Jesus!, op. cit.*, p. 254.

67. Schumacher, *Small Is Beautiful: Economics as if People Mattered*, Harper & Row, New York, 1973, p. 119. See also, Taylor, *Economics and the Gospel*, United Church Press, Philadelphia, Pa., 1973.

68. Messner, *Social Ethics*, Herder & Co., London, 1952, p. 160.

69. Such as Tolstoy's *The Kingdom of God Is Within You,* Noonday Press, New York, 1961.
70. Tolstoy has written dozens of essays on government and Christianity and included this conflicting theme in his early novels such as *War and Peace* and his later ones such as *Resurrection.*
71. Nisbet, *op. cit.,* 1982, vii.
72. *Ibid.,* p. 71.
73. Gospel Order is a phrase which received prominence by its use among the early Quakers. George Fox believed in a communitarian order belonging to the Christian people as a whole by virtue of their inclusion in the New Covenant. (Matthew 5, 18.) He called this Gospel Order and even though he rejected the religious establishment of his time, he understood this community to have form and structure, order and government, while retaining its charismatic and enthusiastic spirit. See Durland, *The Apocalyptic Witness,* Pendle Hill Pamphlets, Wallingford, Pa., 1988.

Chapter Five: *LIVING IN SIN*

1. See Bardell and Durland, "The Bishop of Prato and American Law: Defamation and the Clergy," *Georgetown Law Journal,* Vol. 47, 1958, pp. 384-86. Today the state is encroaching more and more upon church matters but usually where popular support exists.
2. The Reformers refused to use violence directly themselves but, in the manner of the ruling religious authorities in Jerusalem at the time of Jesus, sought state enforced violence as a means of retribution and punishment.
3. Conway (ed.), *The Question Box,* Paulist Press, New York, 1929, p. 427. A 1962 revised edition drops the mention of Quakers but says that the Roman Catholic Church "condemns the pacificism [sic] of those who claim that all wars are incompatible with Christianity. . . ." p. 241.
4. Revelation 13, for example, where church and state are symbolized in the Beasts of the Sea and Land.
5. Stendahl, "The End of Life," *Monograph,* Gustavus Adolphus College, St. Peter, Minn., Jan. 5-6, 1972, pp. 7, 15, 21.
6. See Lindsey, *The Late Great Planet Earth,* Zondevan, Grand Rapids, Mich., 1970, and *The 1980's: Countdown to Armageddon,* Bantam, New York, 1981.
7. The Greek word for "everlasting" coupled with "Hell" can connote age-long in the sense of quality rather than in the sense of time.

8. See Runes (ed.), *Dictionary of Philosophy*, Littlefield, Adams, & Co., Totowa, N.J., 1962, pp. 76, 159.

9. See Fletcher, *Situational Ethics*, Westminster Press, Philadelphia, Pa., 1966, and *Moral Responsibility*, Westminster Press, Philadelphia, Pa., 1966.

10. See note 73, Chapter 4.

11. These provocations were never fully publicized until recently. Rather, Americans were propagandized to believe that Pearl Harbor commenced the "most just of all wars." Morality attached only at the moment of an unannounced war. Since then the U.S. has engaged in undeclared wars.

12. It was agreed with French influence that the principles of self-determination of people did not extend to French colonies in the Pacific.

13. Macquarrie, *Principles of Christian Theology*, Charles Scribners Sons, New York, 1972, p. 335.

14. Brown, *Bury My Heart at Wounded Knee.* Bantam, New York, 1972, p. 1.

15. Augustine coined the phrase "civil theology" as the one of three types of theologies which dealt with public worship, i.e., the worship of the emperor as God. Mary Dyer was hanged in Boston Common in May, 1660, because she chose to return to Massachusetts after being warned that if she did she would be executed. She chose to do so for the sake of others and God's call upon her as she experienced it rather than abandon the principles of her conscience.

16. There was a story to this effect circulating among Christian and Jewish circles while the author and his family lived in Jerusalem in 1983-84.

17. On Reinhold Niebuhr, see, for example, his books: *The Nature and Destiny of Man*, Charles Scribners Sons, 1964, and *Moral Man and Immoral Society*, Charles Scribners Sons, New York, 1960.

18. See Fr. Emmanuel Charles McCarthy's monograph (videotape series), *A Nonviolent Theology of Peace and Justice*, Brockton, Mass.

19. From *The Jewish Sources of the Sermon on the Mount, op. cit.*, pp. 65-67.

20. McCarthy, *op. cit.*

21. "Great Courage Prevailed," *Colorado Springs Sun*, July 3, 1982, p. 8A.

22. From the Walt Disney film, "Snow White and the Seven Dwarfs."

23. When I was an 11-year-old boy, the Marines' Hymn was the only "poetry" I was willing to memorize without being commanded to do so. I did not understand the words then, as I do now, to

be blasphemous, a type of cultural apostasy engaged in by good American people willing to kill the nation's declared enemies on order.

24. Subsequent to this statement, he became a target. From a report in *Parade Magazine* in the early 1980s.

25. "Reagan Lauds Military," *Colorado Springs Sun*, May 16, 1982, p. 4A.

26. "Reagan: Faith Will Beat Communism," *Colorado Springs Sun*, Easter, 1983.

27. Preface, *Biblical Research Handbook*, Covenant Pub. Co., London, 1946.

28. *Ibid.*

29. His Baptist community registered only one objection to my proposed legislation, that I was aware of, as a state legislator between 1966 and 1970, and that was to legitimize public purchase and consumption of alcoholic beverages.

30. Bishop Walter Sullivan along with Catholic Bishops Dingman, Gumbleton and Hunthausen and others have been most active in their opposition to capital punishment and war-making as well.

31. Zahn, *German Catholics and Hitler's Wars*, Sheed & Ward, New York, 1962, pp. 60-61, 86, 92, 144-72.

32. Durland, *No King But Caesar?*, *op. cit.*, p. 78 quoting St. Hippolytus, (c. 225 AD).

33. For an extended interpretation, see Reid (ed.), *Peace in the Nuclear Age: The Bishops' Pastoral Letter in Perspective*, Catholic University Press, Washington, D.C., 1986.

34. "President Urges Preachers to Pray for Soviet Leaders," Colorado Springs *Gazette-Telegraph*, March 7, 1984, p. 3A. See also "Reagan Bible Quotes Stir Critics," *Denver Post*, Feb. 22, 1985, p. 6E.

35. "Reagan Says Grenada Was Turning Point for America," *The Pueblo Chieftain*, Oct. 25, 1984.

36. *Ibid.*

37. *Ibid.*

38. *Ibid.*, and *New York Times*, July 6, 1989, p. 1.

39. Durland, *Monograph*, "Some Papal Statements and Vatican Conduct in Support of Religious, Political, Military and Economic Violence," (1971-1981), 1982. Pope Paul VI addressed 5,000 members of the Italian armed forces, saying, "A well-ordered country should have its army to defend itself." *Catholic Standard and Times*, Philadelphia, Pa., Dec. 15, 1977, p. 2. But see, "Refuse to Serve in Military, Pope Urges," (John Paul II), *Atlanta Constitution*, Feb. 13, 1984, p. 3A.

40. *Ibid.* The pope was reported to have said to Roman Catholic jurists: "It is not possible to construct a society . . . with only the principle of nonviolence. Colorado Springs *Gazette-Telegraph,* (A.P.) Dec. 7, 1980.
41. Quakers, as a Christian religious group, have witnessed to this authentic marriage process. See also Campbell, *Brother to a Dragonfly,* Seabury, New York, 1972.
42. Monograph, "Celibacy in the Early Church," (author unknown), p. 1. See also Herbert, *Priestly Celibacy,* p. 128.
43. *Ibid.,* p.. 2.
44. *Ibid.*
45. Herbert, *op. cit.,* p. 128
46. Approved by Pope Paul VI, dated Oct. 15, 1976, made public Jan. 27, 1977.
47. *Ibid.,* p. 1.
48. *Ibid.*
49. The author has interviewed Christian chaplains in prisons on this subject. Chaplains, whether military or prison, are willing victims of the state, with rare exceptions.
50. "Verdict Flaunts [sic] Purpose of Law," *Colorado Springs Sun (undated).*
51. *Ibid.*
52. DeHaan, *God, Law and Capital Punishment,* Christian Guidance Book, Grand Rapids, Mich., 1974, p. 4.
53. *Ibid.,* p. 7.
54. *Ibid.*
55. McKenzie, "Violence and Kingdom," *Source, No. 10,* Thomas More Assoc., Chicago, Ill.
56. *Times Service,* Nov. 22, 1982.
57. Meanwhile, in the U.S., it received wide publicity with much support except for the section on deterrence.
58. At the third anniversary of the bombing of Hiroshima, Gen. MacArthur's representative was reported to say: "This disaster is your own fault." *Time Magazine,* Aug. 16, 1948.
59. See " 'A' bomb Chaplain: I Was Told it was Necessary," *Sojourners,* Washington, D.C., Reprinted by Center for Peace Studies, Washington, D.C.
60. Perrin, "Surviving Justly is Far More Than Just Surviving," (a book review of Stanley Hauerwas' *Against the Nations) National Catholic Reporter,* 1986.
61. From a letter from the bishop to the author, April 6, 1983.
62. The principal compared the video machines to the "tail-of-the-monkey" and amusement park bumper cars entertainment.

63. From a folk song made popular in the late 50s and early 60s by the Chad Mitchell Trio.

64. Stringfellow's best read books are, *An Ethic for Christians and Other Aliens in a Strange Land*, Word Books, Waco, Texas, 1973, and *Conscience and Obedience: The Politics of Romans 13 and Revelations 13 in Light of the Second Coming*, Word Books, Waco, Texas, 1977.

65. "NATO Says Nuclear Weapons 'Sole Option,'" Colorado Springs *Gazette-Telegraph*, March 7, 1984. See also "How Safe Are We: An Interview with Casper Weinberger," *Parade Magazine*, March 20, 1983, p. 19, and "U.S. Passion is Security," *Colorado Springs Sun*, Nov. 4, 1982.

66. Michaels, "Chaplain's Book Says Peace Activists Speak 'Contrary to Church,'" *National Catholic Reporter*, Jan. 30, 1981.

67. *Ibid.*

68. From *U.S. v. Holladay*, the trial of Martin Holladay for disarming a missile silo, one of many "plowshares" actions.

69. à Kempis, *The Imitation of Christ*, Gardner (ed.), Image Books, New York, 1955, p. 46. The law strives to judge by acts only, not intent. It is not constituted or able to judge inwardly.

70. Orengo, "Serving God and country," *Military Chaplaincy Proposal*, The Project for Review of the Military Chaplaincy (Handen and Sulzman, eds.), Denver, Colo., 1982, p. 58.

71. Zahn, *One Solitary Witness: The Life and Death of Franz Jaeggerstatter*, Beacon Press, Boston, Mass., 1964, pp. 205-6.

72. The University of Colorado is not alone in such ventures. Some religiously identified places of higher education refuse to completely divest.

73. From "Nuclear Stations of the Cross," Brandywine Peace Community vigil at General Electric Corporation's King of Prussia Re-entry Division Plant, April 17, 1987, at which time the author and his wife joined others in holy obedience.

74. Nickalls (ed.) *The Journal of George Fox*, Religious Society of Friends, London, Eng., 1975, pp. 345-46.

75. *Ibid.*, p. 380.

76. See Vanier, *Community and Growth*, Paulist Press, New York, 1979, p. 128.

77. For inspirational words for practical witness Berrigan, D., Wallis, Jegen, Durland and Cordero, *Faith and Resistance*, Abbe Creek Press, Mt. Vernon, Iowa, 1985.

78. Roof, "The Moral Majority Goes Out of Business," Baltimore Sun, June 18, 1989, pp. 1E, 4E comments on the decline of the New Right and Moral Majority movements.

Chapter Six: FORMING COMMUNITY

1. For books and articles on the rapture see McCall and Levett, *Raptured,* Harvest House Pub., Eugene, Ore., 1975; Roberts, "The Prosperity Gospel," *New Covenant,* Vol. II, No. 5, Nov., 1981, and Jewett, *Jesus Against the Rapture,* Westminster Press, Philadelphia, Pa., 1979.
2. Bates, *A Tribulation Map: An Explanation for Those Who Miss the Rapture,* Bible Believers Evangelistic Assoc., Sherman, Texas, 1974.
3. *Ibid.*
4. Lindsey, "Foreword," *The Late Great Planet Earth, op. cit.*
5. Küng, *On Being a Christian,* Doubleday, New York, 1974, p. 31.
6. *Ibid.,* p. 188.
7. See "Living Nonviolence: A Christian Calling," Catholic Peace Fellowship Monograph, New York (undated), pp. 4-5.
8. Ellul, *The Presence of the Kingdom,* Seabury, New York, 1967, p. 36.
9. Baker, "U.S. Passion for Security," *Colorado Springs Sun,* Nov. 4, 1982.
10. A favorite phrase of the suburbanites. For further reading on "the criminal element" see Griffith, "Jesus and the Lawbreakers," *Sojourners,* Aug. 1978, pp. 24-26, and Griffith, "Alternatives to Calling the Police," *The Christian as Victim Conference,* April 1-3, 1982.
11. See Fr. Emmanuel Charles McCarthy's videotape series, *op. cit.,* Brockton, Mass.
12. *Ibid.*
13. *God and Caesar,* Vol. IV, No. 4, Newton, Kansas, Nov. 1978.
14. From the *Catholic Worker* handout entitled "Aims and Purposes."
15. Excerpts from the *Bartimaeus Community Statement of Faith and Lifestyle,* (a working draft, not in general distribution), Section I, pp. 1-2, 5-16.
16. *Bartimaeus Community Statement,* Statement III. The community exists today through its house church.

Chapter Seven: PRACTICING COMMUNITY

1. "Letters to the Editor," Trinidad *Chronicle-News,* Trinidad, Colo., Aug. 29, 1985. I served in the U.S. Army from 1954 to 1967 as enlisted and reserve officer.
2. This letter was received through the public mail.
3. *Trinidad-Plus* newspaper, Raton, New Mexico, Sept. 1985.
4. From "Chaplain of Crew Who Dropped A-Bomb on Hiroshima Now a Pacifist," The Flint Voice, Flint, Mich., March 1980, p. 7.

5. *Sojourners* Magazine, Aug. 1978, pp. 24-26.
6. Berrigan, Philip, "We Are One Family," *Catholic Agitator*, Jan. 2, 1982, p. 3.
7. On Good Friday, April 17, 1987, one hundred people were arrested at an abortion clinic in Philadelphia in a widely publicized event. At the same time, 20 people of the Brandywine Peace Community walked five miles around the General Electric Corporation's King of Prussia Space Division sites praying "The Nuclear Stations of the Cross," composed by one of its members, Bob Smith.
8. This trial ended in numerous convictions.
9. The young man is Martin Holladay, released on parole in 1987 after serving three years of an 11-year prison sentence. The author was an "expert witness" at his trial on international law and civil disobedience, but was prevented from testifying only by the judge.
10. Durland (ed.), *Conscience and the Law*, Center Peace Publishers, Cokedale, Colo., 1982, p. 2.
11. *Ibid.*
12. *Ibid.*
13. *Ibid.*
14. *Ibid.*
15. *Ibid.*, p. 3.
16. Jesus, in fact, knew no borders and thus no trespass to land, as the term is legally applied. For an excellent book regarding the resistance of Jesus to the ways of nations read Myers, *Binding the Strong Man*, to be published by Orbis in late 1989.
17. Schillebeeckx, *Jesus: An Experiment in Christology*, Vintage Books, New York, 1981, p. 243.
18. Ogle, "What is Left for Caesar?" *Theology Today*, Vol. XXXV, No. 3, Science Press, Princeton, N.J., Oct. 1978; Cassidy, *op. cit.*, pp. 57-58; Kaufman, *What Belongs to Caesar?*, Herald Press, Scottsdale, Pa., 1969, pp. 35-38; Dale Brown of the Church of the Brethren Seminary in Elgin, Ill., has been another chief source.
19. *op. cit.*, pp. 252-53, 351, 354.
20. *The Journal of John Woolman*, Citadel Press, Secaucus, N.J., 1972, p. 75.
21. Schlissel, *Conscience in America*, E.P. Dalton Co., New York, 11968, p. 53.
22. Muste, *Of Holy Obedience*, Pendle Hill Pamphlets, No. 64, Wallingford, Pa., 1952. A Quaker, Thomas Kelly, entitled a 1939 William Penn lecture, "Holy Obedience."
23. See *A. J. Muste Memorial Institute Essay Series*, No. 1, New York, 1974, pp. 13-34.

24. Durland, *op. cit.*, p.12.
25. See Forest, *Love is the Measure: A Biography of Dorothy Day*, Paulist Press, Mahwah, N.J., 1986, pp. 166-172.
26. Subsequently a video movie was circulated entitled "In the King of Prussia." The Brandywine Peace Community has conducted vigils and witnesses at G.E. in the Philadelphia area since 1979.
27. Griffith, "Alternatives to Calling the Police," *op. cit.*
28. 417 F. 2d 1002, 1009 (1969) Cert. den. 397 U.S. 910 (1970).
29. Published by the Catholic Peace Fellowship, New York; reprinted in the May 1974 issue of *The Catholic Worker*.
30. *Catholic Worker* Statement of Principles entitled "Going to the Roots."
31. *Ibid.*
32. *Ibid.*
33. See Mathei, "The Earth in Common: A Look at Community Land Trusts," *Sojourners*, Washington, D.C., Nov. 1979, pp. 74-75.
34. The author co-founded this group in 1975, after founding The Community for Creative Non-Violence with two Catholic priests in 1970, and The Center for Peace Studies with Father Richard McSorley, S.J., in 1973. Both organizations are in Washington, D.C.
35. See "Jubilee," *The Interpreters Dictionary of the Bible*, Abingdon Press, Nashville, Tenn., 1962 (Supplement, 1976).
36. Yoder, *op. cit.*, pp. 64-78.
37. See Merton, *The Monastic Journey*, Image Books, New York, 1977, and *The Wisdom of the Desert*, New Directions, New York, 1970.
38. The Author was the co-founder of Irenaeus House Church on Aug. 6, 1980, one of the first church sanctuaries for undocu- mented refugees from Central America, publicly declared on July 4, 1982. The sanctuary movement began on March 23, 1982. Irenaeus became Erimias (wilderness, desert) upon a change of place and people on April 1, 1984.
39. Some resistance groups describe their activities as "campaigns" (i.e. Ground Zero at Submarine Base Bangor, Conscience and Military Tax Campaign, and Brandywine Peace Community's on- going General Electric witnesses in Philadelphia and King of Prussia. These are not witnesses only, but on-going, goal-oriented undertakings. Bijou House in Colorado Springs has been the focal point for a campaign against "Star Wars."

Chapter Eight: CHRISTIAN ADVOCACY FOR THE OPPRESSED

1. p. 1189. This chapter is based on a paper presented to the Third Peace and Theology Colloquium of the General Conference Mennonite Church, Bluffton, Ohio, Oct. 15, 1981.
2. *Ibid.*, p. 1190.
3. *Ibid.*
4. "Utilitarianism," Morris (ed.), *op. cit.*, p. 375.
5. *Ibid.*, pp. 375-76.
6. "The Limits of Jurisprudence," Morris (ed.), *op. cit.*, p. 276.
7. Durland, "Ethics and Legality," *Ethical Issues*, Durland & Bruening, (eds.), Mayfield Pub. Co., Palo Alto, Calif., 1975, p. 23.
8. "An Exposition of the Fundamental Principles of Jurisprudence as a Science of Right," Morris (ed.) *op. cit.*, p. 242.
9. *Ibid.*, pp. 244-45.
10. MacDonald, "Natural Rights," *Human Rights*, A. Melden (ed.), Wadsworth Pub. Co., Belmont, Calif., 1920, p. 50.
11. *Ibid.*, p. 51.
12. "On the Rights of War and Peace," Morris (ed.) *op. cit.*, p. 85.
13. "An Introduction to American Law," *Studying Law*, Vanderbilt (ed.), Washington Square Pub. Co., New York, 1950, p. 382.
14. Durland, *People Pay for Peace*, Center Peace Publishers, Cokedale, Colo., 1985, Part V.
15. MacDonald, *op. cit.*, p. 51.
16. A "right" can be deemed to have accrued or vested "only when litigation could have first been successfully maintained thereunder." *Rowe v. Tucker*, Colo. App., 560 P.2d 843, 846 (1977). If "no action is maintainable" then no right has yet accrued. *Tucker v. Claimant in Death of Gonzales*, Colo. App., 546 P.2d 1271 (1975). For a discussion of human rights and international law see Lillich and Newman, *International Human Rights*, Little Brown, Boston, 1979, specifically "International Covenant on Economic, Social and Cultural Rights," p. 924.
17. Bruening, "Rights: Legal and Moral Parameters," *Ethical Issues*, *op. cit.*, p. 395-96.
18. McClosky, "Rights," *Understanding Moral Philosophy*, J. Rachels, (ed.), Dickinson Publishing Co., Encino, Calif., 1976, p. 300.
19. *Ibid.*
20. *A Theory of Justice*, Harvard University Press, Cambridge, Mass., 1971, p. 135.
21. *Ibid.*, p. 132.
22. Leiser, *Liberty, Justice and Morals*, (2nd Edition) MacMillan Co., New York, 1986, p. 109.

23. *Exousia* (transliterated from the Greek), *Theological Dictionary of the New Testament*, Kittel (ed.), Vol. 2, Eerdmans Pub. Co., Grand Rapids, Mich., 1964, p. 562.
24. Schrey, *The Biblical Doctrine of Justice and Law*, Camelot Press Ltd., London, 1955, p. 129.
25. According to Pope John XXIII in his Encyclical *Pacem in Terris*, these rights are the rights of life, liberty, the right to search for the truth, express opinions, work in a dignified manner, assemble in public, emigrate and immigrate. *National Catholic Reporter*, Vol. 17, No. 39, Sept. 11, 1981, p. 12.
26. Koop, "Pressing the Claims, Interpreting the Cries," *Christian Declaration of Human Rights*, A. Miller (ed.), p. 56.
27. *The Wisdom of Tolstoy*, Rosenzweig (ed.), Book Sales, Inc., New York, 1958, p. 44.
28. Koop, *op. cit.*, p. 144.
29. See Durland, Eugenia, *Voluntary Simplicity*, Alternatives, Forest Park, Ga., 1979, pp. 9-16. *Mishpat* (Justice) and *Tsedeqah* (Righteousness) in Hebrew are clearly related and are responses to Yahwistic righteousness. (Micah 6:1-8.)
30. Achtemeier, "Righteousness in the Old Testament," *Interpreters Dictionary of the Bible*, Vol. 4, Abingdon Press, Nashville, Tenn., 1962, p. 81, paraphrased in part. See also, Harrelson, *The Ten Commandments and Human Rights*, Fortress Press, Philadelphia, Pa., 1980. Hosea speaks of God's deliverance from Egypt as love (11:1.), Micah speaks of it as righteoussness or justice. (6:1-8.)
31. See Roop, "Justice in the Biblical Tradition," (unpublished Associated Mennonite Biblical Seminar paper), Aug. 1972. *Mishpat* and *Tsedeqah* represent different strains of tradition which do not seem to have come together until David after 1000 BC. *Mishpat* is fundamentally judicial, whereas *Tsedeqah* is relational. Jesus did not continue to use them and instead referred to love (*agape*) or mercy (*elios*) possibly more closely related to the Hebrew *Hesed*.

Chapter Nine: SEE THE CONQUERING HERO COMES

1. Berrigan, Philip, "We are One Family," *op. cit.*, p. 2.
2. One of the latest was the Epiphany Plowshares case tried in the Philadelphia Federal Court in 1987, followed by the Paupers' Plowshares trial in the same court. The author was attorney-advisor in the former case for defendant Lin Romano.
3. These values are the highest of the nation-state. See Chapter Eight.

4. Ellul, *In Season, Out of Season,* Harper & Row., Philadelphia, Pa., 1982, p. 58.
5. Berrigan, P., *op. cit.*
6. Ellul, *op. cit.,* p. 59.
7. *Ibid.,* p. 63.
8. *Ibid.,* p. 119.
9. *The Wisdom of Tolstoy, op. cit.,* p. 21.
10. Adapted from Durland, "Christian Theologies of Politics," *Center Peace Journal,* Vol. VII, No. 3, Cokedale, Colo. Nov/Dec 1984, p. 6.
11. *Ibid.*
12. Subjective experience is perhaps more objective than detached objectivism.
13. Durland, *op. cit.,* p. 6.
14. *Ibid.,* p. 7. The historic nonviolent loving service of the ancient, grass-roots Catholic Church was recently dramatized in the film "The Mission" which depicts the risk and sacrifice of Jesuit missionaries in the service of indigenous peoples of Paraguay. Fr. Daniel Berrigan, S.J., was part of the filming of that history.
15. Hauerwas, *Against the Nations, op. cit.,* p. 117.
16. A quote of Hauerwas' from a book review of his *Against the Nations* by Ron Perrin, in the *National Catholic Reporter.*
17. Hauerwas, *op. cit.,* p. 57.

BIBLIOGRAPHY

1. *Journal of George Fox*, Nickalls (ed.), London, 1975.
2. *The Wisdom of Tolstoy*, Rosenzweig (ed.), New York, Philosophical Library, 1968.
3. Durland, *No King But Caesar?*, Scottsdale, Pa., Herald Press, 1975 (paperback edition).
4. Comblin, *The Church and the National Security State*, New York, Orbis Books, 1979.
5. Yoder, *The Politics of Jesus*, Grand Rapids, Eerdmans Publishing Co., 1972.
6. Hauerwas, *Against the Nations*, New York, Winston, 1985.
7. Lind, *Yahweh is a Warrior*, Scottsdale, Pa., Herald Press, 1980.
8. Ellul, *The Politics of God and the Politics of Man*, Grand Rapids, Eerdmans Publishing Co., 1972.
9. Ellul, *The Meaning of the City*, Grand Rapids, Eerdmans Publishing Co., 1970.
10. Bruce, *Israel and the Nations*, Grand Rapids, Eerdmans Publishing Co., 1969.
11. Bright, *The Kingdom of God*, Nashville, Abingdon Press, 1953.
12. Ricoeur, *The Symbolism of Evil*, Boston, Beacon Press, 1969.
13. Mateos, "The Message of Jesus," *Sojourners*, July 1977.
14. Nolan, *Jesus Before Christianity*, Maryknoll, N.Y., Orbis Books, 1978.
15. Berkhof, *Christ and the Powers*, Scottsdale, Pa., Herald Press, 1977.
16. Cassidy, *Jesus, Politics and Society: A Study of Luke's Gospel*, Maryknoll, N.Y., Orbis Books, 1978.
17. Berrigan, Philip, "We Are One Family," *The Catholic Agitator*, Jan. 1982.
18. Kazantzakis, *The Last Temptation of Christ*, New York, Simon & Schuster, 1960.
19. Schillebeeckx, *Ministry: Leadership in the Community of Jesus Christ*, New York, Crossroads Publishing Co., 1981.

20. Gorman, *Abortion and the Early Church*, Downers Grove, Intervarsity Press, 1982.
21. Cadoux, *The Early Church and the World*, Edinbergh, T. & T. Clark, 1925.
22. Küng, *The Church*, New York, Doubleday, 1976.
23. Brown, *Augustine of Hippo*, Berkeley, University of California Press, 1967.
24. Ullmann, *The Growth of Papal Government in the Middle Ages*, London, Methuen & Co., 3rd Ed., 1970.
25. Durland, *The Apocalyptic Witness*, Wallingford, Pa., Pendle Hill Publications, 1988.
26. Nisbet, *The Social Philosophers*, New York, Thomas Y. Cravell Co., 1973.
27. Tolstoy, *The Kingdom of God is Within You*, New York, Noonday Press, 1961.
28. Zahn, *German Catholics and Hitler's Wars*, New York, Sheed & Ward, 1962.
29. Stringfellow, *An Ethic for Christians and Other Aliens in a Strange Land*, Waco, Tex., Word Books, 1973.
30. Stringfellow, *Conscience and Obedience*, Waco, Tex., Word Books, 1977.
31. Zahn, *One Solitary Witness*, Boston, Beacon Press, 1979.
32. Vanier, *Community and Growth*, New York, Paulist Press, 1979.
33. Berrigan, Daniel, Jim Wallis, Mary Evelyn Jagen, William Durland, *Faith and Resistance*, Mt. Vernon, Iowa, Abbe Creek Press, 1979.
34. Jerrett, *Jesus Against the Rapture*, Philadelphia, Westminster Press, 1979.
35. Küng, *On Being a Christian*, New York, Doubleday, 1974.
36. Durland, *Conscience and the Law*, Cokesdale, Col., Center Peace Publishers, 1982.
37. Durland, *People Pay for Peace*, Cokesdale, Col., Center Peace Publishers, 1984.
38. Durland, *The Illegality of War*, Cokesdale, Col., Center Peace Publishers, 1983.
39. Schillebeeckx, *Jesus*, New York, Vintage Books, 1981.

40. *The Journal of John Woolman*, Secaucus, N.J., Citadel Press, 1972.
41. Miller, *A Harsh and Dreadful Love*, New York, Image, 1974.
42. Durland, "Ethic and Morality," *Ethical Issues*, Durland & Bruenning (eds.), Palo Alto, Mayfield Publishing Co., 1975.
43. Durland, Eugenia, *Voluntary Simplicity*, Forest Park, Ga., Alternatives, 1979.
44. Berrigan, Philip, & McAlister, *The Time's Discipline*, Baltimore, Fortkamp Publishing Co., 1989.
45. Ellul, *In Season, Out of Season*, Philadelphia, Harper & Row, 1982.
46. Coy, *A Revolution of the Heart*, Temple University Press, Philadelphia, 1988.
47. Smith, *Bulbs Not Bombs: GE and the Permanent War Economy*, Brandywine Peace Community, Swarthmore, Pa., 1986.
48. Holl, *Jesus in Bad Company*, New York, Holt Rinehart & Winston, 1972.
49. Ullmann, A Short History of the Papacy, New York, Harper & Row, 1972.
50. Berrigan, Daniel, *The Words Our Savior Gave Us*, Templegate, 1978.
51. Douglass, Jim, *The Nonviolent Cross*, Macmillan, 1968.

www.ingramcontent.com/pod-product-compliance
Lightning Source LLC
Chambersburg PA
CBHW060144280326
41932CB00012B/1629